pozwolenia —
mogę "iść" c[...]
sawie. zara[...]
leba i przez pocztę w pudełku
gryzienie Krowieczki Ge[...]
[...]ko[...] to a co tak bar[...] pros
paniuś prefy, które mi już
[...]yjść pozwolicia.) [...] koniec
— W Sobotę było wiele gość
miński, Państwa Siwnicey
Bozewska, Brat pani Drzewicz
[...]iu. — W niedzielę byliśmy
[...]ich, dziś jesteśmy w Sokołow
[...]gutki regularnie a Sza[...]

A Swallow's Shadow

An essay on Chopin's thoughts

Ryszard Przybylski

A Swallow's Shadow

An essay on Chopin's thoughts

Translated by
John Comber

The Fryderyk Chopin Institute

Warszawa 2011

In lieu of flowers on the grave
of Bohdan Wodiczko

'What is best in life
is just weariness and labour.'

IMMANUEL KANT

INTRODUCTION

Notes and words

Apart from the few instances when he was handed some official form to complete or when he jotted something down in his album or sketched the preface for a piano-playing school, Chopin used a pen to write music or letters.

When writing music, he was a composer, since he was working with 'pure sound' and was subject to a great variety of norms, such as the order, pitch and strength of notes. He metamorphosed himself into a musical structure, into musical notation, into a score. To paraphrase Roland Barthes, one might say that at such times he embedded his *why* in his *how to write music*. There is no question that Chopin fulfilled himself in music, and so the 'truest truth' about him resides in his musical works.

When attending to his correspondence, he was not a writer, since he did not craft his words and did not respect any norms of writing or technique, such as composition or genre, as were observed by say Juliusz Słowacki. When tracing letters and words, Chopin was an ordinary person in writing mode. He used language as a tool of communication. He practised linguistic communication. He spontaneously and immediately cast onto paper what he happened to be thinking about. He did not create with his words any normative literary structure.[1]

For clarity's sake, I shall pass over here a number of problems that will be considered later, analysing the bewildering sentences from the preface to his planned piano-playing school. So I shall not enquire what lies behind the notes. I shall not deliber-

---

[1] This reasoning owes much to the thinking of Roland Barthes contained in the study 'Ecrivains et écrivants', in *Essais critiques* (Paris, 1964).

ate whether a musical score is merely notation, in which there is not yet any musical sense, or a finished 'text in the emphatic sense of the word', or 'phenomenal form of music, and not just a "pre-script" for use in musical practice'.[2] Neither shall I expatiate on the imperfection of every utterance, be it in the language of music or in the language of words. Suffice it to state, for the time being, that Chopin poured into his music the essence of his person – very mysterious, but indestructible, elaborated in the literal sense of the word and transported through the notes to eternity. In words, meanwhile, he recorded his thoughts immersed in everyday life, in the murmur of time, light or dark, always hurried, yet in many cases seemingly prepared by lengthy meditation.

Given that music enabled Chopin to isolate the essence of his being from everyday existence, one is hardly surprised that he held it above writing letters. 'But you know that I prefer play-ing to writing', he informed Norbert Kumelski on 18 November 1831 (KS i: 188).* He also preferred writing notes of music to answering letters. And he took great care over the manuscripts of his scores, as he knew that through them he would reveal himself here and there, now and then, everywhere and forever, as long as our world exists. On 18 October 1841, he wrote to Julian Fontana:

---

[2] Carl Dahlhaus, 'Muzyka jako tekst', in *Idea muzyki absolutnej i inne studia* [The idea of absolute music and other studies], tr. Antoni Buchner (Cracow, 1988), 251–255; Ger. orig. 'Musik als text', in Günter Schnitzler (ed.), *Dich-tung und Musik. Kaleidoskop ihrer Beziehungen* (Stuttgart, 1979).

* The following abbreviations are used in this essay: KS = *Korespondencja Fryderyka Chopina* [Corresondence of Fryderyk Chopin], ed. Bronisław Edward Sydow, 2 vols. (Warsaw, 1955); KR = *Korespondencja Fryderyka Chopina z rodziną* [Fryderyk Chopin's correspondence with his family], ed. Krystyna Kobylańska (Warsaw, 1972); KGS = *Korespondencja Fryderyka Chopina z George Sand i z jej dziećmi* [Fryderyk Chopin's correspondence with George Sand and with her children], ed. K. Kobylańska, French texts tr. Julia Hartwig, 2 vols. (Warsaw, 1981); A = *Album Chopina 1829-1831*, ed. Jerzy Maria Smoter (Cracow, 1975). Emphasis in excerpts from Chopin's let-ters is original.

·I ask you, for God's sake, to take care of my manuscript and not crumple it, nor soil it or tear it (everything that you don't know how to do, but I write because I do so love the tedious notes[3] I write). Copy it. *Yours* will stay in Paris. To-morrow you'll receive the Nocturne, and towards the end of the week, the Ballade and Fantasy; I can't quite finish it off. If you're bored with copying, then do it *for the forgiveness of your great sins*, as I'd not like to give this spidery scrawl to any clumsy copyist. I enjoin you once again, because if I had to write these 18 pages again, I'd go mad. Just don't crumple it!!! (KS ii: 44).

He may well have gained this esteem for his 'tedious notes' during his second stay in Vienna. 'Yesterday I also went with Kandler' he wrote to his family on 14 May 1831, 'to the Imperial Library. [...] I don't know if the Bologna library is kept in greater and more systematic order; but imagine my surprise when among the newer manuscripts I see a book in a case with the inscription "Chopin". Quite fat and attractively bound. I'm thinking that I've never heard of any other Cho-pin. There was one Champin – and so I thought that it might have been his name misspelt or something of the sort. Kandler takes it out, I have a look, and it's my hand: Haslinger has given the manuscript of my Variations to the Library. I think to myself: Idiots, as if you had nothing else to keep.' (KR 69). He would soon receive confirmation of the value of his scores from Aloys Fuchs, a notable music collector: 'he showed me', wrote Chopin to his family on 25 June 1831, 'his collection of 400 autographs, among which my bound Rondo for 2 pianos already sits' (KR 72).

---

[3]   In Polish 'nudy' – a pun on 'nuda', meaning 'tedium', and 'nuta', or 'note' (tr.).

Mozart wrote music with ease. Even his great works were created out of hand, 'as one writes a letter'.[4] Chopin found writing a letter heavy going. And establishing the final version of a composition was akin to torture. He loved his 'manuscript flies' (KS ii: 44) precisely because in his case the writing of music was an exceptionally dramatic and wearying act. Here is George Sand.

> His creativity was spontaneous, miraculous; he found it without seeking it, without expecting it. It arrived at his piano suddenly, completely, sublimely, or it sang in his head during a walk, and he would hasten to hear it again by recreating it on his instrument. But then would begin the most heartbreaking labor I have ever witnessed. It was a series of efforts, indecision, and impatience to recapture certain details of the theme he had heard. What had come to him all of a piece, he now over-analyzed in his desire to transcribe it, and his regret at not finding it again 'neat', as he said, threw him into despair. He would shut himself up in his room for days at a time, weeping, pacing, breaking his pens, repeating or changing a single measure a hundred times, writing it and erasing it with equal frequency, and beginning again the next day with desperate perseverance. He would spend six weeks on a page, only to end up writing it just as he had done in his first outpouring.[5]

Joseph Filtsch, meanwhile, was struck by the contradiction between the spontaneity of inspiration, manifesting itself in particular during improvisation, and the laborious process

---

[4]   Alfred Einstein, *Mozart. His Character, His Work*, tr. Arthur Mendel and Nathan Broder (New York, 1962), 142.
[5]   George Sand, *Story of My Life*, group translation, ed. Thelma Jurgrau (Albany, 1991), 1108.

of fixing and writing down the final form of a composition: 'I heard Chopin improvising in the home of George Sand. It is marvellous to listen to him when he is composing in this way: his inspiration is so immediate and complete that he plays without hesitation, as if it had to be just so. But when it comes to writing down and recreating his initial ideas in all their details, he spends days on end in nervous tension and almost alarming desperation. He alters and amends the same phrases continually, pacing to and fro like a madman. What a curious, unfathomable creature!'[6] So Filtsch clearly failed to see that Chopin's metamorphosing of his existence into a score was accompanied by an obsession with the perfect form of a work. Somehow, he did not realise that the drama connected with the choice of a final version, given a certain flaw of character, changed Chopin's creative act into hell. 'You know', he wrote to Jan Matuszyński on 26 December 1830, 'that I am the most *indecisive* creature in the world, and only once in my life have I been able to choose well' (KS i: 162). 'And there is another thing in which I imitate you', he confessed to Tytus Woyciechowski, 'that is, in making sudden decisions' (KS i: 143).

Although, with typical self-irony, Chopin associated this ticket to immortality with paper specked by flies, looking at his 'tedious notes' he might, like Juliusz Słowacki, have whispered:

—

Ta kartka wieki tu będzie płakała
I łez jej stanie...[7]
(This page will weep for centuries
And never want of tears)

—

---

[6]   Quoted in Adam Czartkowski and Zofia Jeżewska, *Fryderyk Chopin* (Warsaw, 1970), 399.
[7]   Juliusz Słowacki, *Dzieła wszystkie* [Complete works], ed. Juliusz Kleiner (Wrocław, 1960), xii: 224.

It seems to have been exactly as Marian Piechal described it in his poem 'Nuty Chopina' [Chopin's notes]:

—

Tu palcem spod klawiszy wydobyte życie,
które w strunach milczących jak krew w żyłach płynie,
ułożone na wieczność w nutowym zeszycie
i zamknięte kluczami w basie i wiolinie.
Tu wreszcie człowiek żywy – żywy jego trud
czeka aż sprawiedliwość z ciszy go odemknie,
aż pod natchnieniem dzioby otworzą się nut
i zmartwychwstanie życie ocalone dźwiękiem.[8]
(Here, teased from the keys with fingers, life,
which flows in the silent strings like blood through veins,
arranged for eternity in a manuscript book
and enclosed by clefs in the bass and the treble.
Here, finally, a man alive – alive his labours,
waiting for justice to open them up,
for the mouths of the notes to open inspired
and life saved by sound to revive.)

—

For this reason, I think that in spite of his 'artistic sufferings', Chopin had no second thoughts about sitting down to write out his scores.

He played no games with immortality when he wrote his letters. He noted detached and hurried remarks on his everyday life. He did not particularly enjoy corresponding. 'Chopin's autographs', we read in the memoirs of Wilhelm von Lenz, 'are rare; he wrote no letters, no notes: "George Sand", he was heard to say, "writes so beautifully, that no one else has any need to

---

[8] *Poezja polska okresu międzywojennego* [Polish poetry of the interwar years] selected and ed. Michał Głowiński and Janusz Sławiński, notes Janusz Stradecki (Wrocław, 1987), 413.

write".'[9] At times, he was extremely irritated by excuses for
tardiness in writing a letter. Maria Wodzińska began one vapid
epistle thus: 'Although you like neither receiving nor writing letters…' (KS i: 261). She was right on the second point alone, as
he did enjoy receiving letters (KR 63, 70). Sometimes, he needed
them like the air that he breathed (KS i: 211). Occasionally, he
would read in the evening everything that had been written to him
(KS i: 187). But he was indeed not fond of writing back, as Felix
Mendelssohn complained: '…and though I know that you never
reply…' (KS i: 278). Such a categorical statement is also wide of
the mark, as he did occasionally reply, especially when obliged
to do so by business, love or conscience. But the complaints of
his acquaintances were justified. 'My dear friend!' wrote Ferdinand Hiller, 'Although I am convinced that this letter will also
go unanswered – just like all the others I have written to you thus
far…' (KS i: 283). Chopin also knew that letters owed, although
burdening one's conscience, paradoxically freeze one's hand.
'My dearest loved ones', he wrote to his family towards the end
of March 1847, 'if one does not write back immediately, later it
is impossible to get around to it, and one's conscience repels one
from the paper instead of making one write' (KR 160).

To a large extent, this was due to that dislike of replying to
letters experienced by many people, and I think Chopin would
have been delighted by Adam Mickiewicz's assertion: 'There
is a peculiar kind of laziness', Tomasz Zan read in a letter addressed to him by Mickiewicz on 3 April 1828, 'for which you
must devise a new Polish word, namely putting something off
from one day to the next. In that way, writing a letter often takes
me half a year…'[10] With Chopin, it sometimes took around
a month. He began the above-cited letter on 28 March and fin-

---

[9]   Wilhelm von Lenz, *The Great Piano Virtuosos of Our Time*, tr. Madeleine
R. Baker (New York: G. Shirmer, 1899), 53.
[10]   Adam Mickiewicz, *Dzieła* [Works], Wydanie Narodowe, xiv: 343.

ished it on 19 April. The phenomenon which he himself called a 'letter writing mania' overcame him perhaps only once in his life (KS i: 109). That was the period of his youthful friendship with Tytus Woyciechowski, in whom he clearly resolved to confide. He usually picked up notepaper only when a particular matter was at hand. Of course, an attempt at conversation was a most particular matter.

Not even his family's complaints could overcome his sluggishness in this respect, although they undoubtedly caused him great embarrassment. 'My dear,' wrote his sister Izabela on 27 November 1831, 'we are well, and your good health pleases us not more than the fact that you've written, as now we sigh at your letters more than before. I don't know if Ludwika wrote you that Mama asks that you set a regular time for writing to us, so as not to delude, or rather deceive, herself so. Though I doubt whether that would help at all, since if you are going to write every two weeks, then Mama will be waiting for a letter a week in advance' (KR 77). The sympathetic Ludwika wrote to him that very same day: 'As for writing, it would make you feel uncomfortable to fix a time and wish to have it fixed. Write when you wish and when you have the mood and the opportunity. Write a lot' (KR 82). A letter from his father of 9 January 1836 was essentially one great call for correspondence. 'I know that you do not like to write; that notwithstanding, My Dear Child, I expect that a word from you would be for them (for your mother and sisters) most gratifying. […] Judge for yourself, My Dear Child, how much a 15-day delay cost us, and if you cannot write yourself for lack of time, then burden Jan [Matuszyński] with it, and add just a few words; the longer your letters, the greater our joy, but even a little news would make us no less content' (KR 110–111). In May that year, his father sent him a little poem in Polish, which, given that father and son generally corresponded in French, should be seen as an unusual occurrence.

—

Drukowałeś, prawda, ale to nie kwita,
Bo za długo do nas list Twój nie zawita.
Żeś zdrów, być to może, lecz o tym nie wiemy
I w niecierpliwości wszyscy zostajemy.
Przerywaj milczenie, pociągnij raz piórem.
A każdy z nas powie: co on robi? już wiem (KR 112).
(You printed, it's true, but that's not enough,
Since your letter has made us wait for too long.
That you're well, that may be, but we haven't a clue
And we're all left impatient for news.
Break your silence, use your pen.
And each of us will say: what's he doing? I know.)

—

His brother-in-law, Antoni Barciński, did not mince his words: 'It is not right to proceed in such a way. Waiting is burdensome. Rouse yourself and mend your ways, write more often, and you will gladden all of us who heartily and sincerely love and adore you' (KR 116). His mother, like any mother would, complained softly, though her sighs certainly afflicted his heart the most. 'Write to us often, for believe me, that when a month goes by without a letter from you, then each of us deceives the other and finds some excuse for why you do not write, so as to comfort one another, but in our souls we all think something different' (KR 116).

His sluggishness or aversion to carrying on correspondence cannot be entirely blamed for his failure to write. There were also more serious reasons.

'Words and sentences', writes Etienne Gilson, 'never keep pace with our thinking, which is quicker than speech, and they cannot define, with the utmost accuracy, meaning, which it is impossible to catch in a verbal net and wriggles away in all directions. That is always the way when, instead of simply speaking to someone, we write the most ordinary letter: "There is so much

18

more I could say to you…", "I haven't the time or the place to explain to you properly…" – and so on'.[11]

The very phenomenon of the recording of our thoughts has been sharply criticised many a time. At the top of his list of the opponents of writing, Chopin could have placed Plato, and at the bottom, his friend Adam Mickiewicz. Chopin knew that a letter is merely a pitiful shadow of our existence, and at times it is not worth picking up a pen to record the mist of our thoughts.

At the age of sixteen, he discovered that a letter can sometimes be simply misleading. 'This letter is like a field', he wrote on 8 July 1825 to Jan Białobłocki, 'in which peas and cabbage are mixed together. There is no logic…' (KS i: 48). This shows that a letter was for him a record of 'the chaos called thought', to use Paul Valéry's apt expression. Quite simply, he did not like to record his own thoughts. 'Dear friend,' he wrote to Auguste Franchomme (incidentally, he began this letter on Saturday 14 September 1833 and finished it four days later), 'Making excuses for my silence would achieve nothing. Would that my thoughts could carry themselves to the post office, without casting them onto paper!' (KS i: 228). When writing the words that were supposed to transmit his thoughts, he often found that they did not correspond to what he was thinking. But the reverse also occurred. Words he had written made him realise that his thoughts should not be transmitted to the addressee. 'I would delete it, but I haven't the time to write another sheet…', he confessed to Dominik Dziewanowski, when he realised that a factual description of his own life might be read as self-praise (KS i: 223). And so he sometimes corrected and deleted, meticulously effacing the letters. He then discovered that a letter is to a large extent a 'monitored conversation' – something that

---

[11] Etienne Gilson, *Lingwistyka a filozofia. Rozważania o stałych filozoficznych języka*, tr. Hanna Rosnerowa (Warsaw, 1975), 206; Fr. orig. *Linguistique et philosophie* (Vrin, 1969).

could have irritated Chopin, who liked to confide in someone close to him, in conversation, face to face.

Only towards the end of his life did he comprehend the real reason for his aversion to writing letters.

Zygmunt Krasiński regarded the dozen or so volumes of his letters as the 'bloody rags' and 'tatters' of his soul. Not without reason, therefore, is his extraordinary correspondence seen as an exact description of thanatological existence and representing an exhaustive depiction of 'the muddy condition of man'.[12] Chopin was the opposite. He knew that a letter was incapable of encompassing the whole wealth of the everyday existence in which man fulfils himself in a particular way, in details and continually. For example, he considered that he was unable to describe all the aspects of his conflict with Mrs Sand. 'That's why I don't write to you,' he informed his sister Ludwika on 10 February 1848, 'since whatever I start, I burn. To write so much! or better still nothing' (KR 173). And so it was impossible to relate in a letter the most important events of his life. 'I shall end,' he informed Wojciech Grzymała on 22 June 1849, 'as it is torture for me to write, even to you. So many things remain behind the pen' (KS ii: 300). Indeed, the most important substance of life remained 'behind the pen'. A letter was only a specious account of one's thoughts.

This all goes to explain why, throughout his life, Chopin wrote but few letters. If we consider that he burned some of those he had begun but not finished (KR 169) and that a sizeable part of those not burned are lost, then it is hardly surprising that we have little reliable testimony to the life of his soul. In truth, they are merely crumbs from his daily bread; but if I want to penetrate his thoughts, then I have no choice but to bore my way into every such crumb with my eyes and my soul.

---

[12] Marek Bieńczyk, *Czarny człowiek. Krasiński wobec śmierci* [Black man. Krasiński and death] (Warsaw, 1991), 175–181.

So why do I chase the shadow of a swallow that has fled into infinity? What can I read from the trail of its flight towards the Land that Truly Exists?

When Chopin wrote a letter, he was expressing in language his experience of the world. Of course, this was only a small part of his wisdom, but it was nevertheless the wisdom of Chopin himself. On such occasions, this secretive man, who masked his thoughts in various ways, 'showed himself' – to use Martin Heidegger's term – in language. He did not say everything, and at times he even lied, especially when writing to his family about his health, but nonetheless he did 'show himself' and 'express himself'. In spite of everything, therefore, we are dealing here with a genuine *Selbstdarstellung*.

We must also remember that his letters were not conceived as works of art. They served him in his everyday affairs, and so in his letters he 'showed' his thoughts spun around by the mill of life. When he wrote a letter, he 'spoke'. And he spoke in the wonderful Polish of the Warsaw intelligentsia – still vivid today.

Adam Mickiewicz called a letter a 'written conversation'.[13] Of course, this is not a dialogue in the true sense of the word, since written discourse precludes it.[14] But it is written 'talking' to another person. Moreover, the language of a letter, at least of a letter by Chopin, is only ostensibly written language. Essentially, what we have here is colloquially recorded spoken language, used principally in everyday life. It was certainly not a literary letter – a work created by an *écrivain* and not an *écrivant*. Chopin's letters, like those of Mickiewicz, are not of that ilk. That was the domain of Słowacki and Krasiński.

Yet the Chopin letter is a paradoxical and mysterious beast. It arose as spoken discourse, but the writing out of that discourse,

---

[13] Mickiewicz, *Dzieła*, xiv: 257.
[14] George Lakoff and Mark Johnson, *Metaphors We Live By* (Chicago, 1980), 87–88.

which precluded dialogue, completely eliminated the 'here and now'. From the moment it was printed, the Chopin letter transcended the time of the sender and the addressee, although it by no means took on the character of a literary text. It is beautiful and wise, yet thanks not to literature, but to the words from which Chopin composed his sentences and to the sentences in which his thoughts congealed. The world of Chopin's letters is not the world of the literary text. It remains the world of his everyday life. These letters do not refer us to a literary *'proposed world* which I could inhabit and wherein I could project one of my ownmost possibilities.'[15] They refer us to Chopin's thoughts, wearied by the torment of life, by the hustle and bustle around people, around his existence. I do not, therefore, pursue any literary analysis, but rather practise noology, since I study the images of thought which – were it not for these letters – would have dispersed into infinity.[16]

A musician is a person who is split, since he has at least two ways of writing down his thoughts. Two ways which have nothing in common, to such an extent that any elucidation of music in words, even a musicologist's professional description, is

---

[15] See Paul Ricoeur's reflections on the world of the text and the world of everyday language in his essay 'The hermeneutical function of distanciation', in *Hermeneutics and the Human Sciences*, tr. and ed. John B. Thompson (Cambridge, 1981); here at 142.

[16] According to André Lalande's dictionary, the term 'noologic' was coined by Jean-Jacques Ampère, who in *Philosophie des sciences* (1834) used it to denote all the scholarly disciplines that deal with the soul. This was also the sense in which it was still used by Etienne Gilson (*Lingwistyka a filozofia*, 157). In *Nomadology: The War Machine* by Gilles Deleuze and Felix Guattari, noology now means 'the study of images of thought and their historicity' (*Colloquia Communia*, 1988/1–3, 247). Deleuze used it in this sense in many studies. In Poland, it was brought to general attention by Bogdan Banasiak in his study *Ogród koczownika. Deleuze – rizomatyka i nomadologia* [The nomad's garden. Deleuze – risomatics and nomadology] (*Colloquia Communia*, 1988/1–3, 255) and the essay 'Samobójstwo filozofii, czyli współczesna filozofia francuska' [The suicide of philosophy, or Contemporary French philosophy] (*Twórczość*, 1989/8, 89).

incapable of penetrating its essence. My efforts concern only the extant words of Chopin. I am aware that in his letters one hears only the murmur of his everyday existence. I am aware that he placed what was most important in his music and communicated to us by means of musical notation. But it is precisely Chopin's thoughts as ground by the mill of life, jotted down between his work on a score and his supper, before leaving for some soirée, after a cup of cocoa drunk on a lonely festive morning, that interest me. I realise his letters provide inexpressibly meagre testimony. And yet they are brimful of the words of Chopin himself. *Ipsissima verba Chopini*. The shadow of a swallow luring us like an eruption of light in the dark of the universe.

CHAPTER I

INITIATION INTO EXISTENCE

The Romantics knew quite a bit about old rites of initiation. Suffice it to say that in the famous prison scene from Part III of *Forefathers' Eve* (*Dziady*), Adam Mickiewicz presented a current Polish version of collective lycanthropy: man changing into wolf. For the Romantic, every experience of youth – the family home, friendship, love, and life in the community – was a step on his initiation into knowledge of the human condition. In the now desacralised world, age-old rites naturally took on new forms, yet the initiation itself remained 'a specific dimension of human existence, since it is inseparable from man's fate'.[17]

Although we do not know what Chopin thought about the initiatory poems and novels of his day, it is clear from the composer's biography that the successive phases in his spiritual maturing conform to the typical Polish model of a young person's introduction to life. This model took shape following the demise of the Polish state, and there is nothing to suggest that at the end of the twentieth century it will suddenly disappear. As with the Vilnius students who were the peers of Mickiewicz, friendship enabled Chopin to understand the function of opposition in man's life, and love proved no more than a prelude to spiritual catastrophe. Through the ritual death of his 'I', he came to experience a crisis of identity. Like many of his peers, Chopin also had to abandon his homeland, and so he ultimately experienced the bitterness of exile, as well.

---

[17] Mircea Eliade, 'Tematy inicjacyjne w wielkich religiach' [Themes of initiation in the great religions], *Znak*, 360–361, pp. 1562–1571.

Let us now attempt to consider how his thoughts behaved when Chopin began to ascend those four steps of youth's initiation into maturity. Elsewhere at this time, initiation led towards light, but in Poland, as one might expect, it often – only too often – led deep down into a dark abyss.

1. The antinomic nature of being

Just before his second departure for Vienna, on the morning of 22 September 1830, Chopin sat down to write a letter to his best friend Tytus Woyciechowski. Tytus lived deep in the provinces, earnestly occupied, despite his young age, with running a country estate.[18] This was a most unusual friendship. In his correspondence with Tytus, Chopin employed such original wordings that some biographers, clearly misunderstanding the language of our Romantic youth, ascribed to him homosexual tendencies. The sender and the addressee were indeed fascinated with one another, but for completely different reasons than are inferred by scholars titillated by the erotic. In this relationship, subtle flights of fancy were counterbalanced by engaging sobriety, and painful uncertainty was forced to admire lightning resolve. In those times, friendship was expressed in the language of love; after all, it is ultimately perhaps indeed a form of love. The correspondence of the Philomaths of Vilnius[19] is teeming with raptures over a friend's beauty, as well as kisses and sighs. In Juliusz Słowacki's *The Thinking Hour* (*Godzina myśli*), a friend appears simply as a paramour. During that period, every young man had a male and a female paramour.

This letter was not sent by post. It was brought by Count Poletyłło, of whose daughter Tytus was secretly enamoured. In the friends' correspondence, she was referred to as 'someone'. 'Everyone talks to me about Olesia, and no one about someone',

---

[18] On Tytus Woyciechowski, see Ludwik Gawroński, 'Tytus Woyciechowski', *Ruch Muzyczny*, 1975/21.

[19] A secret student society at Vilnius University from 1817 to 1823 (tr.).

Chopin reassured his friend in a letter of 31 August that same year (KS i: 134). Tytus, in turn, kept the secret of Chopin's love when the latter had just found his 'ideal'. Indeed, the two young men employed the very same ruse: they ostentatiously adored girls about whom they were completely indifferent.

Tormented by his hidden feelings and aware of his friend's romantic anxieties, Chopin suddenly yearned for a meeting and conversation, be it in Warsaw or in Poturzyn. And that is exactly what he confessed to Tytus in the letter which he placed in Count Poletyłło's pocket. '…for god knows, that to… not the fact that you are far, far away, somewhere there beyond Hrubieszów, I would have bade you come, and I know that you would like (be it only to redeem your other huge transgressions) to bring comfort to others, even if you couldn't abide them, that I might comfort like you, I would do it, but for all that, believe me, there is no remedy, only in Vienna' (KS i: 143). They were about to travel together to Vienna, and Chopin was counting on some real conversations there.

And after this confession, he let fall a notable phrase which in some sense was intended to console, since it expressed the tribulations of both young men as a normal state of human existence:

> you live, you feel, you are lived, you are felt by others, and so you are unhappy-happy. I understand you, I penetrate your soul and… let us embrace, as nothing more can be said (KS i: 143).

This phrase reveals to us the reserves of thought about man and his condition with which Chopin set off on the journey during which his 'I' would undergo a fundamental change. So let us first take a look at the anxiety from which that remarkable thought emerged. Chopin yearned for a meeting and conversation. 'And how sad not to have someone to visit in the morning and share your sorrows and joys with; how abominable when something is weighing on your mind and there is nowhere to set it down' (KS i: 108). A conversation with Tytus would have allowed him to lexicalise the unnamed feelings concealed at the bottom of his soul. To employ his own term, he wished to 'się wyjęzyczyć' (KS i: 209), to place his heart on his tongue, since Tytus at that time was his other 'I', his alter ego, and only his face could wrest from Chopin the deeply concealed and vexing truth.

Romantic friendship was based on the conviction that the existence of 'you' was a priori self-evident. It would never have occurred to young people living in that era that this existence should first be proven. It is our sad century that likes to dabble in such subtleties. Thanks to that conviction, the Romantics succeeded in overcoming the loneliness of the Cartesian *cogito*. The spirit of Tytus was for Chopin just as real as the tree growing outside his window, since he lived in Chopin's 'I' with his most intimate secret. 'And I am glad that my heart has engulfed the secret,' he wrote on 31 August 1830, 'that in me ends what in you begins. And be glad that in me you have a chasm into which you can hurl everything without fear, as if into another you, for your spirit has long since lain there at the very bottom' (KS i: 134). So Chopin regarded Tytus as his other 'I', his alter ego. This secret cemented their friendship, which was clearly built on the emotional act that precedes thinking, on the sensing of a mutual penetration of spirits. '…I penetrate your spirit…', 'your spirit has long since lain there [that is, in the soul of Chopin, who is Tytus's other 'I'] at the very bottom…' Novalis encapsulated a similar experience most succinctly: 'I am you'.[20]

---

[20] Novalis, 'Poetycyzmy 96' [Poeticisms 96], in *Uczniowie z Sais. Proza filozoficzna – studia – fragmenty* [The Novices of Sais. Philosophical prose, studies and fragments], choice and tr. Jerzy Prokopiuk (Warsaw, 1984), 200.

Only this type of experience allowed him to form the notion that the anxiety which was tormenting both him and Tytus was part of human existence: 'you live, you feel, you are lived, you are felt by others, and so you are unhappy-happy'.

So first you live. That means that you are. You exist. The idea was merely stating the obvious: the phenomenon of existence. But Chopin still needed an assertion resulting from a stronger conviction of his existence. After all, we say in Polish: 'Czuję, że żyję' [I feel I'm alive]. For it is impossible to exist without feeling that you are alive, as Chopin would soon come to realise. And so I know that I exist because my mind tells me about it, and I feel that I exist because my senses tell me about it. That much can be read from the two verbs used at first in the active.

Yet this was clearly insufficient for Chopin to be able to define the substance of human existence, and in order to express his idea, he suddenly did something unusual, something he actually rather enjoyed. He violated the language.

'To live' and 'to feel' are intransitive verbs and do not form a passive, since, like the verb 'to be', in the sense of 'to exist', they are the expression of – to quote Etienne Gilson – 'the most fundamental subjective action, that is, an action which is enclosed within the subject itself and does not need a complement in another subject'.[21] And so the verbs 'to live' and 'to feel' are fundamental verbs not because they say something about the subject, but because 'they present the subject to us', as Alfred Gawroński writes about words of this kind, 'as an agent of the primary act, the act of existence'. The active and passive forms, meanwhile, make it possible to 'build synonymous sentences with a different surface structure. Thanks to the correlation of

---

[21] Quoted in Alfred Gawroński, 'Kiedy "być" znaczy "istnieć". Z archeologii pytań metafizycznych' [When 'to be' means 'to exist'. Of the archaeology of metaphysical questions], *Znak – Idee*, 2 (1990), 14–15.

these two forms of sentence, the grammar of language makes it possible – I would even say inclines one – to see the same states or actions from *two different points of view*'.[22] Chopin was clearly interested in availing himself of these possibilities. To exist means to be a subject and an object. To act and to be subject to action. You live and feel, and so you are an agent. You are 'lived' and 'felt' by others, and so you are a patient. You only live when you know that you live for yourself and for others.[23] This conviction moved Chopin away from extreme forms of Romantic individualism. In different variants and approaches, this will wind through all his correspondence, until his death. In a word, for Chopin, existence for oneself was always linked to existence for others.

In respect to the parallelism that integrates the excerpt in question, this utterance should be read in the following way: because you live and feel, you are unhappy. Thus existence in itself is unhappiness. However, because you are 'felt' and 'lived' by others, you can extricate yourself from that gloomy condition. It is not that you are experienced and felt by others, but that you are the life and sentiment of another. Only on this condition can your existence be happy. These subtleties are mere speculation. Although the structure of the text lends them considerable weight, I do not insist on their verity.

---

[22] Gawroński, *Dlaczego Platon wykluczył poetów z państwa? U źródeł współczesnych badań nad językiem* [Why did Plato exclude poets from his republic? At the origins of contemporary research into language], foreword Zygmunt Kubiak (Warsaw, 1984), 235. On the distribution into agent and patient, see Roman Jakobson's study 'Boas' Views on Grammatical Meaning', in *Selected Writings II. Word and Language* (The Hague, 1971).

[23] Later, the Other was supplanted by the Unknown. 'I am speaking of Georg Groddeck,' wrote Freud, 'who is never tired of insisting that what we call our ego behaves essentially passively in life, and that, as he expresses it, we are "lived" by unknown and uncontrollable forces'. In *The Ego and the Id*, tr. Joan Riviere (London, 1927); rev. for *The Standard Edition of the Complete Psychological Works of Sigmund Freud*, ed. James Strachey (New York, 1961), 13.

However, this text testifies beyond all doubt that for Chopin existence had an antinomic character, since the definition of existence comprises two semantically opposed, but equally true, parts. Existence is unhappy-happy. This is an antonym, a pair of words linked by semantic contrast. In this instance, the contrast is particularly distinct, since the opposite of the word 'happiness' is not some separate word, as in the case of beautiful/ugly, but its brutal and unambiguous contradiction: un-happiness. So for Chopin, to exist meant to feel both happiness, all kinds of good fortune and auspiciousness, and also its lack, comprising horror, injury, grief, pain, despair and God knows what else besides.

It was already noted a long, long time ago that certain phenomena which by their very nature appear to be homogeneous are in fact internally contradictory. They have generally been defined by means of antonyms. For example, love is known to be at once both sweet and bitter, *glykypikron*, *dulce amarum*. That is how Sappho described it at the dawn of civilisation. That is how Marsilio Ficino spoke of it during the Renaissance.[24] For us, meanwhile, it is crucial that in Part II of *Forefathers' Eve*, the Polish 'manifesto' of romanticism, Adam Mickiewicz defined existence by means of this very antonym. *Forefathers' Eve* was read by all young Poles in their formative years. Everyone wanted to know the poetry of the Vilnius bard, and Chopin scoured the bookshops of Warsaw in order to lay his hands on some edition of Mickiewicz's works, since his friend Jan Białobłocki, who lived in the remote village of Sokołowo, wished to have the texts at home (KS i: 74). Adam Mickiewicz told Chopin's generation about the mysteries of existence. And here is the first transcendental truth revealed to the people gathered in the cemetery chapel during a supernatural conversation with the spirits of their dead ancestors:

---

[24] See Edgar Wind, *Pagan Mysteries in the Renaissance* (New Haven, 1958), 135.

—

Bo słuchajcie i zważcie u siebie,
że według Bożego rozkazu:
Kto nie doznał goryczy ni razu,
Ten nie dozna słodyczy w niebie.[25]
(For listen and ponder within you,
according to God's vital order:
He who never once bitterness tasted
Ne'er will sweetness encounter in heaven.)

—

The trial of life, the period of a soul's material sojourn, has been presented here as an experience of contradictions, since human existence is clearly of an antinomic character. Human time is filled with dismay, and heaven is open only to those who experienced unhappiness during their earthly existence. The taste of sweetness means nothing without knowing the taste of bitterness. Human time cannot be reduced to pleasures. Existence has a bitter-sweet taste.

And so Chopin took from friendship the conviction that human fate is played out through an interpenetration of 'I' and 'you', and existence itself is filled with painful contradictions. Reading Mickiewicz could only have reinforced this conviction. In those days, such thoughts were a sign of maturing. With them, a young man set out on his way through life, on which he would encounter the next step on his initiation into existence: the passage through the fire of romantic love.

---

[25] Mickiewicz, *Dzieła*, iii:17.

2. The oracular romances of a Pole

In Chopin's times, the word 'romance' had several meanings. First and foremost, it was a literary term, signifying a large epic work with a tortuous plot and dramatic swings of fortune, which usually told of a great love – perhaps a little sad, but certainly not violent. Chivalrous and sentimental novels were romances.[26] That explains why, when recalling his 'Poturzyn adventures' in a letter to Tytus Woyciechowski of 21 August 1830, Chopin wrote: 'I can tell you sincerely that it gives me pleasure to remember it all – your fields left me with a yearning – that birch outside the windows is fixed in my memory. That arbalest! – how romantic!' (KS i: 130). It also explains why, when concluding an account of the difficulties connected with his second trip to Vienna, his parents' plans for him and his passport troubles, Chopin summarised it all succinctly: 'That's the whole romance' (KS i: 141). And it explains why Chopin wrote about the Adagio from the E minor Concerto that it was not 'powerful', but 'more romance-like, calm, melancholic' (KS i: 125). For his love did indeed prove more sad than passionate.

Then, as now, this word was associated with very mundane matters, but in this case there is a difference between former and more contemporary times. For us, a romance is always a passing – albeit perhaps powerful – erotic adventure. In Chopin's times, it signified amorous intoxication, bewitchment, melancholy passion.

---

[26] Euzebiusz Słowacki, *Prawidła wymowy i poezji* [The rules of oratory and poetry] (Vilnius, 1826), 281. On the term 'romance', see Alina Witkowska, preface, in *Polski romans sentymentalny* [The Polish sentimental romance] (Wrocław, 1971), XV–XVII.

During the Romantic era, a young Pole could at times be mad enough to allow himself just a single romance – and not necessarily with a girl. As Maurycy Mochnacki admitted, 'the sole romance of my youth was a mighty, independent Poland'.[27] And most amusingly, it was true. His passionate love for his homeland filled his life to the brim and turned him into a fanatic of political philosophy. This happens in Poland very often, particularly when, instead of a girl, a young Pole falls in love with that mythical many-headed monster – his own nation.

Fortunately, a Romantic young man did sometimes have two romances. Without – God forbid! – neglecting his homeland, for the sake of balance, in accordance with divine and human law, he also bestowed his feelings upon a maiden. In that way, he avoided the wild one-sidedness that leads a man's thoughts onto brigandish pathways, especially during his youth. And so, like Adam Mickiewicz, Fryderyk Chopin underwent a 'normal' romantic initiation into the mysteries of existence: in equal measure he loved both a girl and Poland, thus ensuring himself of not one, but two causes of the 'ruffling' of his 'I'. If by some miracle he managed to avoid the trap that Poland had set for him, he would still have been snared by the girl.

Chopin's girl was Konstancja Gładkowska.[28] She was a singer, trained at the Warsaw Conservatory by Evasio Carlo Soliva. She made her operatic debut in 1830. Her voice graced the composer's farewell concert in the capital, and her ambiguous verse embellished his album.

---

[27] Quoted from Jerzy Szacki, *Historia jedynego romansu. Opowieść o Mochnackim* [The story of a romance. A tale of Mochnacki] (Warsaw, 1958), 7.

[28] See Krystyna Kobylańska, 'Sylwetki wokalistów na tle życia Chopina. Konstancja z Gładkowskich Grabowska' [Profiles of singers against the background of Chopin's life. Konstancja Grabowska, née Gładkowska], *Życie Śpiewacze*, 1948/3. Also Zbigniew Lipowski, 'Muza Chopina' [Chopin's muse], *Ruch Muzyczny*, 1989/20.

The very first mention of Chopin's having been struck by Cupid's arrow bids us assign this sentiment to the realm of rather uncommon experience: '…as I already have, perhaps to my misfortune,' Chopin informed Tytus on 3 October 1829, 'my ideal, whom I faithfully serve, without having talked to her for half a year, of whom I dream, in memory of whom the adagio of my concerto was written, who inspired that little waltz this morning, which I enclose' (KS i: 107). This infatuation did indeed augur misfortune, if only because for six months Chopin could not pluck up the courage to let the girl know that he was seriously interested. So what lay behind that timidity?

The blow was mighty. 'When I consider myself,' he wrote to Tytus on 22 September 1830, 'I feel so sorry that somehow I often lose consciousness. If I have something that interests me before my eyes, horses could trample me and I'd know nothing about it, and I nearly had such an accident on the street the other day; on Sunday, struck by a single unexpected glance in church, just as I was experiencing some delightful torpor, I immediately ran out, and for quarter of an hour I didn't know what had happened to me. And on meeting Doctor Parys, I didn't know how to explain to him my confusion, and I had to blame a dog that had supposedly got caught under my feet and I had stepped over. At times, I go so mad that it's frightful' (KS i: 142). Precisely! During the Romantic era, amorous misery ironically began in a place of worship, beneath the eye of God. Here is an extract from Juliusz Słowacki's *The Thinking Hour*:

—

Bo nieraz wśród ciemnego tłumami kościoła,
Którą z klęczących dziewic natrafiwszy losem,
Wołali na nią silnie niemym duszy głosem;
Wtenczas twarz odwracała od Pańskiego stoła
I pośród tłumu ludzi jej wzrok, w zadziwieniu,
Nieobłędnie rzucony, na twarz dzieci padał,

Jak gdyby na wołanie duszy odpowiadał...[29]
(For sometimes midst a dark church's crowds,
With the soul's mute voice, they called out loudly
To some kneeling virgin whom fate had preferred;
Then she would turn her face from the Lord's table
And her gaze, in surprise, but not distractedly cast
Among the crowd would fall upon the face of children
As if answering the call of the soul...)

—

So Chopin was enslaved by a single glance from a girl; and that helplessness was new to him, since in friendship he was able to guide his emotions. He could restrain and postpone them till later, to enhance his inner joy (KS i: 138). What is more, with Tytus he could fight in some way: '...I know that I love you; I wish you would also love me constantly and more and more, and that's why I scribble so much. It's often the case that someone who wants to make things better actually makes them worse. And I think that in you I can make nothing either better or worse. – The fondness that I have for you will force your heart, through supernatural means, to feel a similar fondness. You are not master of your thoughts, but I am master, and I will not be abandoned like trees allow themselves to lose that greenness which characterises them, which gives them joy and life' (KS i: 140). In his love for a girl, however, he proved completely defenceless and as if paralysed, bewitched, although not possessed. He was afraid of her reaction and trembled at the thought of ridicule.

He also knew that love is a great test for one's 'I'. Here, he writes to Tytus shortly before leaving the country:

I do not, however, mean to stay in Warsaw, and if you have any suspicions of love, as have many people in Warsaw, then

[29] Słowacki, *Dzieła wszystkie*, ii:82–83.

reject them and convince yourself that I can be above everything where my 'I' is concerned, and if I was in love I would
be able to conceal that miserable and impotent fervour for
a few years yet (KS i: 138).

Quite clearly, he was unaware what the concealment of
his feelings might inflict upon him. There is no way of knowing why he considered that revealing his love would bring him
dishonour. Neither do we know if it was 'miserable' by nature
and why it should be hidden, or if it only became 'impotent'
when hidden away in the depths of his heart. Whatever the
case may be, he defined it with a word that presented love as
something slightly comical, since 'fervour' renders amorous
endeavours somewhat less serious. Be that as it may, Chopin
considered that the honour of his 'I' was being tested by the
choice between remaining with his beloved in Warsaw and
journeying abroad to pursue his musical career. But as yet he
had no idea that the balance of his 'I' depended above all on
that singularly tortuous love.

The threat of spiritual crisis was serious, since Chopin was
aware that his complicated feelings had enslaved his thoughts
entirely. 'Just as, involuntarily, something has entered my head
through my eyes and I like to caress it, perhaps most wrongly'
(KS i: 125). And so he took delight in thinking about the love
which – so he supposed – would bring him catastrophe. Like
Gustaw in Part IV of Mickiewicz's *Forefathers' Eve*. So he still
savoured the bitter-sweet taste of existence.

I would gladly reject the thoughts that poison my cheerful-
ness, yet I feel delight in caressing them, I don't know myself
what I am lacking, and perhaps after writing this letter I will
be calmer, since you know how pleasant it is for me to write
to you (KS i: 121).

Yet before leaving the country for the second time, Chopin plucked up the courage and probably confessed to his sweetheart what he felt for her. As custom dictated, some keepsakes were exchanged. As far as we know, Konstancja Gładkowska did not tell him 'no'. It is likely that she allowed him to 'have hope'. And so again uncertainty and dreams. Again the sweetness and bitterness of life. The little poems which she wrote into his album are unequivocally ambiguous:

—

> Przykre losu spełniasz zmiany,
> Ulegać musim potrzebie.
> Pamiętaj, niezapomniany,
> Że w Polsce kochają Ciebie (A 14).[30]
> (Sorry twists of fate you weave,
> Yet yield we must to fortune.
> Remember well, as now you leave,
> In Poland they do love you.)

—

We do not know whether she spoke in the name of all Poland, paying tender tribute to his talent, or whether she was writing on her own behalf alone, pierced by Cupid's arrow. In those days, the third person plural or simply an impersonal form was

---

[30] The second poem, written that same day, 25 October 1830, reads as follows:

—

> 'Ażeby wieniec sławy w niezwiędły zamienić,
> Rzucasz lubych przyjaciół i rodzinę drogą;
> Mogą Cię obcy lepiej nagrodzić, ocenić,
> Lecz od nas kochać mocniej pewno Cię nie mogą'.
> (For to render the laurels of glory immortal,
> You abandon your dear friends and family.
> Yet while others may better appraise and reward you,
> They certainly can't love you better than we.)

—

In Paris, Chopin gave a brief comment to this assurance: 'mogą' ('they can') (KR 287).

often used instead of the first person singular, out of emotional self-restraint. Chopin himself proceeded in this way.

Of course, after Tytus had left to join the uprising in Warsaw, when Chopin remained in Vienna alone, there ensued an explosion of great emotions. Here is his reaction to some snippets of news from Warsaw: '…a certain period', he wrote to Jan Matuszyński, 'saddened me greatly. Is there really at least a little change? Is it not illness? I would easily suppose something of the sort on such a tender creature. Did you not imagine it? Perhaps fright at the 29th? For God forbid that it be on my account. Reassure, say that as long as there's strength enough… that unto death… that after death my ashes will be cast underfoot' (KS i: 162–163). That is just how the Romantic idea of eternal love, unafraid even of the grave, even of eternity, was expressed in those times.[31] The feeling of jealousy also appeared quite soon, although the Russian officers besieging the young lady were swept from the capital during the insurrection. Uncertainty returned, yet in the end Chopin realised that his passion was beginning slowly to wane. 'Her picture before my eyes!' he wrote in his album in April 1831, 'it seems I don't love her, and yet she never leaves my mind' (A 33).

Her image returned once again in Stuttgart, when Chopin took up his album to write out the impressions that thronged his mind at news of the storming of Warsaw. Interestingly, when he thought about his beloved, his fancy did not suggest the idea

---

[31] Cf. Mickiewicz, *Dzieła*, i:153:

—

'I chcę rozmawiać tylko serca biciem,
I westchnieniami, i całowaniami,
I tak rozmawiać godziny, dni, lata,
Do końca świata i po końcu świata'.
(And only through heartbeats I'll talk,
And through sighs, and through kisses,
And converse thus for hours, for days, for years,
Till the end of the world and beyond.)

—

of rape, as in the case of his sisters. 'What has become of her? Where is she? – The poor thing! – Perhaps in Muscovite hands! – A Russian is pushing – strangling – murdering, killing her!' (A 36). So a Russian soldier could have been pushing or even strangling Konstancja, but could not have dishonoured her. Chopin did not imagine such a thing. Like every Romantic 'lover', Konstancja was sacred, and nothing could slight her. The fleeting thought of her death soon evaporated, and Chopin played the role of consoler: 'Ah, my life, I'm here alone – come to me – I'll dry your tears…' (A 36). Thus he embarked on a broken conversation, and began with words which in his letters he reserved for those closest to him, such as his two sisters, Tytus, Jan Matuszyński, Julian Fontana and Wojciech Grzymała: 'My life…'

God only knows how musicians came to take a liking to this expression. In many of Monteverdi's madrigals, the sweetheart is sung of as 'anima mia' or 'mio bene', but the expression 'mia vita' also occurs very often. In the second act of *Orfeo*, to a libretto by Alessandro Striggio, the hero says to Eurydice: 'Tu se' morta, mia vita, ed io respiro'. Similarly, in the conclusion of *L'incoronazione di Poppea*, to a libretto by Gian Francesco Busenelli, Nero sings of his beloved 'mio tesoro', 'mio ben' and 'mio cor', since the lovers cannot find the words to express their feelings, but he also cries out twice 'mia vita'. In Beethoven's letter to the Immortal Beloved, alongside such cries as 'my angel', 'my very self' and 'my all', we also find 'my life'.[32] Nowadays, the sacramental 'my life' can often be heard in pop songs.

This seemingly worn expression betrays Chopin's unusual view on existence, all the more valuable for being uttered without reflection. Words, like dreams, sometimes reveal a thought that lies hidden at the very bottom of one's 'I'. So I shall take a more precise look at this expression.

---

[32] George R. Marek, *Beethoven. Biography of a Genius* (London, 1974), 295–296.

The full uniting of one's 'I' with an Other, which during the Romantic era – as already mentioned – could take place in friendship or in love, occurred not only when one soul absorbed another. 'Because I is someone else', as Artur Rimbaud would later write in a letter to Paul Demeny on 15 May 1871.[33] During the thirties of that extraordinary century, Fryderyk Chopin dared to claim that someone else was his existence. Some Other could not only fill his soul, but could also become his life. In this way, Konstancja, articulated or left unsaid, like the soul of Tytus he had subsumed, ceased to be an object of cognition and became a presence. Notably, in such instances he often wrote the word 'Life' with a capital letter, as if it were meant to replace a name, the sign of a particular person. So to love someone like one's own existence meant more for Chopin than to love him as one's own 'I', since for him the existence of 'I' was more crucial than the 'I' in itself. He held the existence of a being to be more important than the being itself. That is why Chopin was so incredibly earthly. That is why he loved life and people so wisely. Admittedly, I am not convinced that Gładkowska deserved it, but at the end of the day love is not a question of merit; what interests me is Chopin's thoughts, and not that girl's great bungling.

That address to his beloved also had an amusing side. 'Ah, my Life, I'm here alone – come to me – I'll dry your tears, I'll heal your wounds of the present – reminding you of the past. Then, before the Russians arrived. When only a few Muscovites most ardently sought your favours, and you laughed at them, as I was there – [word deleted] I, not Grab[owski]!' (A 36). So at first he wanted to mollify the horrors of the present with recollections of pleasanter times, 'before the Russians arrived', but

---

[33] *Ja to ktoś inny. Korespondencja Artura Rimbauda* [I is someone else. The correspondence of Artur Rimbaud], selection, tr. and ed. Julia Hartwig and Artur Międzyrzecki (Warsaw, 1979), 59.

he immediately remembered that there were Russians in Warsaw before the uprising, and that his sweetheart aroused a certain interest among them.

There is nothing I can do about our magnificent patriots transforming even the erotic into a national affair and often confusing the honour of Poland with the temperament of our young ladies. Thus in the Warsaw of the Congress Kingdom, they were unceasingly under the powerful sway of public opinion. Of course, Russian officers circled nearby, which in the case of Konstancja Gładkowska and her friend Anna Wołkow was not so difficult. After all, officer gentlemen were free to admire the talents of female singers, although, understandably, young Poles, especially civilians, were none too impressed by such a love for music. But most interesting for us is that from his recollections of that Muscovite wooing, Chopin's thoughts immediately leapt to self-admiration. When Chopin was with her, Konstancja laughed at her military admirers. He and only he was her chosen one. Had Józef Grabowski then found himself at her side instead of Chopin, then the Russians would have had the better chance. Chopin was informed that after his departure from Warsaw a sober-minded and financially secure rival had appeared, one who might seriously count on success. Hence our composer tried to ridicule him in his own eyes. As he was uncertain of Konstancja's feelings, he turned Grabowski into a comical mediocrity. That is just what lovers do when their fate has been preordained or when they have sealed their fate themselves.

He took the news of their wedding in rather good heart. When a romantic drama perishes in the flames of history, a man does not have a sense of his own defeat. That explains how rejected lovers in Poland do not often descend into wild frustration. 'Miss Gładkowska', he wrote to Tytus on 12 December 1831 from Paris, 'has married Grabowski, but that does not affect platonic affection' (KS i: 203).[34] He then went on to give a wonderful description of a 'quarrel with Pixis', as if lifted straight out of Molière's *L'école des femmes*. Johann Peter Pixis, aged forty-four at the time, was grooming for his wife a 'very pretty fifteen-year-old lass'. Chopin played the role of the young seducer, resolved to thwart the plans of that lecherous 'old man'. So no despair, but a great deal of laughter.

Thus Chopin's romance with Konstancja proceeded in accordance with the rules of romantic love. Here is Adam Mickiewicz:

> It appears that passion, without losing any of its strength, but running up against increasingly numerous hindrances of law, calculation and decency, and refraining from brute vengeance, has taken on, at least in the north, the character of a sombre and introverted sorrow, as distinct from the pious resignation of mediaeval lovers and the loquacious sentimentality of French and German romances.[35]

This 'introverted sorrow', at times cast deep into the secret hiding places of consciousness, was the work of an equally deeply hidden love. The Romantics were only too familiar with the drama of inexpressible thoughts. They also knew what a pernicious source of frustration is a love not expressed in words. Here is what one of the youngsters says in Słowacki's poem *The Thinking Hour*, written most probably at the end of 1832:

> —
> Szczęśliwy! twoje myśli świetniej w słowach płoną,
> Niż gdy w sercu zamknięte – moje myśli gasną,
> Słów nie cierpią – lecz nieraz w godzinie tajemnic

---

[34] The wedding was held on 31 January 1832 in the Cathedral of Saint John in Warsaw. Chopin must have been informed of the banns. Gładkowska's decision was very sensible, as a question mark had arisen over the continuation of her artistic career in post-Rising Warsaw.

[35] Mickiewicz, *Dzieła*, v:241–242.

Tłumnymi słowy w piersiach jak szatany wrzasną
I wołają, ażebym je wypuścił z ciemnic.
Abym je wywiódł na świat – słów otworzył drogę[36].
(Happy you! your thoughts burn more splendidly in words
Than in a heart concealed – my thoughts expire,
and words cannot abide – but at times in the hour of mysteries
They scream thronged words in my breast like devils
And call me to release them from their darkness.
For me to lead them into the world – to open the path
of words.)

—

Thoughts kept shut inside a heart usually began to expire, and when dying they wreaked havoc in a mind. In Chopin's case, such a situation triggered the ineluctable disintegration of his 'I', and when, one night in Stuttgart, he drew them from his breast and out into the world, when he verbalised his thoughts on paper, it turned out that this 'introverted sorrow' had turned him into a Romantic 'living corpse'.

His romance with Poland brought an equally bitter experience, albeit of a somewhat different kind.

---

[36] Słowacki, *Dzieła wszystkie*, ii:83. The two protagonists of this poem, Ludwik Spitznagel and Juliusz Słowacki, were linked by a secret very similar to that which bound Chopin and Tytus. The former was in love with Aniela Rdułtowska, the latter with Ludwika Śniadecka. 'The difference in nature between Ludwik and Julek can be conceived and denoted in nothing else like in those half-childish feelings of the heart. Ludwik, even though several years his elder, would sooner have had himself chopped into pieces than dare to betray in front of an elder his adoration of her, let alone his feelings, although both feelings and adoration filled his entire soul at that time' (Antoni Edward Odyniec, *Listy z podróży* [Letters from abroad] (Warsaw, 1961), i:455–456). Spitznagel ceased to conceal his passion, but even so the whole thing ended in disaster. During a stay on the Rdułtowskis' estate, 'on the second day at breakfast', we read in a letter of 19 March 1827 sent by Salomea Bécu, Słowacki's mother, to Odyniec, 'with them he was merry, then after breakfast he went to his room and shot himself in the heart. [...] he made no secret of his love for Anielka.' (*W kręgu bliskich poety. Listy rodziny Juliusza Słowackiego* [In the poet's intimate circle. Letters of Juliusz Słowacki's family] (Warsaw, 1960), 214).

As is our Polish way, the homeland appeared at once beside the girl, like a crazed, domineering mother, jealous of her son. It also soon visited upon him the pain of thoughts split between here and there. Initially, he resided here, in Vienna, and longed for there, for Warsaw, but when Poland found herself in great danger, his thoughts suddenly began to dwell there, in the Polish capital. And so melancholy was replaced by the pain of splitting. Here remained only his corporeal shell, and Chopin could have said to his acquaintances in Vienna what a few years later Adam Mickiewicz said to his friends in exile:

—

Gdy tu mój trup w pośrodku was zasiada,

W oczy zagląda wam i głośno gada,

Dusza w ten czas daleka, ach, daleka,

Błąka się i...[37]

(While my corpse among you sits,

Looks you in the eye and talks out loud,

My soul is far, ah, far away,

Wandering and...)

—

...running across the street in his native city, sitting in his room in his parents' home and waiting for his friends at the theatre. 'So write, before you depart [for the front]', he wrote to Jan Matuszyński on Boxing Day 1830, '(*poste-restante* to Vienna), before you leave, call on my Parents, on Cons... [Konstancja]. Stand in for me while you're with them. Call often, may my sisters see you, may they think that you're calling on me and that I'm in the other room; sit down beside them and may they think that I'm sitting behind you. Go to the theatre, and I'll come too' (KS i: 164).

So Chopin began to exist actually not here, but there. 'I don't know what's happening to me. I love you more than life. Write to me. You're in the army! She, in Radom? Have you

---

[37] Mickiewicz, *Dzieła*, i:377.

dug the embankments? Our poor parents. What are my friends doing? I live with you' (KS i: 169). So he began to reside in two places at once: his body in one place, his soul wandering about the other. Vienna, although a specific location, was meaningless, ostensible, alien, even hostile. As for a man who flees into a symbolic reality, for Chopin, the imaginary spaces, which in maturity he would call 'espaces imaginaires', were full of meaning, assimilated, his own. Suddenly, the imagined became the more real. From the point of view of value, the world perceived by the senses became the less significant. Wholly unexpectedly, his romance with his homeland brought with it the conviction that thoughts can free a person from the unbearable material concreteness of the world.

The split was inevitable, but its particularly acute character was determined by rather trivial circumstances.

Since he dwelt there both awake and in his dreams, it is not surprising that he followed the sequence of events back home most diligently. Above all, he assiduously read the Vienna newspapers (KS i: 164). He may also have perused the Polish dailies. From the handful of extant letters, we know that he was even familiar with particular details. For example, he knew which front Jan Matuszyński was heading for. He regretted that the insurgents had not hung the loathed traitor General Aleksander Rożniecki, head of the secret police in the Congress Kingdom. 'But Whiskers (as you already know)', he wrote '– whiskers, cry-baby, it's a pity that abominable musical papa is not ringing. How beautiful that would be, for instance, for the finale to *La gazza*, such a guardian bell…' (KS i: 165). Quite! A brute swinging on a rope to the beat of Rossini's music. Macabre or cruel? Like all his generation, Chopin had a healthy attitude towards the feeling of vengeance. For him, revenge was an act of sacred justice. It was due to an offended conscience. It had nothing to do with bloodthirstiness. So one is hardly surprised at Chopin ruing that, on 29 November,

Rożniecki managed to slither out of Warsaw, although his effigy was indeed hung – on Leszno Street. Chopin's feelings chimed with the sentiments expressed on many printed leaflets, exuding hate for the General, such as 'A lamppost on ul. Leszno talks with Rożniecki', or even the famous offer made somewhat later by the cobbler Tomasz Kmitowski, who promised 'a hundred pairs of shoes with shoe-trees' for whoever caught the scoundrel and brought him to Warsaw.[38]

And then this man, so engrossed in his nation's struggle for existence, suddenly encountered a cavalier disdain for Polishness. The Viennese, inhabitants of the capital of one of the powers that had violated Poland, had formed a certain stereotype of Poles that typifies the attitude of citizens of oppressive states. It most probably arose during Saxon times, a period of Poland's betrayal and fall. In any case, it was well established in Vienna already before the First Partition. In 1770, Franciszek Karpiński found himself in Vienna. 'My residence in Vienna was soured,' he wrote, 'besides my poor health, by the Germans' generalised contempt for my nation. At the town hall there during my stay, one man from the populace wrangled with another and lost his estate that the other had called him a Pole, which for them is the greatest kind of invective'.[39] In 1830, while dining at an Italian trattoria, Chopin overheard: '"Der liebe Gott hat einen Fehler gemacht, dass er die Polen geschaffen hat" [The good Lord made a mistake creating the Poles], and so don't be surprised', he wrote to Matuszyński, 'that I don't know how to write very well what I feel. And don't expect any news from the Pole, since the other man replied: "In Polen ist nicht zu holen" ['There's

---

[38] *Kurier Polski* of 24 February 1831. According to other sources, this cobbler was called Kłopotowski. See Jan Nepomucen Janowski, *Notatki autobiograficzne 1803–1855* [Autobiographical notes] (Wrocław, 1950), 187–188.

[39] Franciszek Karpiński, *Historia mego wieku i ludzi, z którymi żyłem* [The story of my age and the people with whom I lived], ed. Roman Sobol (Warsaw, 1987), 72.

nothing to be got in Poland]. – Scoundrels!' (KS i: 165). In this situation, Chopin's ostentatious accentuation of his Polishness was rather an understandable reflex and would not appear to have been of a mawkish and artificial character, although it might grate today with a sophisticated European.[40] 'Today I'm dining at Mrs Szaszek's,' wrote Chopin in July 1831, 'I'm taking buttons with Polish eagles and a handkerchief with a scythesman. I've written a polonaise, which I have to leave Würfel. I received the portrait of our commander in chief, General Skrzynecki, but awfully impaired and pockmarked from cholera' (KR 75).

Gestures of this kind were compensation for the feeling of guilt that arose as soon as he received the news that an uprising had broken out in Warsaw. At first, he had wished to do what his friends were doing. In such instances, every Pole wants to take up arms; everyone around is looking for guns and sharpening their bayonet's steel on their father's gravestone. At such times, it is a sacred duty to subordinate one's life to the needs of the homeland. Admittedly, in those days Polish society was quite reasonable and showed elegant magnanimity in releasing its musicians from this obligation. Only poets were not let off. Live as you write! But young musicians were reluctant to avail themselves of this exemption. 'The last private thing that I remember about Chopin', wrote Eugeniusz Skrodzki, 'was the letter he wrote to his parents shortly after the events of November 1830 in Warsaw, expressing a burning desire to return home. His father, alarmed at this noble intention, could barely persuade his son that he would more effectively serve his country with his art than by taking up a rifle with too weak a hand' (KR 66). Of course, it was more rational to remain abroad, but there was a price to be paid for such a decision.

It began with irresolution. 'I was supposed to go and listen to Pasta. You know that I have letters from the Saxon court for the

---

[40] E.g. Adam Zamoyski, *Chopin* (London, 2010).

viceroy of Milan. – But how can I go? My parents bid me do as I wish, and I don't like to. To Paris? The locals advise me to wait a while. Return home? – Stay here? – Kill myself?' (KS i: 164). At the same time, a complex of uselessness appears. 'My God, both she and my sisters can serve at least with lints, and I... Were it not for the fact that I would perhaps be a burden now for my father, I would return at once. I curse the day I left, and admit, knowing my disposition, that since Tytus left too much has fallen upon me at once' (KS i: 162). There is a recurring idea throughout Chopin's correspondence that life only has any value when it is useful for others. He had absolutely no interest in living just for himself. Creative artists are often dreadfully egotistic, but Chopin was not of their ilk. And please don't speak to me of any exceptional privileges that he demanded for himself while working. They were not privileges, just essential conditions. In any case, every man's work is sacrosanct and should not be disturbed.

So in Chopin's case, a sense of duty towards the homeland borders on a desire to be useful. This is natural in a man who treated his life as a service to others. But Chopin could not rid himself of the idea that in this instance he should serve his homeland with gun in hand. 'You're going to war', he wrote to Jan Matuszyński. 'Come back a colonel. May you succeed. Why can I not even drum?' (KS i: 170). In an unsent version of this letter, the passage in question reads: 'Why can't I be with you, why can't I be a drummer-boy?!!' (KS i: 168). Goodness me! I can just see him now, as he walks in a hurried march alongside his friends, drumming them to attack. He'd catch his death of cold!

Reflecting on his unusual situation, Chopin arrived at the conclusion that 'in the artistic field' he would serve neither his homeland nor his family by staying in Vienna. 'Not only do they scare off the local audiences', he wrote to Józef Elsner on 29 January 1831, 'with a constant stream of unworthy piano concertos, ruining that kind of music, but above all, what has occurred

51

in Warsaw has altered my situation for the worse, perhaps as much as in Paris it might work to my benefit' (KS i: 170–171). Additionally, Chopin's thoughts were torn between music and the needs of his homeland. Nothing he could have done 'in the artistic field' could have obscured his sense of the uselessness of an artist at a time when Poland found herself in mortal danger. To Chopin's mind, his country did not demand of him fame. It required civic service. The appeals of his father and of Stefan Witwicki tipped the scales towards common sense, but they did not expunge the sense of guilt from his mind.

Johann Malfatti, court physician to the Austrian emperor, was married to a Pole, Helena Ostrowska, and held a great affection for our country. He gave a regal reception to Chopin, and even treated him to special Polish dishes. During musical soirées, there was obviously discussion of that antinomy, which Malfatti regarded as concocted and frivolous. Chopin disagreed entirely. He wrote to Elsner: 'Yet from the day I learned of the events of 29 Nov. up to the present, I have had nothing but worrying fears and longing; and Malfatti vainly endeavours to convince me that every artist is cosmopolitan. Even if that were so, as an artist I am still in the cradle, but as a Pole I've already started my third decade' (KS i: 170).

The romance with the girl left his 'I' in complete disarray. The romance with his homeland, meanwhile, propelled Chopin into a conflict between art and the duties arising from historical existence. His existence was mundane, concrete, corporeal. His art was abstract, raised to the heavens, over and above the passage of time. The blood of his friends, and notes upon paper: for Chopin, the incongruence of these two spheres became both a matter of course and an overwhelming fact. And then he slowly became filled with doubt as to the concrete, palpable value of music. Whatever the case, the great problem of the relationship between music and existence befell him already in Vienna.

3. THE SYMBOLIC DEATH OF THE 'I'

During the Romantic era, when so much attention was devoted to individuality, the youthful 'I' was not diffused by expanding outside itself. It fell into itself, to die of despair. This symbolic death took many different forms. Let us take, for example, François René Chateaubriand. His voracious and impulsive 'I' initially opened itself up to the world and burst into life like wildfire. Thus, as Jean-Pierre Richard writes, his existence took on the form of expanding fiery movement. And only afterwards, when that 'outward-seeking being', to borrow Sainte-Beuve's term, had found what it had been looking for, did disappointment appear and unhappiness arise: his 'I' began to hide within itself.[41]

The instance described by Mickiewicz in Part IV of *Forefathers' Eve* was even more hopeless. Its protagonist was already by nature not an 'outward-seeking being'. The love that he kept from the world did not spur him to conquer the space outside. The beloved was not able to fan from the 'soul's spark' a fire that could have spread out into the world.

—

> Czasem tę iskrę oko niebianki zapali,
> Wtenczas trawi się w sobie, świeci sama sobie
> Jako lampa w rzymskim grobie.[42]
> (Sometimes that spark is lit by a heavenly eye,

---

[41] Jean-Pierre Richard, 'Śmierć i jej postacie' (Fr. orig. 'La mort et ses figures', from *Paysage de Chateaubriand*), tr. Maria Wodzyńska, in Wojciech Karpiński (ed.), *Antologia współczesnej krytyki literackiej we Francji* [Anthology of contemporary literary criticism in France] (Warsaw, 1974), 157.
[42] Mickiewicz, *Dzieła*, ii:62.

Then it wastes away, illuminating itself
Like a lamp in a Roman grave.)

—

And so love drove his thoughts deep inside his 'I'. The fire that they stoked burned hidden and useless. It was smothered within. The fiery Romantic existence turned into something fevered but absurd. The man became a phantom. A living corpse. Thus in shutting his consciousness within the 'depths of his heart', he was at once also triggering a gradual process of the corpsing of his 'I'.[43]

Many people of Chopin's generation went through this ritual of symbolic death, which was typical of Polish romanticism. Chopin himself experienced something of the sort; after all, he was formed by the culture of his times. Of course, he was amused by the prevailing fashion for mawkish sentimentality. In the autumn of 1828, when he was travelling to Berlin, the stagecoach was boarded at Frankfurt an der Oder by 'some German Corinne, full of achs, jas and neins', who amused him most heartily, as she was an incomparable provincial victim of Romantic literature, with Mme de Staël's famous novel to the fore. With his characteristic linguistic flair, he called her a 'romantyczna pupka' or 'Romantic doll' (KS i: 82), although one may suspect here a play on words. Whilst 'pupka' may well be regarded as a Polonised diminutive of the German 'Puppe', meaning 'doll', it is also a diminutive form of the Polish 'pupa', meaning 'bottom'. A similar ambiguity can be heard in Chopin's term 'suszone pupki' for a Pleiad of Parisian composers and musicians, comprising Kalkbrenner, Reicha, Baillot and Cherubini (KS i: 206): dried puppets or dried derrières?

[43] Ryszard Przybylski, *Słowo i milczenie Bohatera Polaków. Studium o „Dziadach"* [The words and silence of the Hero of the Poles. A study of *Forefathers' Eve*] (Warsaw, 1991), 105 (proofs). The prospective publisher, PIW, abandoned the project.

However, there is a difference between an amusing cultural fashion and a genuine and serious experience of youth, from which Mickiewicz summoned knowledge concerning the destiny of man. Chopin learned of how concealed love turns a young man into a 'living corpse' from Mickiewicz's second volume of verse (1823). Admittedly, he had no inkling while reading those poems that in 1831, in some little hotel in Stuttgart, word would become deed, and he himself would turn into a ghost.

Mickiewicz announced to Chopin's generation that imprisoning a 'living' soul within a 'dead' body, within a corpse, rendered man's existence unbearably absurd. Existence then becomes constant suffering, since the soul, still living 'in the world, but no longer for the world', dwells inside the dead 'human form', which, precisely because it is half-rotten and cannot entirely disintegrate into dust, prevents the person from rising to a higher level of development. Juliusz Słowacki called such a creature a 'vital necrotic'. According to Maria Janion and Maria Żmigrodzka, this 'suspended', 'sepulchral' existence, this ostensible life inclined towards death, dead to everything that is 'now', this creature vainly striving to communicate with the world around it, this whole hyperbolic symbolism of the 'living corpse' was, although hazardous, a most eloquent attempt to describe existential despair.[44] Later, in one of his lectures at the Collège de France, delivered on 16 February 1841, Mickiewicz, citing the Ukrainian ethnographer Ivan Vahylevich, reminded his auditorium that according to Slavic beliefs the danger of turning into a 'living corpse' threatened men who were at a turning point, during their passage from youth to maturity: 'A ghost is born, so it is said, with a dual heart and with a dual soul. Until its youth, it lives without knowing itself, without the

---

[44] Maria Janion and Maria Żmigrodzka, 'Fryderyk Chopin wśród bohaterów egzystencji' [Fryderyk Chopin among the heroes of existence], *Res Publica*, 1987/3, 56–57.

awareness of its being, but on reaching a critical period in its life, it begins to feel in its heart the growth of a destructive urge...'[45] In Part IV of *Forefathers' Eve*, Mickiewicz treated the drama of the ghost as a rite of passage. In primitive cultures, this rite enabled a person to obtain a new, more mature, soul. The young soul had to die in order for the 'self' to ascend to a higher level of existence.[46] The situation was similar in Mickiewicz's masterpiece. For a man to mature, the youthful soul, alienated in the form of the Romantic phantasm of the 'living corpse' or the 'ghost', first had to 'express itself', or – as Chopin called it – 'talk itself out', and then... die.

Something of the sort happened to Chopin when, one night at the beginning of September 1831, lodged in a Stuttgart hotel, he picked up his pen and began talking to himself.

Chopin noticed this drawing-near of death, not so much to the body as to the mind, quite early, as soon as he received news of the outbreak of the uprising in Warsaw. His isolation became all the more acute as the thought of death began to wax. On Christmas Eve 1830, it let him feel all its menace.

In order to understand what happened with Chopin that day, we should remember about the specifically Polish cult of Christmas Eve. It is a unique celebration of family ties and of a sacred compassion for every lonely person. Still today, we are capable of crossing three continents and two oceans to spend that evening with our loved ones. Any lonely stranger who knocks on our door that day will find a place set for him at the table. So any Pole who spends that evening alone plunges the very depths of existential horror. And he might even find

[45] Mickiewicz, *Dzieła*, viii:178. Vahylevich wrote under the pen-name Dalibor and published his works in Czech; hence Mickiewicz regarded him as a Czech.

[46] Carl Gustav Jung, 'Odrodzenie' [Rebirth], in *Archetypy i symbole. Pisma wybrane* [Archetypes and symbols. Selected writings], selected, tr. and introd. Jerzy Prokopiuk (Warsaw, 1976), 125–138.

there death. Let us take just one example. Julian Fontana, who was a friend of Chopin's from their childhood, attended the Warsaw Lyceum with him and studied at the Central School of Music with him, who was the copyist of his friend's works and out of his great friendship took care of many matters both big and small, twenty years after Chopin's death, in 1869, took fright at a surge of the despair that undoubtedly lay in wait for him on that holy day and did not wish to live to that sacred moment of the Christmas Eve supper. He was already a wreck of a man. Entirely deaf, suffering from 'consumption of the spinal column', which was eating away at him, hounded by the shame of living off the capital set aside by his late wife's family for his son, he wrote his last letter to his friends and, on the night of 23–24 December, 'asphyxiated himself with carbon monoxide, having also placed a noose around his neck, so as to strangle himself with it when the effects of the stupor faded, making death all the more certain.'[47]

On that extraordinary evening – joyous for some Poles, but ominous, as we can see, for others – Chopin, deprived of his family, worried about the insurrection in Poland, abandoned by Tytus Woyciechowski, who had returned to Poland, heading for the battlefield, found himself among people who could not comprehend what was happening in his heart on that day. Even that Viennese Pole Mrs Konstancja Bayerowa, so close to him thanks to her first name, instead of sitting with him at the Christmas Eve table, invited him to an ordinary reception. Thus Chopin did not partake of a sacred meal with his closest community, but simply ate supper. A little later, he bade farewell to the Czech violinist and composer Josef Slavik, whom he had

[47] Marceli Antoni Szulc (obituary of Fontana from 1870), in *Fryderyk Chopin i utwory jego muzyczne. Przyczynek do życiorysu i oceny kompozycji artysty* [Fryderyk Chopin and his musical works. Towards a biography and an assessment of the artist's compositions] (1873; Cracow, 1986), 229.

met on the street, and – alone – made his way to Saint Stephen's Cathedral. On Boxing Day, he wrote to Jan Matuszyński.

> When I arrived, no one was there yet. Not for the service, but to gaze at that hour at that gigantic building, I stood in the darkest corner at the foot of a Gothic pillar. One cannot describe the magnificence, the grandeur of those enormous vaults – it was quiet – from time to time only the footsteps of the sacristan lighting a lamp in the depths of the cathedral disturbed my lethargy. A grave behind me, a grave below me… Only above me no grave. A gloomy harmony ran through my head… I felt my orphanhood more than ever… (KS i: 163).

Beneath him was certainly the cathedral mortuary, behind him – perhaps the tomb of some dignitary, or an airy grave in which his Warsaw youth was crumbling to dust. The Viennese cathedral became a coffin, in which he was enclosed in a state of half-being, like a 'living corpse'. At that point, doubtless unconsciously, a lethargy complex was born. It is interesting that our Romantics fell into lethargy when they began to feel their own bodies like a corpse or a tomb. 'You guessed correctly', wrote Zygmunt Krasiński to August Cieszkowski on 7 May 1841, 'when you used the word "apathy" – I'm living in lethargy, and revolting against it. […] like Lazarus, I've already begun to rot in a coffin, but my coffin's not of wood, my grave's not of stone, but living like me. I myself am my grave!'[48] Chopin would later define such time spent in the tomb of his own body

---

[48] Zygmunt Krasiński, *Listy do Augusta Cieszkowskiego, Edwarda Jaroszyńskiego, Bronisława Trentowskiego* [Letters to August Cieszkowski, Edward Jaroszyński and Bronisław Trentowski], ed. and introd. Zbigniew Sudolski (Warsaw, 1988), i:41. On the lethargy complex during the Romantic era, see Maria Janion, *Wobec zła* [In the face of evil] (Chotomów, 1989), 96–97. On the lethargy complex in Chopin, see the findings of Krystyna Kobylańska (KR 325–326).

as a 'lifeless state of numbness' or 'lifelessness and indifference' (KS i: 168–169).

These are the borderlands of life and death, the sphere of both being and non-being, a space ruled by phantoms. It is here that the 'I' practises a constant self-negation and observes its own existence as unbroken dying. With Chopin, this state lasted relatively briefly – for about a year. But Zygmunt Krasiński, for example, lived like that from his early youth until his death. 'I'm already dead. I'm a ghost. After the Roman Campaign, my skeleton rode on horseback. I feel like a corpse, but lachrymose and torn. Will I turn into a complete corpse? I'm rotting alive. My body reeks like a dead man's body.' And he ends with an auto-ironic, mocking phrase with a typical Varsovian Russianism: 'Krugom [an utter] corpse am I'.[49] This has a certain resonance, given that in Warsaw still today one can hear a Russian idiom that entered the capital's slang: 'krugom durak' – 'an utter fool'.

Although this process was short-lived for Chopin, the poor chap was clearly irritated by it. When he seized his pen, in order to 'express himself to himself', his description of the experience of his own corpse, as we read in Janion and Żmigrodzka's study, took a burlesque form, far from frenzy or a Romantic play of moods.[50] There is no doubt, therefore, that he thought in terms of the hero of Part IV of *Forefathers' Eve*, but was more ironic and more sensitive to the funny aspects of the situation. He used humour to palliate the horror, although without attempting to conceal the truth.

Stuttgart. A curious thing! This bed to which I'm going might have served more than one dying person already, and today

[49] Krasiński, *Listy do Delfiny Potockiej* [Letters to Delfina Potocka], ed. and introd. Zbigniew Sudolski (Warsaw, 1975), ii:221.
[50] Janion and Żmigrodzka, 'Fryderyk Chopin wśród bohaterów', 52.

it is not repulsive to me! Perhaps more than one corpse lay here, lay for quite some time on this bed? – But where's the corpse that's worse than me? – A corpse also knows nothing of its father, its mother, its sisters, of Tytus! – A corpse also has no lover! – it cannot converse with those around it in its own language! – A corpse as white as I. A corpse as cold as I now feel cold to everything. The corpse has ceased to live… (A 34).

This is a wholly exceptional discourse about a corpse. There are no evasive terms here, no semantic shifts or acrobatics. There is no 'dead man', no 'defunct', no 'body'. We keep hearing the word 'corpse', the sound of which is particularly frightful and terrifying. An abominable thing decays.

But this is a paradoxical corpse, which has not yet died. Like virtually every 'living corpse', he was tormented by the impossibility of communicating with the world around him. Mickiewicz's Phantom spoke of this most eloquently. Mickiewicz himself dreamt of a language of love that would need no words.[51] Chopin, before he found himself in Stuttgart, longed for a conversation that would bring about a true mutual understanding between the interlocutors. He dreamed of a language that would bring two hearts closer together and raise those conversing above the banal speech of society: 'I would not like to travel with you [to Vienna]', he wrote to Tytus Woyciechowski on 18 September 1830. 'I deceive you not, but just as I love you, so that moment would vanish, more pleasurable than thousands of days uniformly spent, in which we would embrace for the first time abroad. I'd be no longer able to wait, to receive, to chatter, as one says when contentment bars access to all cold, forced expressions and one heart converses with another in some divine tongue' (KS i: 138).

---

[51] 'Czemu, chcąc z tobą uczucia podzielać, / Nie mogę duszy prosto w duszę przelać…' (Why, wishing to share my feelings with you, / Can I not simply pour soul into soul…), *Dzieła*, i: 153.

During the Classical era, a 'divine tongue' was poetry. In Romantic times, this term often denoted a tool of communication with 'invisible realms'. And so Chopin knew that he was dealing with a linguistic cliché. Added to this, like Juliusz Słowacki, he could not shake the feeling that language was above all a bodily organ for speech. Hence his cry: 'Divine tongues! What an unfortunate expression, like a divine naval [doubtless at the sight of ancient sculptures of goddesses] or a divine kidney [here, perhaps in a restaurant, when he was served kidneys *a la veneziana*, with onion]; it is dreadfully material-ugly' (KS i: 138). But this all did nothing to dispel his dream of a language in which 'one heart converses with another' and which contains no 'cold, forced expressions'. 'But let us return to that moment in which I see you there', he added. 'Perhaps then I would not contain myself and would blurt out what I always dream of, what is everywhere before my eyes, what I constantly hear and what gives me the greatest pleasure in the world and saddens me the most' (KS i: 138).

And so when he began to talk with himself – since, as a 'living corpse', he could not 'converse' with the world around him – he nonetheless employed a 'divine tongue' and unforced ardent expressions. Finally, he spoke from his own heart to his own heart. I, corpse, will talk with myself.

The continuation of this confession was organised by popular ontological metaphors, which – as we know – allow us to conceive of events, actions, feelings and notions as substances and things. They are based on our experience of physical objects, and in particular of our own body. These metaphors are not present in our everyday language and they mainly shape our idea of the world and of existence.[52] The following appears in Chopin's album.

---

[52] Lakoff and Johnson, *Metaphors*, 3–6.

My corpse has ceased to live, and I have lived my fill. My fill? A corpse sated with life? – Were it sated, it would look well, but it's so wretched, – can life really have such a great effect on one's features, on one's facial expression, on man's outward appearance? – Why do we live such a miserable life, which devours us and serves only to make corpses of us! (A 34).

So first we have the metaphor 'life is nourishment'. To exist is to eat life. One may sample it bit by bit and be an eternal glutton, but one can also eat one's fill of it. Making use of this metaphor, Chopin initially began to make fun of himself. I am a corpse, and so I no longer eat life, but while I lived, I ate. Admittedly, I do not know whether I ate properly. A corpse sated with life should look well, since it ate properly. 'But it's so wretched'. We then have another metaphor, at the other extreme: 'Life is a glutton'. Indeed, man is the food of life, which is suddenly transformed into something like a man-eating Baal. At this point, the linguistic burlesque ends, and Chopin's irony kicks in. With Mickiewicz, a person was turned into a corpse by a consciousness too engrossed in itself, or by thinking that was focussed on thought. With Chopin, it is 'miserable life' that turns people into corpses, which 'devours them'. Human existence is in some way a sacrifice made to 'miserable life'.

Thus Chopin saw the world as a macabre manufactory: 'The clocks from the Stuttgart towers are striking a nocturnal hour. Ah, how many corpses have been made in this moment around the world! – Children's mothers, – mothers' children have perished – how many plans thwarted, how much grief from the corpses in this moment and how much good cheer' (A 34). This ambiguity most probably resulted from the fact that for Chopin the process whereby people became corpses possessed a totally amoral character: 'How many ill-natured guardians – how many beings oppressed by corpses. A good and bad corpse! – Virtue and crime are one!' (A 34). This phantomisation of the world takes place beyond ethics. Kantian stars still shine in the sky, but death has no knowledge of moral imperative. So is it worth living? In this text, that question functions as a hidden musical reprise. The answer, meanwhile, took the form of variations on Sophocles' famous bitter assertion from *Oedipus at Colonus*:

—

Not to be born at all
Is best, far best that can befall,
Next best, when born, with least delay
To trace the backward way.[53]

—

Romantics, especially those who experienced their own corpse, usually kept returning to the idea. Mickiewicz noted it down in Greek in the years when he was creating his incomparable masterpiece 'Gdy tu mój trup w pośrodku was zasiada…' [When here my corpse will sit among you…].[54] With Chopin, it took the following form: 'So it's clear that death is man's best deed! – and what would be his worse? – Birth! being against, opposed to the best deed. So I am right to be angry that I came into the world! – why ever was I not allowed to remain in the inactive world?' (A 34).

Chopin's spirit world, in which – as we can see – souls pre-exist before manifesting themselves in human bodies, is an 'inactive world', a world without events or actions, existing outside life (life which, incidentally, can devour a man or transform him into a superfluous 'living corpse': 'After all, I am inactive anyway! – What will anyone gain from my existence?' (A 34). So the 'living corpse' is rather a being from the spirit world, from the 'inactive world', wandering among people from the miserable, but active, world. It is hardly surprising, therefore, that it

---

[53] Sophocles, *Oedipus at Colonus* (1223–1226), tr. F. Storr (London, n.d.).
[54] Mickiewicz, *Dzieła*, xvi:641.

longs for its transcendent homeland. It is ill at ease here. It should return there. Thus the complex of uselessness created by the political situation was ultimately expressed in existential terms.

The detailed substantiation of this shortcoming took the form of a macabre Romantic situation:

> I'm no use to people, as I have neither calf muscles nor muzzles! – And even if I had, then I would have nothing else besides! – Wherefore calves – when without calves one cannot be! – Does a corpse have calves? – A corpse is just like me (!) like me it has no calves; there's one more similarity. So I am little short of a mathematically strict fraternisation with death (A 34–35).

During the 1970s, Jerzy Andrzejewski carried out something like a telesurvey, asking writers who he suspected were not familiar with Chopin's correspondence to guess the author of this excerpt. The results were not surprising. All the respondents ascribed it to Witold Gombrowicz.[55] Polish intellectuals had grown accustomed to paying tribute to just a single authority – a ritual that substituted for both their knowledge and their sensitivity. For some time, clearly under the influence of France, they had become, to use Chopin's own term, Gombrowiczian 'pupki' [puppets/bottoms], and it did not occur to them that an ironic slant on the macabre was something of a speciality of the Romantic generation. It was conveyed at times in a pompous style, with a fondness for frenzy, à la Zygmunt Krasiński, and at other times with an air of the grotesque, occasionally akin to fairground buffoonery, as in Juliusz Słowacki's incomparable *Piast Dantyszek*.

Chopin did not stint on irony in his experience of his own corpse, doubtless because the horror of this experience was

[55] Jerzy Andrzejewski, *Z dnia na dzień. Dziennik literacki 1972–1978* [From day to day. A literary journal] (Warsaw, 1988), i:296.

acute. Moreover, he always sought the amusing aspects of thorny situations. On this occasion, his comic flair came through in his perverse enumeration of those traits of man which render his existence in society dignified and useful.

So in order to 'be of use to people', one must first possess a gastrocnemius. A full and well-toned calf was admired in Enlightenment-era salons and occasionally clinched the career of a young and enterprising fop. During the Romantic era, it lost its significance, since trousers, which Chateaubriand still regarded as a garment of the hoi polloi, were now covering the whole leg. But in Warsaw, elderly ladies must have muttered about the calves of celebrated salon lions, given that Chopin felt suddenly disadvantaged by nature. Of course, besides calves, in the 'active world' one also needed a muzzle. As we read in Linde's dictionary: 'What is a mouth [*gęba*] in man is a muzzle [*pysk*] in other animals'. A horse has a muzzle. The word 'pysk' is used in Polish when a face is slapped. But Chopin was probably not interested in a salon menagerie. When the word 'pysk' is used in the plural, 'pyski', then it denotes above all cheeks glowing with health. This periphrase contains as much disdain as it does admiration. If we take all of this into account, then it turns out that only a blooming, fine-looking man can 'be of use to people'; in other words, as Chopin wrote in one of his letters, 'something big, grown and burly' (KS i: 209). So what does a 'living corpse' with neither fine calves nor ruddy cheeks, as pitiful as it is 'inactive', dream about?

Furthermore, for Chopin this entire reasoning was 'mathematically strict' proof of 'fraternisation with death'. Thus to some extent the experience of his own corpse took on the character of a schoolboy joke. A corpse has neither fine calves nor ruddy cheeks. I have neither fine calves nor ruddy cheeks. Therefore I am a corpse. QED. Which was to be demonstrated. So schoolboy humour allowed Chopin to play with a phantasm that could easily have paralysed his mind. Clearly, he had not yet closed the lid on his coffin.

Death? 'Today I don't wish for it – unless you feel bad, children. Unless you too wish for nothing better than death! – If not, then I long to see you again – not for my direct, but for my indirect happiness, since I know how you love me' (A 35). This was an apostrophe to his sisters, who he called his children throughout his life, taking the Chopins' female offspring upon himself in the role of father. After all, he was their only brother. They should have felt his male solicitousness and remembered that he came first in the family after their father. This half-joking expression actually betrayed a deep-rooted view on human existence: a person's fate is fulfilled in his family. It was a view for which he would later pay a terrible price.

Let us also point out that Chopin is employing his own terminology here. On the important questions in life – concerning existence (the active and the inactive world) or happiness – Chopin always expressed himself in his own language. He did not refer to any thinkers and took no words from the books he had read, as young people frequently do. His remarks on existence were utterly without pretence, and perhaps for that very reason they are so charming and wise. He sought words for his own thoughts, not read, but experienced, whereas his peers, even Maurycy Mochnacki, usually juggled modish terms with received wisdom.

So he distinguished between direct happiness, which concerns one's own 'I', and indirect happiness, which one feels when bringing cheer to others. Such a distinction could justify both shameless guile and genuine despair. When his own happiness was at stake, he could have taken his own life, so onerous was his state of spiritual lethargy. However, because he knew that his demise would be a horrific blow to his sisters, he decided to carry on living. Only out of love for his sisters did he demur from that irreversible step. And so he thought about suicide.

In youth, this happens quite often, especially when one is aware of non-existence. And it should not be trivialised.

Prior to his metamorphosis into a phantom, some tears were shed.

> An arid tristesse engulfed me long ago. Ah – for a long time I could not cry. – How good I feel… wistful! Wistful and good! – What feeling is that? Good and wistful. – When one is wistful, it is not good; and yet pleasant! – It is a curious state – But a corpse just the same. It feels at once both good and bad. It takes itself to a happier life and feels good; it regrets leaving the past life and feels wistful. A corpse must feel like I felt when I stopped crying (A 35).

Thus his decay resembled the 'curious state' of sentimental escapists, immersed in dreams of the happy life of yesterday, since the present time of the phantom was a time of hurt. And only in the future could he count on consolation. This experience gave rise to a charming sense of yearning, a therapeutic remedy concocted by the novels and the lyric poetry of the sentimental era, soothing any strong spiritual disturbances. Thus the 'living corpse' first flopped down onto an elegant Enlightenment-era chaise longue before sinking into the 'joyful sadness' or 'delectable tears' that were typical of Romantic heroes, as described during the 1820s in sentimental novels. In any case, he was overcome with a feeling that was as conventional as it was genuine, as pleasant as it was melancholic, which the English termed at that time the 'joy of grief'. So Chopin was still sensing the bitter-sweet taste of existence.

In spite of everything, his confession is moving, since he felt sentimental longing (the word 'wistful' is repeated five times) as a lethargy of consciousness. And in this respect he resembles the protagonist of Part IV of Mickiewicz's *Forefathers'*

Eve. He wallowed a little in his own unhappiness, mollified by the sentimental remedies for allaying despair. He consented a little to the immobilisation of his awareness, intoxicated by the bitter-sweet wine of life.

This acute anxiety ended with an experience that he expressed in a way that Mickiewicz himself would not have misprized:

> It was clearly some fleeting death of my feelings – for a moment, I died for my heart! Or rather, for a moment, my heart died for me (A 35).

And so there is no doubt that he distinguished his 'I' from his 'heart'.

Of course, 'I' is abstract in the extreme, although it is paradoxically felt as something quite concrete. There is no image of one's 'I' without a personal rite, which usually comes about spontaneously, albeit influenced by the lifestyle that holds sway during a particular period.[56] And so, as was the custom at that time, Chopin's 'I' comprised above all 'feelings'. These should not be identified with Mickiewicz's 'feeling', signifying – as Teresa Kostkiewiczowa writes – non-transmittable inner experiences. In the programmatic ballad 'Romantyczność' [Romanticity], 'feeling' is identical to Plato's 'eye of the soul', and so to 'inner vision', which takes in supersensory, non-physical reality.[57] Chopin's 'feelings' were a reaction to the

---

[56] See Helmuth Plessner, *Pytanie o conditio humana. Wybór pism* [The question of the human condition. Selected writings] (Warsaw, 1988), 288; also Lakoff and Johnson, 233–235.

[57] Teresa Kostkiewiczowa, 'Poezja i czułe serce. Szkic o sensach „czucia" w świadomości poetyckiej oświecenia i Mickiewicza' [Poetry and a tender heart. A sketch about the meanings of 'feeling' in the poetic awareness of the Enlightenment and Mickiewicz], in Maria Żmigrodzka (ed.), *Studia romantyczne* [Romantic studies] (Wrocław, 1973), 100, 105–106.

material world and to historical existence. They enabled him to acknowledge himself in his distinct being. So in his 'I', Chopin simply felt his own continued existence. Moreover, youth is particularly sensitive when it comes to its 'I', and generally in respect to 'inner' psychological problems. 'At this time of life, a person finally discovers his distinctive and inimitable nature'.[58]

The word 'heart', in turn, was not for Chopin a linguistic cliché, although during the Romantic era it was used like a worn sixpence. It is impossible to forget the instruction he issued on his death bed. He requested that his heart be removed and taken to Warsaw. He had been raised on Mickiewicz, in whose oeuvre, as in the Bible, the heart symbolised that which was most personal in man, unique, intended only for oneself. The heart was a man in hiding, *homo absconditus*, a mysterious bastion of identity. When looking at the bloody heart of the protagonist of Part II of *Forefathers' Eve*, palpitating in a breast rent asunder, we are looking at a person's wide-open tabernacle, usually closed and inaccessible.[59] One way or another, Chopin knew that besides his 'I', there also existed within him a 'heart', a mysterious and undefined spiritual element, difficult to grasp, like every thing in itself, like every unknowable centre.

The metamorphosis into a 'living corpse' evidently disturbed the balance between his 'I' and his 'heart'. For a moment, Chopin experienced the annihilation of his 'I', and his sense of existence broke off. His 'I' died, although he knew that there still existed that mysterious element of his identity: his 'heart'. 'For a moment, I died for my heart'. At that moment, he existed without living. Yet this experience was so indistinct and so ambiguous that he immediately came to the opposite

---

[58] Igor S. Kon, *Odkrycie „ja"* [The discovery of the 'self'], tr. Larysa Siniugina (Warsaw, 1987), 204–206.
[59] See Przybylski, 'Epifania bohatera Polaków' [Epiphany of the hero of the Poles], *Res Publica*, 1987/5, 37.

conclusion, that what had been annihilated was the hidden centre of his identity, his 'heart', although he did not lose the sense of the continued existence of his 'I'. 'Or rather, for a moment, my heart died for me'.

Contained in the phantasm of the 'living corpse' was Chopin's experience of losing his identity whilst retaining the awareness of the existence of his 'I'. And so he experienced the boring out of the essence from his person. When a person's 'heart' dies, he becomes a 'living corpse'. Hence Chopin gained the conviction that his existence was deprived of meaning. He began to sense his own existence as something needless and absurd. The spiritual crisis he experienced in that Stuttgart hotel concerned not his views on life, but rather the structure of his consciousness. True despair arises not out of a confusion of ideas, but from the horror of existence.

Such despair descends upon a person quite suddenly; but it is fortunately short-lived. Chopin stressed this quite clearly. A 'fleeting death' of feelings signifies not so much their immediate death as their death 'for a moment', as he reiterated. So he asked himself: 'Why not forever?' The state of a 'living corpse' weighed upon him so much that he added: 'Perhaps I'd find it more bearable' (A 35).

Chopin would not have been Chopin had he not furnished this crisis with mocking remarks. The irony of his first reflection involved the altering of a popular expression. 'Alone, alone – (—) Ah, my orphanhood is indescribable. My sensibility can barely endure it. My heart is all but breaking from the amusements and great pleasures it has experienced over this last year' (A 35). A heart usually breaks from grief or despair. From amusement, our hearts leap, since Poles love to dance. Over the course of that year, 1831, Chopin experienced feelings that justified the common use of the idiom. By replacing pain and despair with amusement and pleasures, Chopin began a linguistic game that was indicative of his distance in respect to the spiritual drama he was experiencing.

The irony of his second remark was of a wholly different nature, as it revealed, in a wholly unexpected way, the political aspect of Chopin's existential drama. The modern-era states of Europe established exceptionally stringent controls over their subjects, one of which was the generalised implementation of passports. Quite simply, a passport became the document of one's official existence. Without a passport, one could not exist in what one might call 'international life'. In order to travel to a foreign land, one had to possess a document issued by one's own Leviathan. In this way, state authorities gained control over human beings, at least in this vale of tears – a control that was utterly unlawful, antagonistic and oppressive, especially if it was not an emanation of the sovereign laws of a society, as it generally was not. And Chopin's metamorphosis into a 'living corpse' was formally and officially rubber-stamped by an oppressive state. I have no passport, therefore I do not exist. I am a corpse. 'Next month my passport expires – I cannot live abroad – or at least I cannot live officially. As a consequence, I will be even more like a corpse' (A 35). And so everything conspired to turn him into a phantom, even the principles that govern modern-day forms of the political life of societies.

Of course, the experience of one's corpse has a universal character and reminds us of a truth that takes on great importance in times when a contempt for matter begins to dally with people's minds in a blatantly indecent manner. It teaches a person that he is a 'thinking body'.[60] After all, while living, we are constantly dying, continually disintegrating. So this experience reminds

---

[60] This expression ('thinking body') is borrowed from Osip Mandelstam. It appears in a poem written on 21 July 1935 in Voronezh, in exile. Incipit: 'Не мучнистой бабочкою белой' [Not as a mealy white butterfly], in Собрание сочинений [Collected writings] (Moscow, 1994), iii:88.

us of the somatic character of human existence. It initiates us into an existential drama brought about by our body. Here is Mircea Eliade.

> Initiation is death, and any death that is consciously assumed may become an initiation. But a 'symbolic death' (ritual, initiatory) is not just suffering, torment, illness and so on – it is also the experiencing of our own corpse, reconciling ourselves to a simple fact about which we had forgotten: not only are we passers-by, but we are also continually decaying, and we have to accept the corpse that is our body, reconcile ourselves to the idea that we are also that corpse.[61]

So in that Stuttgart hotel, Chopin experienced the terrifying majesty and the repulsive misery of feeling and thinking matter. I think in my body. I feel in my body. This experience was something of an acid test of a person's awareness. It forced him to experience death before death. 'Man tastes death several times before he dies,' wrote Zygmunt Krasiński to Juliusz Słowacki on 18 June 1841, 'learning eternal peace while his energies constantly wane! Doubtless vice versa, when lying in his coffin, he learns there another life – through imperturbability and silence, he steels himself for movement and for some new turmoil. – The world is based on contradictions'.[62] The Romantic experiencing of existence was also based on contradictions, and the notions of life and death merged with one another to such an extent that it is difficult, today, to fathom whether Chopin was thinking of life while recording his experience of dying or was thinking of death while talking about his life. The Romantics

[61] Mircea Eliade, 'Z dzienników' [From the diaries] (21 February 1955), *Znak*, 400 (1988), 30.
[62] *Korespondencja Juliusza Słowackiego* [The correspondence of Juliusz Słowacki], ed. Eugeniusz Sawrymowicz (Wrocław, 1963), ii:287.

– especially those with health problems – soon lost themselves in death's black cloud.

If they believed in God, then they were tormented by the thought of living at a time when His image was becoming blurred in human souls. If they confessed the religion of nature, then they were racked by the conviction of the desacralisation of life. The further from the sacred, from the divine, that society grows, the more 'living corpses' there are. In the summer of 1799, Friedrich Hölderlin wrote to Susette Gontard:

> Every day I have to summon the divinity that's been lost. When I think about great people in great times, how they kindled the sacred fire and turned everything dead, of wood, all the straw of this world into a divine flame with which they soared into the heavens, and then I think about how often I wander like a barely flickering lamp and have to beg for a drop of oil to illumine, if only for a moment, this night that surrounds me, then, you see, some curious shiver runs through me and I silently invoke those terrible words: living corpse.[63]

This was something of an impasse, since a 'living corpse', the dead 'human form', prevented the soul from returning to its heavenly home. On the morning of 4 June 1824, Eugène Delacroix, the only man apart from Wojciech Grzymała with whom Chopin talked heart to heart towards the end of his life, picked up a notebook and wrote down the following confession:

> I live in company with a body, my silent companion, constant and exacting. He it is who establishes the individuality, the

---

[63] Friedrich Hölderlin, *Pod brzemieniem mego losu. Listy – Hyperion* [Under the yoke of my fate. Letters – Hyperion], tr. and ed. Anna Milska and Wanda Markowska (Warsaw, 1976), 192.

mark of the weakness of our race. My spirit has wings, but my body, her brutal gaoler, is severe. He knows that though she be free it is only to be enslaved again, weakling that she is. In her prison she forgets herself and only rarely does she glimpse the pure blue of her celestial home. Unhappy fate, to yearn unceasingly for my release, I who am a spirit immured in this mean vessel of clay! [...] It seems to me that the body may well be the machinery that restricts the soul, which is more universal. The soul must pass through the brain as through a mill, where it is hammered and stamped with the seal of our contemptible natures. But how unbearable is the burden of this living corpse![64]

The horror of this burden was described in detail by Zygmunt Krasiński. From Marek Bieńczyk's treatise *Czarny człowiek* [Black man], we learn that the poet, dogged by illness and neurosis, continuously observed his own dying. He sensed that his body was in a state of decay, and eventually he became obsessed with negating himself. He lamented that although no longer alive, he was still unable to die; that for all eternity he would be observing his death and decay. And so, focussing his awareness on his dead subjectivity, he essentially banished his existence from being. Whatever one might say about this absurd situation, for Krasiński it was his daily reality. Instead of hauling his awareness out of this negativity, his imagination, latching onto the impulses of his body, which he always felt to be a 'living corpse', thrust Krasiński into the contemplation of dying. Thus the experience of his corpse ousted the idea of cognitive activity. Krasiński was able to perceive, but understood less and less. He was unable to settle in life and to grasp the sense of his own existence. Philosophical ideas could not extricate him from

---

[64] Eugène Delacroix, *The Journal of Eugene Delacroix*, tr. Lucy Norton, ed. Hubert Wellington (1951; London, 2006), 45.

74

this turmoil. At times, his constant communing with death drove him to such irritation that even his faith could not console him.[65]

So during this era, a ghost was a being that was very frequently encountered. Even the simplest folk could turn into phantoms, just like Tadeusz Józef Chamski, an ordinary soldier condemned to an émigré's fate, a 'good honest Catholic Pole' suspecting every democrat of spying for Russia, as touching as he was repulsive. Like most Polish freedom fighters, he wrote poetry. Cobbling verse together is a grave Polish illness, and if foreigners were familiar with our – actually beautiful – language, then we might be seen around the world as a nation of incorrigible scribblers. So Chamski slogged away for several months at a time over his heroic epic about General Jan Skrzynecki. For the entire year 1834, 'he did nothing but work on his *Janaida*, sufficiently indefatigably and laboriously that the following year, 1835, he completed it. That is, he completed the rough version of all the books of the *Janaida*, but at the same time he so exhausted himself in body and mind through work and lack of sleep, so enfeebled himself morally, tormented by the spectre of increasingly black hallucinations and sombre thoughts, that he grew haggard and yellow, became a recluse, sought only loneliness, constantly sighed, often wept, and usually did not know what he craved or what he was doing and became a virtual ghost.' He described his phantom state quite lucidly. 'In this state of stupefaction, he could not understand himself, since he was not ill, but out of weakness could barely stand, was conscious, but felt drowsy, and he could barely comprehend what he was reading or what anyone was saying if quickly or a little unclearly'.[66] He returned to normality when he 'forgot himself'

---

[65]   Marek Bieńczyk, *Czarny człowiek. Krasiński wobec śmierci* [Black man. Krasiński and death] (Warsaw, 1991), 69–98.

[66]   Tadeusz Józef Chamski, *Opis krótki lat upłynionych* [Brief description of years gone by], ed. and introd. Robert Bielecki (Warsaw, 1989), 323.

and began to dance every day till he dropped. He transfixed his phantom not with a ring of aspen, but with dance. A true Pole!

In keeping with the biblical account of the creation of man, Polish Romantics had bodies made of clay. It was a poor and brittle construction, in which, for a limited time, dwelt the essence of man: his soul. According to the Neoplatonic interpretation of this pericope, the swallow's clay nest is treated as the soul's prison. The Romantics were rather contemptuous of matter. Chopin remained unimbued with this Platonic madness. He valued a person's corporeality and did not treat the biblical metaphor with deadly gravity. In order to suppress his fear of the consequences of his illnesses, he effected a certain semantic acrobatic feat. 'For the love of God', he wrote to Jan Matuszyński in November 1830, 'don't be rash, as we're of the same clay, and you know how many times I've already fallen apart. – My clay won't dissolve in this rain now, inside it's 90 degrees Réaumur. You could – ah! no, you couldn't – probably make a house for a kitten from my clay' (KS i: 154). He knew his body's weaknesses, but from his early youth he valued his clay hut and, unlike our Romantics, did not consider it a wretched abode for his 'I'. Hence, neither was the 'living corpse' a decaying prison of the soul. It was rather a degraded form of 'thinking body', which in moments of despair felt only the absurdity and insubstantiality of its existence.

4. The city of his youth in ruins

When news reached Stuttgart of the defeat of the uprising in Poland, Chopin knew nothing about either the capitulation agreement between the Polish army and the staff of General Ivan Paskievich or the pact regulating the way in which the enemy forces were to enter Warsaw. He was deeply convinced that the capital had been taken by storm. So those dozen or so bewildering lines written into his album were created by his fevered imagination, animated by news that was as desperate as it was terrifying. It is quite simply the record of a phantasmal vision of the city's capture by enemy troops. On this occasion, Chopin set down on paper what he saw in his imagination. This is attested by the words 'I see' that escaped him at the moment when his memory was worried about the fate of a friend. 'I see Marceli captured' (A 36). In a similar way, he 'saw' other friends and all the members of his family. Each of the figures invoked by his mind appeared to him in circumstances that arose in his imagination. Marceli Celiński was not actually caught by the Russians. Wilhelm Kolberg did not perish on the ramparts. His sisters were not raped. His mother was not killed. These images were not formed by his knowledge, since Chopin actually knew very little.

So the vision of Warsaw's fall owed much to ignorance, but it was by no means the work of naive awareness. So it did not occur before the thought. On the contrary, it was born of the thought that fled Stuttgart to wander around the ramparts of the capital, around its streets and houses. Phantasmal images, arising in a disordered and unpredictable manner, now poured into the fissure between here and there. Unsurprisingly, therefore, the pages of Chopin's album give the impression of recording the convulsions of his consciousness.

Passing over a number of admittedly fascinating details, I shall begin my analysis of this text with the cry that was wrenched from him not by his imagination, but by information in the press about the results of the early morning storming of Warsaw on 6 November 1831: 'Sowiński, that good old soul, in the hands of those brutes!' (A 36). This information was given by the Prussian *Gazeta Rządowa* on the basis of unverified rumours and was replicated by other European newspapers. In the Polish version, it read as follows: 'The Russian forces displayed incredible bravery in taking the entrenchments by storm. At the village of Czystem, four Polish regiments were partly cut down and partly taken prisoner. Among the prisoners are the heavily wounded General Sowiński and the instigator of the insurrection of 17/29 November last year, the commander of the insurgents who attacked the Belvedere, Piotr Wysocki. The latter shot himself, so it is said, on being captured'.[67]

Neither piece of news was correct. In order to protect their commander from the revenge of the Russians who were intensely seeking him, the captured officers of 10th Rgt spread the false news that Wysocki had perished.[68] He was indeed wounded and so fell into enemy hands, but he did not commit suicide. General Sowiński, meanwhile, was not seized, but died in his entrenchment. So Chopin cried out in pain at the moment when false information from the battlefield had not yet been corrected.

It is understandable that any news about Sowiński must have concerned him. The general and his wife, Katarzyna, were very close friends of the Chopin family, and Fryderyk had known him since he was a boy.

---

[67] *Tygodnik Petersburski*, 1831/71.
[68] Tomasz Świtkowski, *O wzięciu Woli dnia 6 września 1831 roku* [On the capture of Wola on 6 September 1831] (Paris, 1833), 23.

Sowiński's military career was rich and meritorious.[69] It began in 1794. On the very first day of the insurrection, he led his colleagues from the Knights' School onto the streets of the insurgent city. In the company of Chopin's father, he doubtless recounted interesting memories and reflections. During Napoleon's Russian campaign, in 1812, he lost a leg in the Battle of Mozhaysk and thereafter walked with a crutch. In 1820, following his return from imprisonment to Warsaw, a decree from the emperor of Russia and king of Poland called into existence a military college, known as the Apprentice School, and Sowiński was appointed its commander, with the rank of colonel. Fryderyk's father, Mikołaj Chopin, taught French at the college, and only lost the post after the defeat of the uprising, when the school, like the university, was closed by the Russian authorities. So these two families maintained lively social contacts with one another. Chopin performed in the colonel's home as a child, when Warsaw was gripped with admiration for its 'Wunderkind'. Sowiński was a great music lover. In one of the letters he wrote from the entrenchments in the Wola district of Warsaw, he confessed to his wife that he missed listening to music.[70]

When the uprising broke out, he behaved with restraint, to say the least. He did not let his pupils out onto the street, as he considered that they ought not participate in irresponsible disorder on the part of hot-headed youths.[71] As we know, this was the position adopted by many high-ranking Polish officers. General Józef Chłopicki, the later commander in chief and dictator of the uprising, stated that it was not an insurrection, but

[69] See Czesław Kłak, *Polski Leonidas. Rzecz o legendzie historycznej i literackiej generała Józefa Sowińskiego* [The Polish Leonidas. On the historical and literary legend of General Józef Sowiński] (Warsaw, 1986), 5–102.
[70] Ibid, 163.
[71] Juliusz Stanisław Harbut, *Noc listopadowa* [November Night] (Warsaw, 1926), 218. Wacław Tokarz, *Sprzysiężenie Wysockiego i Noc listopadowa* [Wysocki's conspiracy and the November Night] (Warsaw, 1980), 232–233.

a 'simpletons' brawl'. We can be sure that Mikołaj Chopin was of a similar mind and branded the November Night as a great act of stupidity.[72] Soon, however, when the uprising began to express the will of the entire nation, the colonel, like many military dignitaries, changed his mind and joined the action. He was appointed commander of the artillery of Warsaw garrison. On 23 August 1831, the day he wrote that letter to his wife, he advanced to the rank of brigadier general.

During the Russian storming of Wola, which began at 5 a.m. on 6 September 1831, he defended the key redoubt no. 56. 'Continually fighting in the chief battery,' wrote Major Tomasz Świtkowski, who, literally one minute before the situation he described, ordered the wounded Piotr Wysocki to be taken to the nearby church, 'he did his duty as commander and soldier; he never deserted the gun, although all the artillerymen had been shot; he used rank-and-file soldiers to carry the charges; although this went slowly and awkwardly, he nevertheless shot at the enemy; when the Russians eventually began to rush his main battery, Sowiński and his soldiers with rifle in hand resisted the foe: but pressed by the greater enemy forces, standing at his gun, he refused the offered pardon, and, transfixed by bayonets, he rendered up his life.'[73]

The cry that Chopin emitted in Stuttgart was not just a sign of his pain. It also carried information about his attitude towards Poland's enemies: 'Sowiński, that good old soul, in the hands of those brutes [*szelmy*]!' In the dictionary of Samuel Linde, a caricature of whom was drawn by Chopin while he had the privilege of being one of his pupils, the word 'szelma' signified a cheat. So that no one would be left in any doubt, Linde gave

---

[72] This is speculation, but solidly grounded. Mikołaj Chopin worked with Col. Sowiński at the Apprentice School, and he was hostile towards any kind of movement stirred up by the democratic 'monster'. See KR 83–84.

[73] Świtkowski, *O wzięciu*, 22.

the analogous Russian word *плут* and the German *der Betrüger*. Thus Chopin used the word 'szelma' for a banker acquaintance when he did something untoward (KS i: 333) and for bloodsucking publishers (KS i: 347).

The backward-looking Linde did not peruse the contemporary press or new literature. His documentation did not go beyond the eighteenth century. Moreover, his monumental dictionary was completed in 1814. In Romantic times, the word 'szelma' took on a completely different meaning. Let us remember that Chopin's text was written in 1831. The following year saw the publication of Part III of *Forefathers' Eve*, in which this word did not mean a rogue or cheat. In the Ball scene, the Right Side, or the true Polish patriots and noble Russians, looking at the Left Side, that is, the Russian civil-military bureaucracy and Polish turncoats, twice sings this eloquent, but blunt, refrain:

—

> Ach, szelmy, łotry, ach, łajdaki!
> Żeby ich piorun trzasł.
> (Ah, brutes, rogues, ah, blackguards!
> May lightning strike them down.)

—

One might think that this was referring to cheats. After all, there were plenty of thieves and bribe-takers in the Russian administration in Lithuania, besides the rogues and scoundrels. But no! Elsewhere, the Right Side explains exactly how it understands the word:

—

> Te szelmy z rana piją krew,
> A po obiedzie róm.[74]
> (Those brutes drink blood in the morning,
> And after dinner rum.)

—

---

[74] Mickiewicz, *Dzieła*, iii:239, 241, 244.

The Russian *szelma* could have been a cheat, but when he was carrying out his duties as administrator in a subjugated country, he became a bloodthirsty phantom. The Russian *szelma* was a monster. One could say 'Oh, you *szelma*' about a good-natured fibber, as Chopin called Tytus Woyciechowski (KS i: 131). But when the epithet was bestowed on a Russian, then everyone knew that no joke was implied. Novosiltsov himself was well aware of the fact. Anna Gorecka, wife of an eminent fabulist, was an ardent patriot. Here is an excerpt from a memoir of those times: 'Although, under Alexander I, people were not punished for the slightest word out of place, it was enough that there were such figures as Novosiltsov and Baikov whom Mrs Gorecka put it to most bluntly: and on one occasion, when Novosiltsov, aware of her principles, visited her on her sickbed, and she politely enquired about his health, he replied: "Well, nought can afflict the Muscovite brute".'[75] Chopin would not have grieved had Sowiński merely been caught by cheats. He cried out of terror because the general had ended up in the hands of bloodthirsty villains. Such horrendous accounts were given by our military men and civilian politicians of imprisonment in Russia that this news could well have left Chopin not only indignant, but also terrified.

Polish units began to leave their positions in the evening of 7 September. They headed towards the right bank of the Vistula. The unconditional capitulation of the city was agreed during the night of 7/8 September and signed in the morning by General Kazimierz Małachowski. By ceding the left bank of Warsaw, the insurrectionary forces were gaining time, which made it possible to evacuate all the Polish troops to the Praga district. The wooden homes on the outskirts of the city went up in flames.

---

[75] Gabriela Güntherów Puzynina, *W Wilnie i w dworach litewskich. Pamiętnik z lat 1815–1843* [In Vilnius and in Lithuanian manors. Journal from the years 1815–1843], ed. Adam Czartkowski and Henryk Mościcki (Chotomów, 1988), 115.

Political activists, members of parliament and anyone who felt threatened joined the soldiers. The Russian army began to occupy the city from the north and the west. At the city gates, the municipal authorities welcomed the victors with bread and salt.

Raymond Durand, French consul in Warsaw, was a sober observer of political and economic life in the Congress Kingdom, and he followed the events of the uprising in the same matter-of-fact way. He was a well-known figure in Warsaw and the subject of much gossip. Chopin repeated one such rumour in a letter to Tytus Woyciechowski.[76] Contrary to popular opinion, Durand was favourable to the Poles. He was familiar with imperial villainy and was also disgusted by the stupidity of the Polish capitulators. So there is no reason to doubt the veracity of his report of 14 September 1831. 'The occupation of the city was carried out, as already mentioned, with the utmost order. [...] I need not speak, minister, of the almost universal sadness that set in following so many needless victims. Equally inevitable is the mutual offence, which only time and the nobleness of the tsar may dispel. However, these moods do not in the least prevent the utmost gratitude for their solicitous sparing of the city. The Cossacks plundered several homes in distant suburbs, and a number of thefts even occurred in more frequented districts. Yet strict

---

[76] 'Among diplomatic news, the latest is that Mr Durand, the former French consul who protested against Philippe and wished to enter Russian service, has been recalled to France, and a new tricolour consul, not yet even known by name among diplomats, has already arrived in his place' (KS i: 141). It turns out that Warsaw was quite well informed about diplomatic life. Following the July Revolution in France, for some time the consul was indeed thinking of demonstratively relinquishing his post. Hence Chopin's 'former consul'. Durand's family ultimately talked him out of it, and 'with great joy' he remained in Warsaw, assuring the new regime of his complete loyalty. (See Robert Bielecki, introd. to Raymond Durand. *Depesze z powstańczej Warszawy 1830–1831. Raporty konsula francuskiego w Królestwie Polskim* [Dispatches from insurrectionary Warsaw 1830–1831. Reports of the French consul in the Kingdom of Poland], tr., introd. and ed. R. Bielecki (Warsaw, 1980), 19–20).

edicts put an end to this disorder and security was restored.'[77] Naturally, the streets on which the Russians installed themselves looked like one great military camp. As we read in the memoirs of Fryderyk Skarbek, Chopin's godfather, 'Bivouacs and pickets, nocturnal fires burning on all the squares, taken up with straw, hay and wood, and midst it all soldiers, horses, cannons and guns stacked up. […] Of the more notable residents, no one on the streets; everyone shut in their houses.'[78] If Chopin's family were shut inside their home on Krakowskie Przedmieście, then they could have watched from the windows as the soldiers kept warm by their fires, but within their own four walls they felt completely safe, particularly since they lived in the palace of General Wincenty Krasiński, the most faithful of the Russian tsar's loyal servants. Of course, a few days later, the systematic repression began. The time came for arrests and terror, for the wholesale destruction of education and culture. Dishonoured and cruelly defeated, Warsaw was cut off from Europe. Meanwhile, a season of notorious 'Moscow balls' was inaugurated, attracting the families of individuals arrested or exiled, constrained by fear for the fate of their loved ones.[79] Yet none of the excesses that generally occur in such circumstances was noted during the

---

[77] Durand, *Depesze*, 238–239. Durand was perhaps not socially active in Warsaw. As Stefan Witwicki wrote: 'Russia has continually sought to keep consuls arriving in Warsaw away from the Poles. Those gentlemen, not mixing at all among Polish society and not understanding the native tongue, can know only what they hear from the Muscovite officials. For instance, the French consul (Mr Durand) has yet to strike up a sincere acquaintance with any Polish home or with any Polish family throughout his entire lengthy stay in Warsaw.' Stefan Witwicki, 'Moskale w Polsce' [The Russians in Poland] (1832), in *Zbiór pism pomniejszych* [Collected minor texts] (Leipzig, 1878), ii:50. Yet although the Russians did indeed endeavour to misinform the diplomatic corps, Durand was highly intelligent and was not content with the 'Russian pulp'.

[78] Fryderyk Skarbek, *Pamiętniki* [Memoirs] (1878), quoted in Jerzy Skowronek and Irena Tessaro-Kosimowa, *Warszawa w powstaniu listopadowym* [Warsaw during the November Rising] (Warsaw, 1980), 205–206.

[79] Mickiewicz, *Dzieła*, iii:311; Witwicki, 'Moskale', 34.

Russian army's capture of Warsaw. One horrific incident did take place outside the city, on a deserted battleground.[80] 'The leaders of the Russian army', we read in the memoirs of Natalia Kicka, whom Chopin occasionally accompanied during musical soirées in her grandmother's celebrated salon, 'postponed their entry into Warsaw and the occupying of her streets until 8 September. This was required in order to maintain discipline among the troops. General Toll [who led the capture] promised soldiers they would be allowed to run riot in Warsaw. Paskievich [chief commander of the whole campaign] preferred to rule over our beautiful capital than over a pile of rubble. Entering by night, the plundering that General Toll had promised the Russian troops would have been unavoidable. Looting would have been followed by conflagration, and the Russians, I repeat, wished to rule over a beautiful Warsaw, which they found so alluring.'[81] The Russians behaved properly.[82] During both the capture of the city and its occupation, the tsar's officers, especially those loyal to their commanders, took care to ensure that the Russian soldiers not turn into a rowdy, marauding horde.

Chopin knew nothing whatsoever about all this. At the news of Warsaw's capture, his imagination was immediately overrun by a vision of slaughter in the Praga district of the city. He thought that the events of thirty years previously were being repeated. This is quite understandable. No one in Warsaw awaiting the storming by Paskievich's army could resist associations with the year 1794. After all, traumatic experiences usually come flooding back in analogous circumstances. On 20 August 1831, while Varsovians were busy building defensive entrenchments, Klementyna Hoffmanowa, so loved in the Chopin family, wrote

---

[80] Klementyna Tańska-Hoffmanowa, *Pamiętniki* [Diaries] (Berlin, 1849), i:216.

[81] Natalia Kicka, *Pamiętniki* [Memoirs] (Warsaw, 1972), 324.

[82] Witwicki, 'Moskale', 34. At times, Russian officers were full of goodwill and admiration for the Poles. See Puzynina, *W Wilnie*, 163.

in her diary: 'Now many people think that Warsaw will defend itself until it drops: I am perfectly calm, trusting God that he will want to look after our city. If bullets fly, then we will doubtless take shelter in the cellars: if the worst comes to the worst, it will still be Paskievich and not Suvorov.'[83]

Paskievich was indeed different to Suvorov, the commander in chief of the Russian forces that stormed the right bank of the Vistula in Warsaw in 1794. Both were brilliant strategists, but in contrast to Paskievich, a composed and even-tempered man, Suvorov was known for his volatile, combustible character. His staff, at times even exposing themselves to abuse, took great care to ensure that his bloodthirsty orders, issued in a state of drunkenness, were not implemented. He was a typical Russian merciful brute. Anyone familiar with Russian history will know that an oxymoron of this kind is no literary invention. 'The Russians in Praga', we read in the memoirs of Jędrzej Kitowicz, 'ran wild with fire and sword, sparing no one: the Cossacks even carried little children around the streets on spears. However, not all Praga went up in flames, and not all the citizens were slain by the enemy's sword: only three streets were burned, those along which the Russians entered, as General Shuvarov, who had command over the Russian army, did not

---

[83] Tańska-Hoffmanowa, *Pamiętniki*, i:209. This author, well-known at that time, was a very close friend of Chopin. When travelling through Ojców on his first journey to Vienna, Chopin put up there in the same cottage where Mrs Tańska had stayed in 1824 during her journey around Poland – trumpeted in the press. Her description of Ojców was published in *Rozrywki dla Dzieci*, a periodical that was familiar to the Chopins, as it published an obituary of Emilia. So the composer was aware of following in the famous writer's footsteps, and was proud of the fact (KR 48–49). In the years 1831–1833, Chopin's sister Ludwika was a member of the Patriotic Union of Polish Women, of which Tańska-Hoffmanowa was chief patroness. General Sowińska's wife also worked for this most deserving organisation. See Janina Siwkowska, *Nokturn, czyli Rodzina Fryderyka Chopina i Warszawa w latach 1832–1881* [Nocturne, or Fryderyk Chopin's family and Warsaw in the years 1832–1881] (Warsaw, 1986), i:20–32.

allow anything more to be burned than what had been torched during the initial surge, having given his men a short time for such bestial pleasures'.[84] But this was a real slaughter. Here is a description compiled by Henryk Mościcki from the accounts of those who survived. 'No one was spared. Infants pulled from their mothers' breasts were taken on lances, "so they wouldn't grow to avenge", and thrown into burning houses. Growing boys were taken alive, to be transported deep into Russia and there, according to some truly diabolical idea, brought up to be enemies of their own homeland. Nuns in the Bernardine convent were raped and butchered, [...] poor wretches were dragged out of their homes to be dealt an elaborate death amid drunken amusement. [...] Soon, the public squares were savagely strewn with naked corpses hacked to pieces, crammed into the mud in one horrifying mass, shapeless clusters and piles of bodies of soldiers, civilians, Jews, priests, monks, women and children, here and there still twitching with spasms of life.'[85] The most appalling scenes occurred along the left bank of the Vistula, before the eyes of the population, terrified and powerless, which on that day thrust this massacre into the national memory.

Remembrance of this event in the composer's family must have been quite vivid, since Mikołaj Chopin was a soldier in the Kościuszko Rising. Some scholars have admittedly questioned this fact, but their reasoning is really quite paltry. As Alfred de Vigny wrote in his *Servitude and Grandeur of Arms*:

Family recitals have the especial excellence that they en-
grave themselves on the mind much more deeply than does
the written word; they live with the life of their venerable

[84] Jędrzej Kitowicz, *Pamiętniki, czyli Historia polska* [Memoirs, or A history of Poland], ed. Przemysława Matuszewska (Warsaw, 1971), 615.
[85] Henryk Mościcki, 'Szturm i rzeź Pragi w r. 1794' [The storming and massacre of Praga in 1794], in *Pod berłem carów* [Under tsarist rule] (Warsaw, 1924), 18–20.

narrator, and they project our existence back into the past, just as a prophet's imagination can project it forward into the future.[86]

If I, although born eight years after the Bolshevik War, can still enumerate the skirmishes, battles, camps, engagements and forays of my father and his colleagues from the 1920 campaign, then Chopin, although born sixteen years after the Praga massacre, must have been familiar with his father's experiences from that tragic year 1794. When everything in Warsaw was moving towards an eruption, Mikołaj Chopin booked a seat on a stagecoach. He was heartily fed up with us Poles, as I find hardly surprising, and wished to return to his native France. But when the uprising began and the populace poured out onto the streets to the tolling of bells, he was swept away by the euphoria. So he joined the voluntary Warsaw militia and soon earned the rank of lieutenant. When Suvorov's army, which had moved along the right bank of the Vistula, was nearing the Praga district, Fryderyk's father was stationed there with his unit in one of the hastily erected fortifications. Like all the Polish troops deployed along the Praga entrenchments, he was doomed to death, since even those who survived the fighting, even those who were wounded, were later ruthlessly cut down. On the night prior to the Russians' storming of the city, which took place in the morning of 4 November 1794, Mikołaj Chopin received an order to give up his position to his neighbours and take his unit across to the left bank of the river. Were it not for that, then Fryderyk Chopin would not have been born. This anonymous Frenchman would have perished childless in a collective grave. A vivid depiction of the Praga massacre has been passed down to us by two splendid artists. The first picture is the work of

[86] Alfred de Vigny, *Servitude and Grandeur of Arms* tr. Roger Gard, (1835; London, 1996), 7.

Jan Piotr Norblin, a Frenchman who came to Poland in 1774, worked here for us and ultimately – as Mieczysław Porębski writes – became a witting participant in that great historical cause. He chronicled our history in the years 1791–1794, from the passing of the Third of May Constitution to the death of Poland on the battlefield at Maciejowice. His invaluable and moving cycle of pictures included a drawing entitled *The Praga Massacre*, which Porębski describes: 'The spacious interior of a poor suburban chamber is the scene of horrific acts. Raped women, murdered adults and children, even a dog, the body of which lies in the middle, are the victims of a horrifying slaughter machine. The artist depicts it most starkly. The murderers act in broad daylight.'[87] One soldier holds an infant by the leg before smashing it against the stove. Another pulls a man along the floor, then the next murderer thrusts a bayonet into his back. Witnessing all of this, the mother of the family swoons in distraction. Two soldiers rape a girl. And it all takes place amid corpses lying in their own blood.

Aleksander Orłowski, another marvellous chronicler of Poland's rise and fall, portrayed the same subject somewhat differently. 'With Norblin, the scene of the Praga massacre became a shocking act of protest. An analogous scene depicted by Orłowski is merely an anecdotal account of soldierly merciless-ness, in the face of which even a purse offered by a murdered Jew is futile.'[88] One is immediately struck how the defenceless people are surrounded by a mass of soldiers. A man hugging a boy, clearly in a spontaneous gesture of protection, is mur-dered by several soldiers at once – with bayonet and sword. Several also fall upon a woman with an infant in her arms and

---

[87] Mieczysław Porębski, *Malowane dzieje* [Painted history] (Warsaw, 1962), 38. In his Parisian exile, Chopin maintained social contacts with Jan Piotr Nor-blin's son, the cellist Ludwik Piotr.
[88] Ibid, 44.

a little child at her skirt. Some look for money. Others destroy everything that can be destroyed.

Similar horrors took possession of Chopin's imagination at the moment when he wrote the words 'the enemy's at the door'. He 'saw' then all his loved ones as victims at the mercy of the rabid Russian army. So Chopin's text is a typical product of imagination, which began to work under the influence of the traumatic experiences of Warsaw from the year 1794.

Since we are considering phantasmal reality, I shall allow myself to soften a little those horrors that befell Chopin and to use at first some words from Bertolt Brecht's comic *Threepenny Opera*. Fryderyk saw his sisters as 'victims of soldierly wantonness': 'Perhaps my sisters have succumbed to the fury of riotous Muscovite villainy' (A 36), he wrote in his notebook. Since the earliest times, in every era, in all lands and in all civilisations, women have been raped in conquered cities. So Chopin could well have imagined the worst, particularly since he was aware of the events of 1794. Indeed, the same thing was feared in Warsaw itself. On 8 September 1831, when the Russians were setting up their bivouacs on the Warsaw streets, Natalia Kicka, already mentioned here, who found refuge in the home of the Austrian consul on ul. Miodowa, decided to call on Princess Anna Czartoryska on ul. Nowy Świat. Understandably, she feared being seized by the soldiers and raped. 'On leaving the home of Mrs Oechsner,' we read in her memoirs, 'I took with me her butler, an old campaigner. He concealed two loaded pistols in his pockets. I asked him to keep a close watch over me. The Russian troops had already occupied some streets. Miodowa was still free of them. Passing by the Capuchins', I entered the church and said a prayer, preparing myself for possible death. On rising, I turned to my companion and said: "If some Russian should approach me, remember, shoot at me. Aim well, may your hand not tremble. Remember, I ask this of you. I prefer to be killed on the spot than violated".'[89] Kicka wrongly ascribed her survival to the widow's weeds she was wearing after the death of her husband, an army general. Quite simply, Paskievich, for various reasons, seized Warsaw in a different way to Suvorov, and his troops were exceptionally disciplined. This time, rapes were out of the question. But Chopin could not have known this, and images of wrecked homes and raped girls appeared before his eyes.

He invoked his mother twice, on each occasion due to entirely different associations. First, there was the news that during its capture of the city the Russian army had bombarded and then passed through Powązki cemetery, where in 1827 the Chopins had buried their youngest offspring, Emilia. 'Mother,' we read in the notebook, 'my suffering, affectionate mother, you survived your daughter only to have Muscovy come and oppress you over her bones. Ah, Powązki! – Did they respect her tomb? A thousand more trampled bodies crushed her grave' (A 36). So his mother appeared to him in the aura of a martyr, who lived to see the desecration of her daughter's grave, trampled by the boots of marauding enemy soldiers. The cemetery itself appeared like a ghastly, monstrous morgue. The Russian artillery opened the graves not for resurrection but to take new bodies. Killed soldiers fell upon the rotted bones in their coffins, blown out by bombs into the light of day.

Justyna Chopin appeared to Fryderyk for the second time in connection with the mother of Konstancja Gładkowska. We know nothing today about this wife of the steward of the Royal Castle, but Chopin must have known something. She seems to have had a dreadful reputation in the capital's patriotic circles and must have served the Russians in some way, given that Chopin enquired of Jan Matuszyński on learning of the outbreak of the 'hour of revenge' and the bloody reckoning

---

[89] Kicka, *Pamiętniki*, 323.

with generals on the night of 29/30 November 1830: 'Did they not hang her mother?' (KS i: 165). Even bearing in mind the rather normal dislike felt by men for their sweethearts' mothers, there must have been something pertinent here. Did she really merit the scaffold? 'You have a mother?' he began a conversation with Konstancja, 'And such a bad one!' He then immediately added: 'I have such a good one! – Or perhaps I've no longer got a mother at all. Perhaps a Russian has killed her... murdered her – my sisters helpless, there's no one to pick up our Mother' (A 36–37). So he created an image that could have been lifted straight from the drawings of Norblin and Orłowski, just slightly modified. His sisters are defending themselves against rape. His mother has been murdered. His father is paralysed by grief to such an extent that he is unable to lift his wife's body from the floor. 'Nie wie sobie rady'. This incomparable expression, deeply rooted in old Polish, shows Mikołaj Chopin in a truly extraordinary light. In the sixteenth century, during the era of Jan Kochanowski, the word 'rada' meant reason, prudence, conviction or idea. Thus if someone 'nie wie sobie rady', then he was in a state of spiritual prostration, with no idea what to do in a matter concerning himself. Chopin was familiar with the content of this expression and had experienced it profoundly himself. In April 1831, he did not know what to do with himself, whether to live or to die. Hence, on 1 May he wrote in the same album: 'I feel odd, I feel sad, – [rady sobie nie wiem] – why I'm alone' (A 33). So the deep significance of this expression betrayed an immobilisation of his thoughts. A paralysis of his mind. And that, for the son, was a measure of his father's collapse.

In Fryderyk's phantasmal vision, Mikołaj Chopin is truly remarkable. He is the only one not threatened by insults, wounding or death. He is threatened only by hunger. As in the case of General Sowiński, the term defining the father which today any good psychoanalyst would elicit from the son during a session of immediate associations is 'good-natured' or 'kind-hearted'. In those days, this was a respectable term, carrying none of that ironic indulgence which it has somehow acquired somewhere along the way. When Chopin said that someone was 'good-natured', he had in mind, first and foremost, that he was honest. That is how he described both his sister Izabela (KS i: 327) and also Julian Fontana (KS i: 310, 312). 'My poor father! – my kind-hearted father, perhaps hungry, with no money to buy bread for my mother!' So this is a man worthy of veneration, like every noble elder. Thus Chopin is soon overcome with bitterness: 'Oh father, such pleasures in your later years' (A 36). His father's humiliation involved no more than powerlessness. He was spared the death that raged all around, but was unable to defend his daughters or his wife. So Chopin first 'saw' the rape and murder that was rampant in the family home, and amidst those horrors his father appeared to him as someone condemned to the shame of powerlessness. Thus he raised a lament over the unmerited degradation of the Protector of the Family. In this daydream, he revealed his father's great obsession: the conviction that a man's duty is to ensure his family of bread and safety. It was a precept that he adopted from his parent.

Now that we have examined the phantasmal vision of his family's fortunes, let us try to grasp how Chopin 'saw' Poland's foes.

Throughout the text, he described them consistently with one word alone: 'Moskale'. This name was in common use at that time. In Linde's dictionary, 'Moskal' or 'Moskwicin' signified a subject in the state of the Russian tsars. 'The nations under Russian rule are given the general name Moskali'. This explanation was imprecise, and even misleading, since it would mean that a Lithuanian from the annexed territories should be called 'Moskal'. The above-mentioned eighteenth-century memoirist Jędrzej Kitowicz understood 'Moskal' to signify a Russian or even a Russian soldier who could have belonged to one of the numerous nationalities which peopled that vast empire, and yet he would not have dared to have referred in this way to a Pole from Podolia. The question was quite straightforward. For a very long time, Poles had distinguished between Rus, which was part of the Republic of Poland-Lithuania, and Moscow, or the Grand Duchy of Moscow. When that duchy became Russia, it began to be called Moscow. As we read in Hugo Kołłątaj's *Uwagi nad teraźniejszym położeniem tej części ziemi polskiej, którą od pokoju tylżyckiego zaczęto zwać Księstwem*, 'Russians do not like to be called Moskali, since that name cannot be applied to the whole Russian empire, but only to that land which lies between the Oka and Volga rivers. When, however, the princes of Muscovy had the fortune to bring so many Slavic nations under their rule and long retained that one name, all the other countries incorporated in the Duchy of Moscow went under the same name among foreigners'.[90] The words 'Moskal' and 'Rosjanin' were still being used interchangeably by Maurycy Mochnacki.[91] From the time of the last Partition, or at least during the time when Chopin was growing up and attending school, this word took on a pejorative shade of meaning. All kinds of atrocities began to be associated with the Moskal, cupidity and boorishness the least of them. For some, it was a derogatory name, although it is difficult to gauge how much contempt smouldered within it and how much hatred. Suffice it to recall the excerpts quoted above from Kitowicz or Kicka. In 1819, Julian Ursyn Niemcewicz,

---

[90] Hugo Kołłątaj, *Uwagi nad teraźniejszym położeniem tej części ziemi polskiej, której od pokoju tylżyckiego zaczęto zwać Księstwem Warszawskim* [Remarks on the present situation of that part of Polish territory which since the Treaty of Tilsit has begun to be called the Duchy of Warsaw] (Leipzig, 1808), 66.

[91] See Maurycy Mochnacki, 'Kilka listów do Wydawcy w niektórych przedmiotach narodowego powstania' [A few letters to publishers on some aspects of the national uprising] (1832), in *Dzieła* [Works], iv:*Pisma rozmaite* [Miscellanea] (Poznań, 1863), 94–95.

a former aide to Tadeusz Kościuszko, captured by the Russians following the Battle of Maciejowice in 1794 and imprisoned in St Petersburg, published the book *Dzieje panowania Zygmunta III* [The reign of Sigismund III]. It was censured by Józef Kalasanty Szaniawski, a former Jacobin who in the Congress Kingdom held high office and earned universal contempt among Poles. 'Szaniawski', as Kajetan Koźmian writes, 'began his office by satisfying the complaints of the imperial commissar: unable to stop the printing of *Historia panowania Zygmunta III*, where only the epithet Moskwicin was used for a Russian, he ordered the pages to be pasted over with little pieces of paper bearing the word Rosjanin'.[92] In journalism and poetry from the November Rising period, a Moskal is also portrayed as the complete opposite of a Pole. He was a man of Asia, whereas the Pole was a man of Europe. For Chopin's friend Stefan Witwicki, 'Moskale in Poland' meant 'Asia has invaded Europe again'. And so when Chopin's thoughts were occupied with the Russian commander of the Polish campaign, there appeared in his Stuttgart notebook the proud sentence: 'Paskievich – a pup from Mogilev, – captures the seat of the foremost monarchs of Europe?' (A 36). The Moskal became a champion of enslavement, whilst the Pole was a knight of freedom. So Moskal was a name defining a man from a foreign and hateful spiritual realm.

—

Kto powiedział, że Moskale
Są to bracia nas Lechitów,
Temu pierwszy w łeb wypalę
Przed kościołem Karmelitów.
Kto nie uczuł w gnuśnym bycie
Naszych kajdan, praw zniewagi,
To jak zdrajcy wydrę życie

---

[92] Kajetan Koźmian, *Pamiętniki* [Journal], ed. Marian Kaczmarek and Kazimierz Pecold (Wrocław, 1972), iii:102.

Na niemszczonych kościach Pragi[93]
(Whoever might one day have said
The Russians were our like,
I'd be the first to shoot him dead
Outside the Carmelites'.
Whoever in our listless chains
The laws of outrage still ignores,
On Praga's unavenged remains
I'll end the traitor's earthly course.)
—

Such were the words of the famous insurrectionary song that my mother was still teaching me when I was eight, so lengthy was its career in the national primer. The new, Romantic meaning of the word 'Moskal', which departed from Linde's explanations, is perhaps best defined by Adam Mickiewicz in his article 'O partii polskiej' [On the Polish party], published in the Parisian *Pielgrzym Polski* in 1833: 'On the other hand, the [European] cabinets rely on [tsar] Nicholas: he is the visible head of their Church: and for that reason the peoples of all our enemies, of all the enemies of freedom, are regarded as Moskale'.[94]

And so for Chopin, as for the whole Romantic generation, a Moskal was a man who helped create a political system based on deception, oppression, murder and aggression. He was an enemy destroying a civilisation built on the principles of freedom and a respect for the rights of the individual. Hence, for Chopin the defeat of the uprising signified the beginning of the end of that civilisation: 'Moskal ruler of the world?' he asked himself with trepidation (A 36). He was clearly aggrieved at that civilisation for not understanding the meaning of our insurrection, the prin-

[93] Rajnold Suchodolski, 'Polonez' [Polonaise], in Andrzej Zieliński (ed.) *Poezja powstania listopadowego* [Poetry of the November Rising] (Wrocław, 1971), 36.
[94] Mickiewicz, *Dzieła*, vi:93.

ciples of the 'Polish party', the principles of the 'Polish religion of freedom', as Mickiewicz would have put it. 'God, God! Move the earth, may it swallow up the people of this century. May the cruellest suffering beset the French, who did not come to our aid' (A 37). This cry may be interpreted as an example of typically bizarre Polish grievances against the West for once again placing its shallow political interests before the moral duty of a European state. Yet more than anything, this would appear to have been an expression of his repulsion at the spiritual indifference which – if anyone should ask – afflicted the new bourgeois nations to a greater degree than anyone would care to remember today. It is telling that Chopin considered that France had a duty to help us; such was the strength within him of the myth of the French as a nation in possession of some political morality. So the French- man is portrayed as a traitor, and the Russian as a rapist, rogue, fire-raiser and murderer. Merciless and cruel.

So now we know the significance of this word, we can set about analysing the most riveting fragment of the notes made in Stuttgart – those three extraordinary sentences addressed directly to God.

The Poles have two marvellous texts in which their (justi- fied) grievances with the Creator are expressed. Both were born of despair. In both cases, the furious scream came from the souls of people who we regard – quite rightly – as the spiritual leaders of our nation. In both cases, the accusations – for these are ac- cusations arising from an outraged sense of justice – are of a very similar character. Both arose not in Poland, but abroad. They were written during the same period, when, through the combined ef- forts of foreign monsters and home-bred fools, we found ourselves once again in the outermost circle of the political hell of Europe. Still today, they stick like a thorn in the soul of every Pole.

One of them was written in 1832, in Dresden. This is the conclusion of the Great Improvisation, in which Konrad,

the protagonist of Part III of Adam Mickiewicz's *Forefathers'*
Eve, describes his phantasmal flight into the heavens, a typically
Romantic flight towards transcendence on Platonic 'wings of the
soul'. Once his imagination had assured him that he was standing before God, this rather unpleasant bard posed the Creator
several fundamental questions and demanded of Him what one
might call plenipotentiary powers in connection with the Polish
question. There is no doubt that he was puffed up with hubris
and not of sound mind, but his impatience at the silence and
indifference of God was as justified as it was lofty. Driven to
his wits' end, he turns to threats:

—

Odezwij się, – bo strzelę przeciw Twej naturze;
Jeśli jej w gruzy nie zburzę,
To wstrząsnę całym państw Twoich obszarem;
Bo wystrzelę głos w całe obręby stworzenia:
Ten głos, który z pokoleń pójdzie w pokolenia:
Krzyknę, żeś Ty nie ojcem świata, ale…[95]
(Speak, – or I'll shoot at Your nature;
If I don't smash it to pieces,
I'll shake all your dominions;
Or I'll shoot a voice into the whole of creation:
That voice, which will pass from generation to generation:
I'll cry that You're not the father of the world, but…)

—

And at this moment, when he has refrained from uttering
the blasphemous word aloud, the devil, who happens to be in
the vicinity, completes the thought for him: 'but… the Tsar!'
No matter that Konrad did not speak the word 'tsar' with his
own lips, since he thought it deep in his heart, since in his soul
he transformed the God of love into the organiser of the Russian system of violence and lawlessness, because in the same

---

[95] Mickiewicz, *Dzieła*, ii:167.

Forefathers' Eve the Russian tsar appears as the proxy of Infernal Evil on earth. For Mickiewicz, the 'tsarist system' was truly the Evil Spirit of Europe. So in Konrad's accusations, God has revealed Himself as an insensitive monster, a henchman of evil and injustice, a perpetrator of ill deeds and murders.

The second text was written in the year 1831, in Stuttgart. It expresses the same suspicion that the world is governed not by the good God of Judaeo-Christian civilisation, but by a gnostic Evil Archon of the World: Moskal. In contrast to Konrad, at the news of the capture of Warsaw and the defeat of Poland, Chopin did not refrain from blasphemy and wrote down a thought just as furious as that of the Hero of the Poles: 'Oh God, you are! – You are and you take no revenge! – Have you not yet had enough of the Muscovite crimes – or – or you are Moscow yourself!' (A 36).

First let us deal for a moment with the punctuation of this text, since it has some connection with the character of the accusation.

Chopin was educated during a period when the Polish language textbook used in schools was the famous *Gramatyka języka polskiego* by the Piarist Onufry Kopczyński, published in 1817, after the death of its author, who had contributed greatly to Polish culture. His system of punctuation required that each written text also be recited aloud, hence it was later known as a rhetorical-intonational system. 'Never disregard', wrote Kopczyński, 'the very close similarity between speech and music. Written in music are separate signs for notes higher and lower, quicker and slower; there are signs of punctuation, that is, pauses, shorter or longer. All of this is in verbal speech, and it should all be marked in writing, as well.'[96] Thus, according to Kopczyński, the dash, with which Chopin's text is crawling,

---

[96] Onufry Kopczyński, *Gramatyka języka polskiego* [A Polish grammar] (Warsaw, 1819), 261. See also Konrad Górski, 'Interpunkcja w „Panu Tadeuszu"' [Punctuation in *Pan Tadeusz*], *Pamiętnik Literacki*, 59/2 (1968).

discharges the function of a musical rest, to which, understandably, our composer was particularly alive. One is justified in suspecting that even in a text intended for himself and for silent reading, he immediately placed a dash wherever his thoughts paused for expression. Sometimes even after an exclamation mark. And he did this because each of the successive thoughts, which were indeed most emphatic, had to 'resound' to him. There is no question that when writing out words, which for him could not be soundless notions, Chopin heard their sound with his internal ear. Thus such pauses marked out the successive cries of his thoughts.

Chopin's accusation consists of several points. Firstly, in a short phrase, he transmitted the idea – neither grievance nor astonishment – that God, who observed Poland's tragedy, truly existed: 'Oh God you are!' In this sentence, the words 'you are' mean 'you are, therefore you know'. Poland is falling into an abyss. God knows this and still has the temerity to exist. Similar astonishment is expressed by Mrs Rollison in *Forefathers' Eve*. God has the nerve to rule over a world of horrendous injustice. He tolerates the activities of foul murderers.

—

Syn! wyrzucili z okna, z klasztoru, na bruki.
Me dziecię, mój jedynak! mój ojciec-żywiciel –
A ten żyje, i Pan Bóg jest, i jest Zbawiciel!
(My son! they've thrown from the window, from the
                                    monastery, onto the street.
My child, my only child! my father-provider –
And He lives, and the Lord God is, and is Saviour!)

—

Next Chopin pictures the Creator as the Old Testament God of vengeance. Since he exists, perhaps he exists only as an avenger. So why does he not send down vengeance upon the enemies of Poland? 'You are and you take no revenge!'

The idea of a God of forgiveness did not even occur to Chopin. So he was able to join the group of philomaths from Part III of *Forefathers' Eve* imprisoned 'in the Basilian monastery, converted into a prison of state' and sing with them:

—

Tak! zemsta, zemsta, zemsta na wroga,
Z Bogiem i choćby mimo Boga![97]
(Yes! revenge, revenge, revenge on the foe,
With God or be it in spite of God!)

—

After a pause, which this time allowed him to soften the cry of indignation, God was seen as a heartless monster. The long sentence, which is not a cry, but a caustic 'mutterance' concluded with a bolt of lightning, includes an idea on which Chopin's generation was raised. Widely read in Warsaw was Jan Paweł Woronicz's famous poem 'Hymn to God' ['Hymn do Boga'], in which Poland's misfortunes were treated as punishment for unspecified sins. We are guilty of some transgressions against God and so deserve the monstrous deeds of our enemies.[98] Chopin seems to have agreed with this, but at the same time he thought that even if God was punishing us justifiably, did he not exaggerate on 8 September 1831? Does that day not attest His bloodthirstiness? He wrote: 'Have you not yet had enough of the Muscovite crimes' without a question mark, although the syntax implies such a sign. Chopin's thoughts were suddenly interrupted by some dreadful suspicion. So he placed a dash,

---

[97] Mickiewicz, *Dzieła*, iii:147.
[98] Jan Paweł Woronicz, 'Hymn do Boga', in *Poezje* [Poetry] (Cracow, 1832), ii:18:

—

'Więc gdy nie możesz karać bez przyczyny,
Los nasz być musi płodem naszej winy'.
(If you cannot punish without cause,
Then our fate must derive from our guilt.)

—

to suspend them. This was followed by the word 'or', which indicates that Chopin already knew the answer. But it was so horrendous that his thoughts froze again, out of fright. So he placed another dash, to avoid screaming out that truth for at least a moment. But eventually everything snapped within him. He phrased a brief, unambiguous and monstrous accusation: 'or you are Moscow yourself!'

Thus God is an aggressor and a murderer, since that is how Chopin saw Moskal. He is also the protector of evil and injustice, a savage and inhuman Asian, since that was how his generation saw Moskal. This is not the God of the unjustly suffering servant. In any case, Chopin, like Konrad in *Forefathers' Eve*, questioned here the good and just God of Judaeo-Christian civilisation. And, as it was for Konrad, this accusation was based on the excessive suffering of his nation.

This is one of Chopin's many utterances about God. We have no right to make any generalisations. We also have no right to draw from this text any conclusions regarding the character of Chopin's religiosity. After all, it was written in a state of despair. It arose out of the flames that were consuming the world of his youth. And that may explain why it returns to us in times of disaster and cataclysm. For in Stuttgart, Chopin committed to paper the doubt that appeared as a logical conclusion from the traumatic experience of a nation excessively tormented by endless defeat and suffering.

This doubting was in some sense prepared for by the spiritual life of pre-rising Warsaw. As we know, Varsovians read Woronicz's famous 'Hymn to God'. This poem was written in 1805 and expresses the uneasiness of conscience that engulfed our forebears after the Polish state was obliterated. We can learn what this poem meant for the generation to which Chopin belonged from Maurycy Mochnacki's masterpiece of literary criticism 'Woronicz', published in the *Kurier Polski* of 15 January 1830.

For Romantic youths, it was a work 'unparalleled in the whole of Polish literature'.[99]

This hymn was a Pole's meditation on the doubt that once gripped the Psalmist:

—

'I say to God my Rock, "Why have you forgotten me?
Why must I go about mourning, oppressed by the enemy?"
My bones suffer mortal agony as my foes taunt me, saying
to me all day long, "Where is your God?"'

(Psalm 42, 9–10)

—

In Woronicz, it reads as follows:

—

Pamięć naszą uczciwą, głośną w poprzek świata,
Jak skorupą garncarską, o kamień stłuczoną,
Pogwizdując wędrowiec depcze i pomiata.
A patrząc na bram naszych postać okopconą,
Potrząsa głową i pyta zdumiany:
„I gdzież ich teraz ów Bóg zawołany?...".[100]
(Our honest memory that resounds through the world,
Like an earthenware pot, smashed 'gainst a stone,
Is trampled and kicked by a wayfarer, whistling.
And seeing the blackened form of our gates,
He shakes his head and asks in amazement:
'And where now is that God they invoke?')

That 'invoked God' denoted the famous God of the Poles, who, in spite of their devotion and attachment, in His unfathomable dimension decided to send down upon them, as upon Job,

---

[99] Maurycy Mochnacki, *Pisma po raz pierwszy edycją książkową objęte* [Writings. First edition in book form], ed. A. Śliwiński (Lviv, 1910), 232.

[100] For more on this subject, see Ryszard Przybylski, *Klasycyzm, czyli prawdziwy koniec Królestwa Polskiego* [Classicism, or The real demise of the Congress Kingdom] (Warsaw, 1983), 213–214.

a whole avalanche of torments. Consequently, young people from Chopin's generation, who went into raptures over this poem, posed themselves the question: what does this experience mean? The suspicion must have occurred to them that God was excessively cruel. Hence, Chopin also cried: 'Have you not yet had enough of the Muscovite crimes'. Who are you, if you respond to devotion and love with horrendous castigation? This distressing question tormented many Poles at that time. It must also have exercised Chopin, as well, given his explosion of grievances and accusations at the news of Warsaw's capture. In some way, this was a natural reaction on the part of a Warsaw intellectual, though stamped with the boldness that is peculiar to exceptional people alone. On the day after the Russian troops entered Warsaw – this took place, as we may recall, on 8 September 1831 – the famous poet and professor of literature Kazimierz Brodziński, to whose university lectures *le tout Varsovie* hastened prior to the uprising, wrote a poem entitled '9 września 1831', which includes the following lines:

—

Boże! Boże! gdzieś się podział,
Osławiony nasz obrońca?
Któż się, w Tobie ufny, spodział,
Że do tego przyjdziem końca?
Coś umyślił z nieszczęsnymi,
Żeś nas rzucił bez sposobu?
Aniś chciał nas mieć wolnymi?
Aniś wszystkim otwarł grobu![101]
(God! God! where have you got to,
Our notorious defender?
Who 'mongst those who trust in you
Expected us to come to this?

---

[101] Kazimierz Brodziński, *Poezje* [Poetry], ed. Czesław Zgorzelski (Wrocław, 1950), ii:138.

What plans for us unfortunates,
That you've abandoned us helpless?
You neither wished to make us free?
Nor opened for us all the grave!)

—

Brodziński failed to understand how a good Father could punish innocent children, but he did not dare accuse Him of a predilection for cruelty. He asked. He asked, because he could not get his head around the idea that God could be the tsar or Moskal. Such an idea could only have occurred to people in whose souls despair had smothered the sentimental god-fearing nature typical of Poles.

In this extraordinary text, Chopin also addressed his own attitude towards the uprising. He uttered only three sentences on this subject, but, to a calm and diligent reader, they speak volumes.

The questions that arose in the immediate wake of Tytus's departure to take part in the insurrection now occurred to him again; the same questions that Doctor Johann Malfatti posed him in Vienna. Despite his extremely earnest attitude towards his art, Chopin still considered that even the exceptional talent that everyone around him talked about did not exempt him from the obligation which at times of historical ordeal weighed upon every Pole. Nearly all his friends were out on the battlefield, and so nothing could stifle within him the sense of guilt. It was a debt that could not be paid in music, even in music that expressed the spirit of Polishness and brought glory to our homeland around the world, as our patriots did indeed demand of him. This anxiety could only have been quelled by a deed on a par with those of his peers and friends. 'Ah, why could I not kill at least one Moskal! –' (A 36). I can just picture him as he fixes the bayonet to his rifle and runs a Moskal through. Yet he felt that he ought to have left for the uprising and killed the enemy, like his friends. And so,

105

immediately after this thought occurred to him, he remembered his close friend, who on learning of the outbreak of the insurrection bade farewell to him and returned from Vienna to Poland: 'Oh Tytus – Tytus!' (A 36). His friends were killing, and so he too should kill. Like the whole of his generation, like the students and cadets of Warsaw, Chopin was raised on Adam Mickiewicz's 'Ode to Youth' ['Oda do młodości']. Consequently, he harboured the conviction that murder should be met with murder.

—

Gwałt niech się gwałtem odciska,
A ze słabością łamać uczmy się za młodu![102]
(Let violence be met with violence,
And let us conquer our weakness while young!)

—

So the shame of inactivity preyed on his mind. The fall of Warsaw, which should have put an end to those constant pangs of conscience, in fact only heightened them.

The thought of his miserable art again reared its head. 'And I'm here idle – and I'm here with bare hands – only occasionally groaning, hurting at the piano – I despair…' (A 37). Even the masterpieces he wrought from the piano could not assuage the conscience of this boy brought up in a community which, at a time of war, opposes writing implements with a bayonet, a keyboard with a rifle. His parents were rational and prudent, especially his mother, who – like every Polish woman – knew that her son, on hearing the clamour of fighting for his homeland's freedom, would be dreaming of skirmishes by day and by night. Were he to kneel before a cross, he would cast the kneeler aside. Were he to sit at the piano, he would cast the music aside. If he failed to find a rifle, he would grab a hoe and tilt with it at the black sun of despotism. Everyone still considered that he was a national treasure, that fate had predestined him for the

---

[102] Mickiewicz, i:103.

loftiest goals, that his only duty was to make the most of his genius. Yet the entry in his album shows that even the defeat of the uprising could not induce him to reconcile himself with that perfectly reasonable idea, although – as we shall see – in many other things Chopin displayed quite exceptional good sense. Also, that all our boys are very similar to one another, in the nineteenth century and today. A fine sturdy specimen will still risk his life to triumph or perish, and a frail constitution will sink in complexes.

So Chopin left Stuttgart with contradictory feelings. He did not know what to do next. '…hurting at the piano – I despair', he wrote in his notebook. Then he made a pause, in which, as in a maelstrom, his helplessness swirled, and asked himself: '– i cóż nada?' (A 37). This expression, again drawn from the depths of the Polish language, meant 'and what might help me?', 'and who might advise me?'.

He was helped, of course, by life. With the Poles, after every historical convulsion, some enter the earth, for eternal peace, others go underground, to fight and to fret, and still others go to Paris, to live like normal people and create. At that time, Chopin had behind him Warsaw, the city of his youth, and in front of him Paris, the city of his mature years. But from Stuttgart, where he experienced both the ritual death of his 'I' and also another end to Poland, he took to Paris the same old anxiety. He was still unable to verbalise his thoughts, since he still had none of his nearest and dearest close by. On Christmas Day 1831, he wrote to Tytus: 'I'd like you here, you'd not believe how sad I am here that I've no one to express myself to' (KS i: 209). He dwelled on the borderlands between life and death, where phantoms lurk. '…outwardly, I'm cheerful, especially among my own (I call Poles "my own"), but inside something's murdering me – some forebodings, anxieties, dreams or sleeplessness – longing – indifference – a desire for life, and a moment later a desire for death…' (KS i: 210–211).

So Chopin took to Paris several unusual complexes. He went there with grievances against God, who hovered like Moskal over the humiliated city of his youth with a knout in his hand. These sentiments would later give rise to a vision of an insensitive and ruthless God. He dragged there his grievances against France – a feeling that would turn him into a shrewd observer of the intellectual and political life of the French. And he hauled there his suspicion that music was powerless in the face of the historical experiences of his nation and the specific dramas of existence. So the Chopin who first set foot on the Parisian streets was a man with an irresistible inclination to flee into the realm of his imagination. And yet, after all, music is an imaginary realm, albeit filled with most substantial sound.

CHAPTER II

SETTING HIS LIFE IN ORDER

On arriving in Paris, Chopin faced a most serious task, which – it would later emerge – he discharged both swiftly and soberly. He actually found himself in the situation of the ambitious heroes of Balzac: he had to conquer Paris. Convinced that achieving this aim would solve most of his problems, he immediately set about reinventing himself, since he knew that the image he projected to Parisians would go a long way towards determining his artistic career.

He also knew that the situation of an artist was dependent upon social conditions. For this reason, he resolved to conquer above all the 'upper echelons' of Paris, which at that time determined a musician's public success. When happenstance enabled him to present his talent in the salons, immediately after his victory, and in a relatively short space of time, he created a suggestive, and rather costly, lifestyle for himself, which demanded excellent attire, an elegant abode and well-organised public performances. This was an essential setting to his innate charm and natural refinement. As a consequence, Chopin had to fill his days with continuous toil, since he had no 'initial capital'. In order to keep up his image in the minds of the elite, Chopin had to earn systematically. So he busied himself interminably with his compositions and also gave lessons. George Sand, who observed him at close quarters for many years, was of the opinion that he worked like a nigger, even when he was suffering (KGS ii: 70).

Whilst observing a particular lifestyle, he also imposed certain norms of behaviour on others – norms which began to hold sway among the people around him, as well. Anyone who

110

wished to enter his circle had to conform to certain rules. The order in his life was guaranteed by a peculiar system of information, comprising easily recognisable signs. Thus in ordering his life, Chopin at the same time created his world. That world could be ignored, but not wrecked. Anyone who penetrated it immediately became subordinated to the Centre, even if he were a genius. Balzac never forgave Chopin for that.

Let us examine the three forms that transformed Chopin's life into an harmonious whole: attire, apartment and public appearance. These were the three signs by which he could be identified. Only Chopin dresses that way. Only the Ariel of the piano could live like that. Here comes the one and only Messenger of the Gods onto the stage. I have no doubt whom I am looking at and whose playing I am listening to.

1. THE ATTIRE OF A SPIRITUAL ARISTOCRAT

People have made use of the symbolism of colours in every era, and fashion has naturally not omitted to exploit it. But in the first half of the nineteenth century, the colour of one's attire carried primarily information about one's political views. There would be nothing out of the ordinary in this, were it not for the truly universal knowledge of the semiotics of colours that was characteristic of that period. This could be encountered in various social milieux and in various places. Here are three examples of the semiotic actions of ladies of that time.

On 24 May 1829, in Warsaw, the Russian emperor was crowned King of Poland. Nicholas I could not abide the Poles. He saw the ceremony itself as 'senseless torture', but since the turbulent moods had to be allayed and, above all, the favour of that part of the aristocracy which was to form the royal court had to be somehow won, it was decided to give a sign of Russian magnanimity. So Tsarina Alexandra made the short journey from the Royal Castle to the Cathedral of St John (where the ceremony took place) in a separate open carriage – at a slow and dignified pace, of course, so that the people of Warsaw could get a good look at her. As Julian Ursyn Niemcewicz relates, she was dressed 'in national colours'.[103] That meant in white and amaranth. Thus the white-amaranth dress of the Russian tsarina was to curry Varsovians' favour for the hated, imposed ruler who, on the strength of the Vienna Congress of 1815, had become monarch of the little state known as the Kingdom of

---

[103] Julian Ursyn Niemcewicz, *Pamiętniki czasów moich* [Memoirs of my times], ed. J. Dihm (Warsaw, 1957), ii:303.

112

Poland. The information contained in Tsarina Alexandra's dress was the operatic clemency of the despot, *la clemenza dello zar*.

After the fall of the November Rising, during which the tsar was dethroned by the Insurrectionary Seym, a substantial part of the Polish army decided to enter exile. People marched in columns of fifty to a hundred through Germany to France. Active along the route were German Associations for Poles in Need and in Transit (Vereine zur Hilfsbedürftigen und Durchrei-senden Polen). Local residents spontaneously showed them huge kindness, feeding them and clothing them at their own expense. Locals and exiles sometimes drank together, out of enthusiasm and despair, which drew high-minded protests from puritanical supporters of a brotherhood of free peoples.[104] On 17 February 1832, when a group of exiles was passing through Frankfurt am Main, the proprietress of a very exclusive and expensive brothel, in which a room cost 500 guldens, in some irrational transport, or perhaps reckoning on some good publicity, offered several dozen Polish officers a free night's accommodation in her es-tablishment. The invited officers were gathered together in the drawing-room of the bordello, which resembled some magnifi-cent palace. 'Soon', as we read in the journal of Józef Alfons Petrykowski, 'the side door opened and a butler announced in French: "Voici les mesdemoiselles". Although in accepting these amusing and unexpected invitations, each of us felt a certain repulsion, or at least some sort of disdain, when we espied the 46 young ladies dressed in white dresses with amaranth sashes and bands, that is, when we saw the national colours adorning the loveliest creatures in the world, we could not but feel some sudden emotion, not respect or esteem, but some extraordinary

---

[104] See Piotr Roguski, *Tułacz polski nad Renem. Literatura i sprawa polska w Niemczech w latach 1831–1845* [The Polish émigré in Germany. Literature and the Polish question in Germany during the years 1831–1845] (Warsaw, 1981), 41–42.

wonder.'[105] On this occasion, the white-amaranth dress was a sign of the brotherhood of peoples and of admiration for noble freedom fighters, who, after a splendid reception, turned their attentions to 'the loveliest creatures in the world' – doubtless with respect and great contentment.

On 13 December 1836, at a musical soirée given by Chopin, where the guests included the marquis Astolphe de Custine, the singer Adolphe Nourrit, the writer Eugène Sue, Ferenc Liszt and several Poles, George Sand, so one diarist wrote, appeared in 'fantastical attire'. She was yet to launch her full-blown offensive on Chopin. The writer, who clearly enjoyed wearing original outfits, decided to express her view on the Polish question that was exercising the French artistic elite at that time. Besides, any excuse is good for presenting a new creation. Women are even capable of using a funeral to such ends. It should be borne in mind, as well, that in those days many people were under the impression that the Polish colours were white and crimson, possibly on account of border signs. In 1825, when Gabriela Günther (Puzynina), a resident of Lithuania (clearly well versed in the various shades of red), crossed the border between the Russian empire and the Congress Kingdom at Terespol, 'the bridge over the Bug was painted half in black with vermilion stripes from Russia and in white with crimson from the Kingdom side'. So Mrs Sand also appeared at that soirée in a white dress, which 'she had tied around with a broad crimson sash: the oddly-cut white jacket also had crimson facings and buttons. Her black hair, parted in the middle of her head, fell in curls on either side of her face and was bound above her brow with

---

[105] Józef Alfons Petrykowski, *Tułactwo Polaków we Francji. Dziennik emigranta* [Exiled Poles in France. An émigré's journal], introd. and ed. Anna Owsińska (Cracow, 1974), i:72. This incident was brought to my attention by Józef Bachórz. See Maria Janion and Marta Zielińska (eds.), *Style zachowań romantycznych* [Styles of Romantic behaviour] (Warsaw, 1986), 191–192.

a golden band.'[106] On this occasion, a creation in the Polish national colours expressed the opinions of a French democrat.

So in three different cities of Europe, in three very different milieux, one could employ the same colour sign, legible and clear, for three different purposes, albeit all of them political. At that time, politics had even taken over the world of colours. Just please don't explain this phenomenon in terms of female vanity. Sex has nothing to do with it. In any case, men, especially military men and politicians, can be just as vain as women. Towards the end of 1831, when Chopin arrived in Paris, the semiotics of dress was flourishing there. Thus the newcomer's first information about politics in the French capital came from fashion and colour. And Chopin proved a proficient interpreter of those signs. 'The school of medicine,' he wrote to Tytus Woyciechowski on 25 December 1831, 'the so-called "*jeune France*" (who wear little beards and have certain rules for the tying of scarves), remember that here each political party dresses differently – one speaks here of the exaggerated. – The Carlists have green waistcoats; the Republican Napoleonists, in other words that *jeune France*, red; the Saint-Simoniens, or new Christians, forming a separate religion, with a huge number of proselytes already, who are also for equality, wear blue, etc. etc.' (KS i: 208).

It is perfectly understandable that such an observant man immediately turned to his own style of dress and endeavoured to mark it with suitable significance, although he was certainly not concerned solely with transmitting information.

In Chopin's day, male attire had taken on the features of a uniform. On one of the pages of Chateaubriand's *Journal d'outre tombe*, written while he was still in exile, we read that in 1792 the world suddenly turned grey. That was a year of the indisputable triumph of the townsfolk. The jacket appeared – hitherto the last

---

[106] Puzynina, *W Wilnie*, 79. On Sand's dress, see Józef Brzowski, *Dziennik* [Journal], quoted in Czartkowski and Jeżewska, *Fryderyk Chopin*, 213.

garment worn by a condemned man. Pantaloons, shoes and under-wear, the same worn by everyone, filled the world with a gloomy uniformity. Dress began to blur the boundaries between social classes. A cutter would be told: as cheap, comfortable and vulgar as possible. Bodily curves began to be blurred at all costs. The dark hues of the frock coats straightened out the torso. The overcoat was born – the best way of obliterating attire, a true uniform of the phalanstery of the townsfolk, an efflorescence of egalitarian culture. But how to find a gentleman beneath that rough and oval shell? How to find form in a paltry cloth shop?[107]

So fashion during the Romantic era was to a large extent a reaction to the drive towards an aesthetic egalitarianism that accompanied the victory of the third estate. A cult for diversity was born, undoubtedly linked to a new-found esteem for the individual. Elegant models were launched. Original garments were admired and individual ideas valued. There also appeared the dandy, a special breed of coxcomb and popinjay, which brought a Romantic frenzy to fashion.[108] During the first years of the reign of Louis Philippe, when Chopin was elaborating his style of dress, part of public opinion in Paris associated the 'fashionable man' with the dandy. Since he was the opposite of Chopin's ideal, let us take a closer look at him now.

He first appeared as a variety of *petit-maître*. Although, as Balzac accurately wrote, the etymology of this name is uncer-tain, we do know that in the seventeenth century it was used to describe impertinent courtiers. In the Age of Reason, Diderot

---

[107] See Roger Kempf, *Dandies. Baudelaire et C-ie* (Paris, 1977), 171.
[108] Recent works have warned against an uncritical acceptance of the im-ages of dandyism that were created in the 1840s by Jules Barbey d'Aurevilly and Charles Baudelaire. And indeed, these were rather projections of the writers' own dreams and yearnings than a picture of historical reality. Baudelaire, for example, made Delacroix an ideal dandy, although the great artist actually had an aversion to that tribe. On the specific dandyism of Barbey d'Aurevilly, see Pierre Colla, *L'Univers tragique de Barbey d'Aurevilly* (Brussels, 1965), 14–18.

gave this name to various kinds of pretentious loudmouth, 'drunk on self-love'. The *petit-maître*, as in the eighteenth century, now had three different incarnations and appeared in society as *le muscadin*, *le merveilleux* or *l'incroyable*. Thus Paris could admire whole bunches of eccentrics distinguished by their attire. Quite often, this was a sign of particular political views, usually anachronistic and always ill-perceived. Stendhal's Lucien Leuven was branded a *muscadin*, because he flaunted his aristocratic sympathies. Also still distinguished were such types as *le fat*, *le fashionable* and *le lion*.[109]

All these names were in common use; and interestingly they were also employed in musical life to define the style of a work or a performance. In the spring of 1834, Chopin and his German pianist friend Friedrich Hiller travelled to Aachen for the Lower Rhine Festival organised by Felix Mendelssohn. Mendelssohn had first met Chopin in December 1831, in Paris, on his way back to Germany from London, and the reunion in Aachen made a great impression on him. He noted the dazzling innovation of Chopin's compositions and playing, but added: 'They both suffer a little from the Parisian love of despair and emotional exaggeration, too often losing sight of time and sobriety and of true musical thought.' Since Mendelssohn tended towards the opposite extreme, they complemented each other and learned from one another, although he admitted to feeling 'like an old schoolmaster faced by a couple of "mirliflores" or "incroyables".'[110] So he saw them in some way as musical dandies, affecting melancholy and

---

[109] Domna C. Stanton, *The Aristocrat as Art. A Study of Honnete Homme and the Dandy in Seventeenth- and Nineteenth-Century French Literature* (New York, 1980), 54–59. There was a great deal of terminological confusion in the press of the day. Some, for instance, saw the 'lion' as a species of dandy, while for others he was the exact opposite. It was also written that the dandy wanted to show himself and the 'lion' wanted to look at himself. In other words, a snobbish idler was juxtaposed with an interesting personality.

[110] Quoted in Zamoyski, *Chopin*, 110.

exaggerated originality, mixed with a certain insouciance. A *mirli-flore* is simply a fop, whereas an *incroyable* was associated above all with an eccentric. We do not know what and how the two guests from Paris played to deserve such an appraisal. A delicate *rubato* might have been enough for Mendelssohn to qualify Chopin as one of Paris's artistic young blades.

The lawgivers of the world of fashion insisted that behind every type of popinjay stood a man with a specific aesthetic attitude to life. That was true, yet this whole company can be divided into two groups: advocates of provocative elegance and fanatics of refined elegance. Thus in Chopin's day, the 'fashionable man', *l'homme à la mode*, simply tried to please or else, in accordance with the formula of Jules Barbey d'Aurevilly, to please while being unpleasant, *plaire en déplaisant*. A dandy drew attention to himself with attire that was either particularly elegant or provocatively original. Naturally, that is how things looked in Paris. In Vienna, many a dazzling dandy cruised around in a tilbury, and all of them, even the most exquisitely elegant, obviously caused a sensation against the background of the commonly accepted bourgeois elegance in that city. The Viennese townsman, whilst observing the fashions, was by no means a 'fashionable man' in the Parisian sense. That explains, for instance, why Franz Schubert was never faced with a choice between elegance and extravagance. He dressed like everyone: decently. 'This man', wrote Hoffmann von Fallersleben, on seeing him for the first time in some Grinzing wine tavern – is no different from the ordinary Viennese, speaks in Viennese, and like every Viennese wears elegant linen, a clean frock coat and a shining hat'.[111] Chateaubriand would call this attire the uniform of an urban phalansterian.

---

[111] Quoted in Tadeusz Marek, *Schubert* (Cracow, 1955), 210. In hard times, Schubert shared part of his wardrobe with his closest friends, and any sort of fashion, refined or provocative, was far from his thoughts. All he wanted was to be dressed relatively decently.

All the Polish creative artists in Paris at the beginning of the thirties who had a few pennies to spare had to make the choice between distinction and provocation. In order to gain a more suggestive portrait of Chopin, let us now turn our attentions to a brilliant Polish bard who had no hesitation in choosing *l'art de plaire en déplaisant*, a fashion that aroused in the composer of the mazurkas aversion, to say the least. For obvious reasons, this art was based on exaggeration. According to Yoko Nishikawa, Parisian dandies adopted above all certain details from English fashion, which they held as a model, and quickly lapsed into exaggeration. In France, this was immediately associated with the essence of dandyism.[112] To some Englishmen, this exaggeration seemed ludicrous. Here is what Lady Morgan wrote in her book *La France en 1829 et 1830*.

> Self-conceit [*la fatuité*] was so little to the taste and habits
> of the intelligent and studious youth of that country, and is
> so little suited to the ideas of equality that reign here, that
> *le merveilleux*, as the Parisian dandy is known, is seen here
> as something funny rather than as a model. [...] In spite of
> the care taken over his toilet, and contrary to the suppositions
> of journalists, he always looks *endimanché* [in his Sunday
> best], since he exaggerates in all aspects of fashion, from the
> knot of his tie to the laces of his shoes.[113]

This exaggeration in attire was accompanied by an ostentatious impertinence in behaviour. Balzac discovered this very quickly and described it in articles published in *La Mode* and in the novels of manners he was writing at that time.[114] Provocative insolence was employed as part of a 'strategy of stupefaction'.

---

[112] Yoko Nishikawa, *Balzac et le dandysme* (Kyoto, 1977), 70.

[113] Ibid., 69–70.

[114] Ibid., 82, 106.

It always appeared just before or just after some captivating performance. Such a contrast dumbfounded the society, and the dandy began to be seen as a mysterious chasm of contradictions. The society was not without blame. Lucien Leuven tried to be well-mannered and polite – until, that is, he understood that vulgarity would bring him esteem that was commensurate with his insolence. Even the more spiritual Barbey d'Aurevilly considered that impertinence was the sister of charm. This was inherited from Byron. In any case, the dandy was convinced that without extravagance, manifested in his dress, among other things, his person would not acquire significance.

L'art de plaire en déplaisant is regarded as the expression of a typically Romantic aesthetic of contrast. This applies particularly to France, where Victor Hugo, in the programmatic preface to his play *Cromwell* (1827), recommended to Romantic art not so much the mixing as the combining of opposites: good with evil, beauty with ugliness, the lofty with the grotesque. According to Domna C. Stanton, the very principle of pleasing in displeasing contained a typically Romantic paradox, which confused cause and effect. This fundamental ambivalence opened up within the system of dandyism scope for many possible variants. Out of the many different signs, the dandy could choose those which he himself found pleasant but which revolted those who beheld them, or vice versa, choose those which disgusted him but delighted others. He could arrange them in various proportions, creating his own variant of the system.[115] The dandy was aggressive. He rejected the aesthetic of persuasion and imposed himself upon onlookers in a violent way. He sought to conquer. But his success, understandably, depended on his financial means.

It is not surprising, then, that in 1832, when Juliusz Słowacki, a poet who could combine the angelically sublime with the terrifyingly macabre, came to choose a model of elegance, he plumped

---

[115] Stanton, *The Aristocrat as Art*, 146–157.

for *l'art de plaire en déplaisant*. Let us take a close look at him, since he was the complete opposite of Chopin.

He wanted to provoke. His dress was to be defiant, and his behaviour impertinent. On 7 March 1832, he wrote to his mother from Paris:

> So now in the morning I am a man of letters – I correct proofs, write and copy out; and in the evening, from half past nine, I become *un Dandy*, an English *petit-maître* – and I admit that I like it: I try to ensure that in the evening no one can guess what I am in the morning – and in the morning that nothing remains of my evening *fatuité*.[116]

So initially the aim was that his dandyism be only a pose adopted in society and that vanity, although assumed, not begin – God forbid! – to eat away at his poetical soul. Cora and Nelly, acquaintances of Miss Pinard, the daughter of his Paris publisher, regarded him as Oswald, the hero of de Staël's novel *Corinne*. And that was not to his liking. 'After reading through Mr Bulwer's romance *Pelham*, I have turned away a little from Oswaldian musings towards dandyism…' he informed his mother on 30 July that year.[117]

Edward Bulwer-Lytton's novel *Pelham, or the Adventures of a Gentleman* (1828) was hugely popular all across Europe at that time. This is attested by the fact that in 1834–1835 Alexander Pushkin sat down to write a work entitled *A Russian Pelham*.[118] In France alone, between 1828 and 1849, it was given eight editions. The Parisian critics received it as a handbook of dandyism. Pelham's dandyism involved above all an ostenta-

---

[116] *Korespondencja Juliusza Słowackiego*, i:99.

[117] Ibid, i:127.

[118] Alexander Pushkin, *Полное собрание сочинений* [Complete collected works] (Moscow and St Petersburg, 1949), vi:594–598, 772–776; Eng. tr. in *Complete Prose Fiction*, tr. Paul Debreczeny (Stanford, 1983), 462–464.

tious fight against vulgarity in all its manifestations, including the traditional amusements of English aristocrats. Pelham was the antithesis of the 'barbaric' Englishman. In his dress and his comportment, he preferred 'French manners', although he discovered that his reserved and impudent 'English face' brought him celebrity and respect. That must have pleased Słowacki. Admittedly, staid attire was not his cup of tea. But at that time he would not have been satisfied even by the outfit of Beau Brummell himself, who was then considered to be the ideal embodiment of elegance. 'His chief aim', wrote the first biographer of the greatest dandy of the nineteenth century, William Jesse, 'was to avoid anything marked'.[119] Brummell disdained extravagance, because it hinted at vulgarity. When a gentleman attracted attention on the street through his outward appearance, he died as a dandy.

Słowacki was not interested in hidden refinement. He wanted his dress and his manners to irk. On 12 July 1832, he went for a walk. '…just today', he wrote to his mother in the above-mentioned letter, 'I succeeded in my role in the Tuileries gardens: for the first time, my attire turned the ladies' eyes – as I had white galligaskins, a white cashmere waistcoat, in huge, multicoloured flowers, like ladies' dresses of old, and my shirt collar turned out – add to this a cane with gilded head and polished gloves, and you'll have Julek… One of my friends even heard a lady saying: "What a lovely costume". And I approached the company of Ludwik Platter and having said a few words walked away, certain that they said about me: "*Quel fat insupportable!*".'[120]

So like every dandy, he practised street theatre. The role of the shocking apparition was played by the floral waistcoat.

---

[119] William Jesse, *Beau Brummell* (London, 1844), i:59. Quoted in Stanton, *The Aristocrat as Art*, 41.
[120] *Korespondencja Juliusza Słowackiego*, i:127–128.

Since the famous premiere of *Hernani*, the waistcoat had become a special sign of the dress of all kinds of dandy-provocateur.[121] In Słowacki's extravagant outfit, particular significance was taken on by that patch of coloured blooms. One detail was taken from Byron, most probably after perusing numerous lithographs of the lord: the 'turned-out shirt collar'. It was just spread more widely, and Słowacki never tied it up with a scarf or a tie. This novelty has enjoyed a remarkable career in Poland. Still today, youngsters who cannot bear a 'horse-collar' wear a shirt with a 'Słowacki collar'.

However, the poet's entire creation could only arouse laughter or anger. The word *fat*, which he so wished to hear from the Polish company in the Tuileries, had long been familiar in the *grand monde*. During the seventeenth century, it signified a pretentious and arrogant nincompoop. In the nineteenth century, its meaning altered somewhat. Of course, *le fat* continued to be puffed up and conceited, but he also began to be a popinjay. At that time, he was generally identified with the dandy, although some theorists of fashion, such as Horace Raisson in *Code civil. Manuel complet de la politesse* (1828), treated him as a degenerate metamorphosis of the dandy.[122] He was suspected of triviality. 'For me,' wrote the editor of a weekly chronicle in *La Mode*, 'that self-importance is more impertinent than the open contempt which a commoner [*roturier*] aroused in a true and brave nobleman in the times when there still existed townsfolk, gentry and peasantry.'[123]

---

[121] See Théophile Gautier, 'Legenda czerwonej kamizelki' [Fr. orig. 'La légende du gilet rouge'], in Joanna Guze (ed.), *Pisarze i artyści romantyczni. Szkice – wspomnienia – groteski* [Romantic writers and artists. Sketches, recollections and grotesques] (Warsaw, 1975), 37–44.

[122] Stanton, *The Aristocrat as Art*, 54.

[123] Quoted in Nishikawa, *Balzac et le dandysme*, 78.

And it was this triviality of attire that for Słowacki was to stir repugnance, thanks to which *le fat* suddenly became a knight of romanticism, tilting at the generally accepted norms.[124]

So why did he become a dandy in the first place? Well, he was always proud that his mother took care over his good manners. Kremenets generally ensured its young residents of a worldly education, as natives of Vilnius would not let him forget, proud, above all, of their knowledge and contemptuous of airs and graces and elegant balls. So in his dandy phase, Słowacki drew on his Kremenetsian urbanity, avoiding Vilnian slovenliness like the plague. 'And you will doubtless ask me, mama,' he continued in the same letter, 'why I do it. Well, on becoming a poet, I wish to escape the reproof that sets out our kind as neglected and casual... and I do not wish to be refused entry to a gaming house, like Mickiewicz, because the servants took him for a lackey and gave the reply that his scarf was wrongly tied...'[125] So this was emblematic of his battle with the 'Lithuanian god'. At one Parisian soirée given by Prince Adam Czartoryski, he took a close look at Mickiewicz and described him in a letter to his family of 4 October 1832: 'You could not imagine how lewd he looks with his crumpled shirt collar and in a grimy frock coat'.[126]

It was this concern for elegance that triggered his interest in dandyism, but his choice of the attitude *plaire en déplaisant* was determined by his tendency for frenzy. The 'English air', *l'air anglais*, appeared by way of contrast. Thus he paraded his haughtiness and poise, his sang-froid, which was juxtaposed with French hot-bloodedness and southern impulsiveness. It was

---

[124] This most probably explains Barbey d'Aurevilly's motto to his essay *De dandysme et de George Brummell*: 'Of a fop, by a fop, for fops', with this kind of dandy replacing the words 'the people' from the well-known Anglo-Saxon left-wing watchword.

[125] *Korespondencja Juliusza Słowackiego*, i:128.

[126] Ibid, 144.

his clothing that was to shout. He himself, in every situation, should remain impassive and cool. That, indeed, is how he remained on his way to a duel.[127]

This dandy's most eloquent provocation was an outfit presented in society during a trip around the Alps organised by the Wodziński clan, which took place from 31 July to 20 August 1834. It is not irrelevant to these considerations that the group of travellers included Maria Wodzińska, a sixteen-year-old girl whom Słowacki loved at that time with a very, and I mean very, literary love. Two years later, on 9 September 1836, Fryderyk Chopin would propose to her and be accepted. So this young woman encountered two different types of 'fashionable man' in what might be called a very intimate way. Her admirers were a dandy and a gentleman.

Of course, Słowacki reckoned on causing a shock. And he reckoned right. His appearance made such an impression on the Wodziński ladies that he went down in the family legend, passed down through the generations. Years later, Maria's nephew, born after the poet's death, in 1852, would write: 'Dandyism – that sickness of the era to which Słowacki also succumbed. Several decades later, the refined oddness of attire and the overcoat with cape, lined with green silk, from which the poet would not be parted during the time of that trip to Tell's grotto and chapel, aroused merely an ironic smile on Maria's now age-worn countenance...'[128] So he was still eliciting distaste. But most interesting for us here is the fact that in this legend Słowacki represented a stark contrast to Chopin in the field of fashion. 'Short, with a slight stoop, a mighty skull on a frail chest, of swarthy complexion, with eyes now burning with the glow of smouldering

---

[127] Ibid, 128–462.
[128] A. Wodziński, 'Maria W[odzińska]', *Kurier Warszawski*, 21 January 1897. Reprinted in Jerzy Starnawski, *Juliusz Słowacki we wspomnieniach współczesnych* [Juliusz Słowacki as recalled by his peers] (Wrocław, 1956), 62–63.

coals, now piercing with a cold steel blade, a vulturine nose, sensuous lips, quite gracefully defined, though occasionally twisted with sarcasm – like Chopin, with whom, incidentally, he had more than one common feature of physical and spiritual similarity, but without his refinement and good taste – they took great care over all outward forms and appearances, in his posture, movements and dress he sought to imitate the dandies of those times.'[129]

That outfit of Słowacki's which was recalled years later looked as follows: 'That you might picture me well, Mama,' he wrote in a letter from Geneva of 21 August 1834, 'I must describe to you my fantastical dress. I had a linen tunic, embroidered with green silk or yarn, a black leather belt, white galligaskins, a black and white straw hat, quite low, with huge wings and tied around with a purple ribbon – to this, thick-soled shoes – and a walking stick taller than me, white with an iron spike, such as highlanders ordinarily use. In this outfit, I looked so young that I was given 15 years of age'.[130] Neither shepherd boy nor harlequin. With this pretentious motley look, Słowacki joined the dandies' campaign against black. It was technicolour theatre, but even the clothes of Théophile Gautier sometimes looked like a fantastical stage costume. As Julia Hartwig writes in her book about Nerval, the Bohemia of the Impasse du Doyenné adored outfits from the era of Henri IV.[131] Although Eugène Sue admittedly propagated refined elegance, he himself dressed garishly and at times looked like a Mediterranean market.

When profound religiosity appeared in Słowacki's life and work, he abandoned the strategy of dandy-provocateur. Overnight, he became *un fashionable*, who could please even

[129] A. W[odziński], 'O Marii Wodzińskiej' [On Maria Wodzińska], *Przegląd Polski* (1912). Reprinted in Starnawski, *Juliusz Słowacki*, 63.

[130] *Korespondencja Juliusza Słowackiego*, i:253.

[131] Julia Hartwig, *Gerard de Nerval* (Warsaw, 1972), 125–148.

the fiercest enemy of extravagance. With his elegance, he began to resemble Chopin. 'Know now', he wrote to his mother from Paris on 16 May 1842, 'that I dress myself always with quite considerable elegance – as I once promised myself in my youth, out of fear that the negligence common to my occupation might one day overcome me... So I always take a good tailor, [which] saves me unnecessary expense – I most often wear black, with small exceptions in my galligaskins or my waistcoat – never almost entirely in black, as that smacks of the cloth... I also have one original trait, that I always wear pale yellow-white gloves – that is my luxury, but not very costly – as all my clothes are clean, I never soil them quickly. I also wear most often patent leather shoes – which is no luxury at all... I always try to be dressed in such a way that I might be able to go anywhere without changing – and never such that I be seen to have dressed up deliberately... That is my policy on dress.'[132] The times of revolt against the 'uncolouristic civilisation', the times of battling for Romantic red against Classical grey, had passed.[133] It was a triumph for Eugène Chapus, a theorist of elegant fashion, who in 1830, in his *Théorie de l'élegance*, had recommended first and foremost black. Admittedly, Baudelaire would soon turn black into a symbol of the spiritual poverty of contemporary times.[134]

Słowacki accepted it, although he endeavoured to incorporate into it some unusual colouristic accents. Essentially, just one detail remained from his dandyism. Those pale yellow gloves. Ten years before, in 1830, lemon yellow gloves from Bodier or Boivin were considered by dandies to be a badge of their caste. Many protagonists of prose works by Balzac and Stendhal wore them quite simply as a characteristic sign. Balzac even wrote

---

[132] *Korespondencja Juliusza Słowackiego*, i:483.
[133] Gautier, *Legenda*, 38–40.
[134] Kempf, *Dandies*, 177–178.

a short *Étude de moeurs sur les gants*. For some time, dandies were known as 'yellow-gloved corsairs', *corsaires à gants jaunes*.[135] Słowacki turned his back on dandyish piracy and the gloves now served him as a splash of colour in a carefully assembled composition, which – as Brummell recommended – would be noticed only by a true connoisseur.

When, however, mystic visions appeared in his life, the 'fashionable man' ultimately turned into the 'inner man' of the New Testament. Provocation and ostentation, dress and colour, lost their meaning. As he wrote to his mother from Paris on 2 August 1842:

> So you see, my dear, that the world of glossy gloves and waxed floors has completely disappeared from my eyes – for what can one get from it… It is vain theatre for playful minds, for fleeting words – and today I need to be inwardly a man, as perfect and good as I can.[136]

Soon, he would be producing a thoroughgoing critique of fashion and accusing the nineteenth century of despiritualisation. 'Fashion is agreeing to something not justified in the soul, such as wearing low or tall hats… etc. It is different when clothing derives from the soul, e.g. people of the early times of the globe, among whom beauty was leonine nature, dressed well when they donned hats bristling with long hairs, which rendered people more like lions.' Even 'in Voltaire's day, when the whole might of man was considered to reside in his head – that part

---

[135] Michel Lemaire, *Le dandysme. De Baudelaire à Mallarmée* (Montreil, 1978), 63. Brummell's gloves were also unusual, but their dandyism, as Barbey d'Aurevilly wrote, resided in the fact that they were made by four different glovers. One of them worked just on the thumb, the others on the remaining fingers.

[136] *Korespondencja Juliusza Słowackiego*, i:492.

of the human body was aptly augmented with a wig made of huge curls'.[137]

Decisions taken at the beginning of the thirties, taking account of the demands of Parisian fashion, placed Chopin among the ranks of the robust opponents of Słowacki. I would just ask you not to say that this matter, particularly at a time of a painful national defeat, was not exercising the minds of our exiles. Fortunately, we have elegance in our blood. In the very depths of hell, during the Warsaw Rising of 1944, girls and boys embellished their improvised uniforms with fashionable accessories, and only in the sewers did this all lose its meaning. Maurycy Mochnacki, for example, had but few pennies in his pocket, living in the French provinces, in Metz, and yet he took care over his dress and appearance. As Michał Podczaszyński informed the writer's mother in a letter of 6 March 1832, 'Maurycek, ever the *charmant*, has now become a great *élégant*. Always well groomed. I tie a scarf around his neck, I trim the greater part of his side whiskers and his chin. Unrecognisable, the lad.'[138] So as soon as Chopin had put a little money together, he thought not so much, of course, about a decent outfit – in his case, sloppy attire was unthinkable – as about the style of his wardrobe, to which he sought to impart a specific eloquence, easily legible in respect to the system of value and appraisal that held sway in contemporary fashion.

As we have seen, the terminology here was rather confused. Quite simply, some theorists, especially those working with the daily *La Mode*, insisted that the dandy was not an elegant man. During the forties, this standpoint was debated by Barbey d'Aurevilly, but at the time when Chopin was deliberating his 'policy on dress', to use Słowacki's expression,

---

[137] Słowacki, *Dzieła wszystkie*, xv:486.
[138] Maurycy Mochnacki, *Dzieła* [Works] (Poznań, 1863), i:72.

the views of the *La Mode* group, with Balzac to the fore, could not be ignored.

As Rose Fortassier wrote, *La Mode*, backed by the Duc du Berry, treated elegance as something of a *laissez-passer*, a ticket to the new aristocracy, which was adopting English models. Birth began to draw riches, and those two domains attracted talent, which enhanced elegance with the products of its imagination. In his *Traité de la vie élégante*, Balzac oppugned the idea that one was born elegant, like one was born a poet. He stated that elegance could be acquired. His treatise, which was written prior to the 1830 Revolution, was ahead of its time, and its premises were not fully appreciated until after the triumph of the bourgeoisie, when the elegance of the aristocracy began to be distinguished from the fads of the popinjay.[139] I might add that such insight could only have been shown by a townie with a complex of low birth, posing as an aristocrat, who was also a brilliant artist.

And here is a nineteenth-century aphorism from his extraordinary *Traité...* 'Dandyism is a heresy of the elegant life. In essence, it is faking fashion. The *dandy* is a man who has become a piece of boudoir furniture, a particularly fancy mannequin. He can lounge on a sofa and deftly suck the tip of his walking stick, but a thinking creature... Never ever! The man who sees only fashion in fashion is a fool'.[140] As Yoko Nishikawa has perspicaciously noted, dandyism was thus defined as a revolt against the authority that 'elegant life' always represented. In light of this, one should ask what Balzac considered to be 'elegant life'.

He made many fascinating remarks on this subject, but for understandable reasons I shall concentrate here only on those

---

[139] Rose Fortassier, *Les Mondains de la Comédie humaine. Étude historique et psychologique* (Lille, 1980), 36–37.
[140] Quoted in Nishikawa, 68.

observations which concern creative artists. This prose genius asserted that the fashion of each social group expresses completely different content. He distinguished 'elegant life' from the elegance that is manifest in the dress and comportment of a particular person. Every individual can be classified and coded. Speak, walk around, eat, dress, and I will tell you who you are. 'Elegant life' is led only by people who do nothing. Their elegance is the expression of their material success. Besides high-ranking state functionaries, princes, prelates and generals, this group also includes dandies, whose special sign is the tilbury, a box at the opera or meals in cafés. In the rubric 'social function', Balzac places nothing against the dandy. People who work, so Balzac continues, lead a 'busy life' (*la vie occupée*). Although Chopin worked, we shall not explore this category, so as not to muddy matters. People who think, meanwhile, lead an 'artistic life'. By their names, in the rubric 'social function', we find the comment: 'beyond criteria'. And also 'beyond criteria' is the elegance of the artist.

From this, one surmises that the elegance of a do-nothing, *un homme qui ne fait rien*, expresses his material success, whereas the elegance of an artist expresses the profundity of his inner life, his consciousness, his soul. The 'boudoir furniture' dandy is certainly not an artist, who – as we read in Balzac – is a complete exception: 'his idleness is work, and his work is rest'. The artist 'is elegant and sloppy in alternation. Depending on his preference, he will now don a farmer's shirt, now plump for a tailcoat worn by a fashionable man. He cannot stand norms. He imposes the norms.'[141] For Balzac, the elegance of the artist, just like his sloppiness, is an expression of his spiritual freedom.

Thus in the early 1830s the artist, with his elegance, began to signal his belonging to the new stratum, to the aristocracy of

---

[141] Ibid, 72–77.

spirit, infinitely superior, in every respect, to the aristocracy of birth. If he flaunted his dandyism, then he deprived himself of the possibility of manifesting his distinctness, since the provocation of the fairground could not be reconciled with aristocratic loftiness.

Consequently, having rejected the principle of *l'art de plaire en déplaisant*, Chopin realised Balzac's vision of the artist's social elevation to a degree of which the author of *Traité de la vie élégante* could only dream.

He was one of those people who manifest their care over their appearance and their sense of distinction at an early age. In a man, if this feature does not emerge between his fourteenth and seventeenth years, then it never will appear, unless it is artificially induced by circumstances. A boy who knows a pair of well-cut trousers when he sees them and is able to name at least five kinds of material from which suits are made will undoubtedly be elegant as an adult.

In 1825, at the age of fifteen, in a letter to Jan Białobłocki, Chopin suddenly inserted among friendly banter the following piece of news: 'I have new culottes from the royal court... well made (though that's actually not true), a new neckerchief, or to use another term, since you might not understand that one, a cravat, for X pounds, zhe ne me suvyan plue combyan, zhe lay payay avec larzhon ey la man de ma shair sur Louise' (KS i: 49).[142] Since he already knew when culottes were poorly cut, he himself was cut out to be a distinguished person. Three years later, he was clearly already dreaming of unusual attire, since in a letter written to Tytus Woyciechowski on 27 December 1828 from Warsaw, he informed his friend: '*Rondo à la Krakowiak* finished in score. Introduction original, more so than myself in a fancy frock coat' (KS i: 86). He also paid

---

[142] '...I don't remember how much, I paid for it with the money and the hand of my dear sister Ludwika'.

attention to women's outfits, something which – as we know – the vast majority of men, particularly 'real' men, cannot boast of. When he was twenty, he could discern that Miss Henriette Sontag looked better in morning dress than in an evening gown (KS i: 128). In his mature years, he displayed a remarkable understanding of Mrs Sand's gowns. His objective attention to the details of her attire was quite affecting. 'Madame's dress', he wrote to his companion from Paris on 2 December 1844, 'is of black levantine, of the finest quality. *I chose it myself* in accordance with your recommendations. – The seamstress took it with your instructions. She considers the material to be very beautiful, modest, but suitable. I think you will be satisfied. The seamstress seemed very intelligent. The material was selected from among ten others. It costs nine francs per metre, and so of the best quality – I expect it will be perfect; the seamstress, who wishes to do her job well, has everything planned' (KGS i: 157). He also noted trifles in the dress of his acquaintances, and made jokes on this account. As George Sand wrote to Charles Duvernet in January 1844:

> Chopin instructed me to tell you that Mr Serre [a journalist] must be an active and a shrewd man, since he noticed that he does not wear straps on his trousers. According to him, this is a sign that he has torn off the unnecessary tethers and marches forward like the devil (KGS ii: 154).

It is understandable that such a person, as soon as finances allowed, became an *élégant*. He always had his own tailor, shoemaker and glover. In the late thirties, he was outfitted by Mr Dautremont. During that same period, his hats were made by Mr Dupont. When he was getting ready to return to Paris following his first sojourn at Nohant, he gave Julian Fontana a whole list of instructions regarding new clothes:

I forgot to ask you to place an order for a hat with my Dupont on your street. He has my measurements and knows what light hats I need. Let him give it this year's form unexaggerated, since I don't know anymore how you dress nowadays. Apart from that, go across to *Dautremont*, my tailor on the boulevard, and have him immediately make me some grey trousers. Choose yourself a *dark grey colour* – winter trousers, something decent, with no stripes, smooth and stretchy. You're an Englishman, you know what I need. He'll be glad to hear I'm travelling up (KS i: 363).

From this we learn that he paid attention to what was currently being worn and observed an English moderation in colours and patterns. He appears to have changed his hat every year. In any case, Fontana received a similar instruction two years later, in 1841 (KS ii: 47).

At that time, two details of male dress became the metonym of the dandy: waistcoat and gloves. Instead of saying 'here comes a dandy', people would say, for example, 'here comes a cashmere waistcoat'. Consequently, an elegant gentleman who had made it known that he did not belong to that tribe was particularly attentive to this item of clothing, since the dandy liked to show off the wealth and variety of his waistcoats. He did so quite ostentatiously. Balzac's Charles Grandet had grey, white and black waistcoats. Some resembled beetles, some were flecked with gold, some sparkled, while others were dull, with a stiff or turn-down collar. Some had gold buttons or buckles right up to the neck. A dandy could stupefy everyone around with his waistcoat. Let us not forget about Słowacki's, with its huge multicoloured flowers, for example. And so Chopin ordered a 'black, modest velvet waistcoat, but with a small, discreet pattern, something very modestly elegant. If there aren't any decent ones, then a material (that is, silk) one, black, modestly beautiful. I'm relying on you. Not very wide, just so' (KS i: 363). He was clearly scared stiff of anything gaudy. Since dandies were for some time also associated with gloves, he also took care over this detail. Pale colours were then *de rigueur*. Chopin opted for immaculate white (KS i: 223), thereby renouncing refined pale shades, such as the lemon or 'misty rose' favoured by the dandies.

Of course, he took great care over every element of his dress. After all, that is what elegance involves. He thought about his footwear, even when in Nohant (KS i: 351, 354). In this area, he impressed the great *élégant* that was Eugène Delacroix. 'Dear friend', he wrote to Chopin around the turn of 1844 and 1845, 'I forgot to ask you yesterday for a favour – to write in your name to Mr Brown, the shoemaker, with a request that he come to me during the next few days around 9 a.m. (rue Notre-Dame-de-Lorette 54). Perhaps with your recommendation he would deign to make me some shoes. I have written to him without success and decided to ask you for support prior to your departure' (KS ii: 124). We know little, meanwhile, about Chopin's neckwear. Dandies worked marvels with ties and cravats. Around 1830, *Art de la toilette* listed seventy-two ways of tying a tie.[143] Then every dandy should have devised a seventy-third. But this detail of attire was also greatly respected by advocates of the toned-down, *fashionable*, style, since it was like a sign of originality in the grey and uniform world. Horace Raisson wrote the study *De la cravate considérée dans ses attributions morales, littéraires, politiques, militaires, religieuses* (1828), and Balzac produced the treatise *De la cravate considérée en elle-même et dans ses rapports avec la société et les individus* (1830). So there were clearly defined rules for wearing ties. Did Chopin observe them? Most certainly, when he appeared at the court, donning a white tie (KGS ii: 96). On a daily basis, 'he wore long, wide ties that covered his linen', recalled F. Henry Peru, a pupil of

---

[143] Kempf, *Dandies*, 179.

Chopin's from the last years of his life.[144] Chopin also appreciated good soap and scented water (KS ii: 20). And he was not
indifferent to working attire. When alone and composing, he
obviously thought about comfort, but also about appearance,
since he might receive friends dressed like that. 'Go to the Palais Royal, as well', we read in a crossed-out passage of a letter to Fontana from 17 June 1841, 'and buy me at number 37
(I think) in the gallery on the theatre side a shirt *en toile écrue*
for 14 fr.[ancs], a *blouse de chasse fermée par-devant, forme de
chemise*. If not 37, then 47 or 27, an ordinary tailor. The shop
looks like this. [Here Chopin drew a plan with notes: entrance,
gallery, corridor]. There is one who has such shirts. I bought
one from him a week ago: mother-of-pearl buttons, well sewn,
two breast pockets, etc.' (KS ii: 22–23). He may well have been
wearing such a shirt when George Sand drew the well-known
portraits *Chopin at work* (1841) and *Chopin at his desk* (1841).
Pupils would not have seen him in this garment. 'And his shiny
shoes?' recalled Georges Mathias. 'The shiniest I've ever seen!
He had a very small foot. And he usually wore a waisted frock
coat, done up right to the top, cut to the latest fashion. He wore
only what was most elegant and refined. One always had the
impression that everything was straight from the needle.'[145]

Wilhelm Lenz, a musician two years older than Chopin,
decided to take lessons from our hero. So he journeyed to Paris
in 1842 and went to his acquaintance Ferenc Liszt for protection,
since Chopin was known to be inaccessible. Many callers left
empty-handed. Liszt wrote for him two words on his visiting
card: '*Laissez-passer*', and signed it. With that recommendation,
Lenz went to Chopin's home. 'I gave Liszt's card to the servant
in the anteroom;' we read in Lenz's memoirs, 'a man-servant
is an article of luxury in Paris, a *rarissima avis* in the home

---

[144] Quoted in Czartkowski and Jeżewska, *Fryderyk Chopin*, 426.
[145] Ibid, 391.

of an artist. The servant said that M. Chopin was not in Paris. I did not allow myself to be put out, and repeated: "Deliver this card, I will attend to the rest." Chopin soon came out to me, the card in his hand; a young man, of middle height, slim, haggard, with a sad, though very expressive countenance, and elegant Parisian bearing – stood before me. I have seldom, if ever, met with an apparition so entirely engaging.'[146] Lenz soon grasped that Chopin could not abide any extravagant attire, in contrast to Liszt, who reacted to a lack of taste with a laugh. One morning, Liszt suggested to Lenz that they go for a walk. He noticed at once that the young newcomer was wearing a quite peculiar overcoat. It turned out that Lenz had bought it in Hamburg, because he liked it very much and it fitted him nicely. It was velvet imitating tiger-skin. Nowadays, American kitchen hands run around Paris in such apparel. So Lenz's pretentiousness knew no bounds, but even many years later he appeared not to understand Liszt's impatience. The brilliant Hungarian's fine irony was ravishing. 'With him, you'll turn heads in Paris', he said, before adding, like some Renaissance prince: 'I alone can walk around with a man dressed like that'.

Chopin would have done anything to rid himself of the company of that tiger-skin. A comparison with Friedrich Kalkbrenner speaks volumes about Chopin's elegance. And contemporary pianists willingly compared those two famous masters. 'Chopin was *very* distinguished', wrote Lenz, 'not like dead-and-gone Kalkbrenner, as a peacock [...] but as a *great artist* [...] in his manners, in his whole outward appearance'.[147] So one recognised immediately that he was an aristocrat of spirit. 'I also recall from concerts at Erard's', writes Georges Mathias, 'his meetings with Kalkbrenner, the conversations between these two people who were simply poles apart. One trait that

---

[146] Lenz, *The Great Piano Virtuosos*, 48.
[147] Ibid, 29.

they did have in common was that they both behaved like true gentlemen. Ah, there was one more similarity between them: they both wore clothes buttoned up to the neck, in keeping with the fashion of the day, except that Chopin's buttons were black, and Kalkbrenner always wore gold buttons.'[148] Elegant black and pretentious gold. Sometimes, a detail says as much about a man's elegance as the overall effect. When one observes the rules of fashion, a detail becomes quite irreplaceable for assessing the character of a person's elegance.

This ostentatious refinement was part of a deliberate social strategy, aimed at maintaining the artistic position he had attained in Paris at the beginning of the thirties. Chopin turned his dress and his comportment into a clear sign, conceived in such as way that anyone beholding him would feel admiration and respect. The sign as fashionable, 'supreme elegance', adopted from the milieu that Chopin resolved to conquer and subjugate, yet marked with personal details. Thus Chopin's outfit was his armour in the battle for position among the 'upper echelons' of Paris.

Only a victorious battle guaranteed him a 'career'. He was well aware of this, although he was under no illusion as to the spiritual values of that milieu. Of course, he liked and esteemed some of its representatives, since they were in some respect exceptional people. Yet there is no doubt that he considered it essential to win over that elite. In mid January 1833, he wrote from Paris to Dominik Dziewanowski:

> I've entered the finest society, I sit among ambassadors,
> princes and ministers; and I don't even know by what mir-
> acle, as I've certainly not forced my way up. For me, today,
> it is the most necessary thing, as thence apparently issues
> good taste; at once you possess great talent if you have been
> heard at the British or Austrian embassy, at once you play bet-

---

[148] Quoted in Czartkowski and Jeżewska, 408.

ter if the Princess de Vaudemont was protecting you. Is protecting – I cannot write, because the *old lady* died a week ago; and she was a lady in the mould of the late Zielonkowa or chatelaine Połaniecka, who occasionally hosted the court, did a great deal of good and hid many aristocrats during the first revolution; the former lady, following the *July days*, was at the court, the last of the family of the elder Lady Montmorency (the owner of a host of white and black bitches, canaries and parrots and proprietress of the funniest monkey in the local *grand monde*, which, during the soirées she gave, used to bite other countesses) (KS i: 223).

Of course, dandies could be found among this elite, as well, and with a tendency towards extravagance, but the binding rule was naturally distinction. In these circles, a 'heresy of elegance' was seen as a vagary. An artist-dandy, however great and famous, would have aroused aversion and could not have counted on success. In order to conquer this elite, Chopin had to adopt the rules of fashion that obtained there.

The reigning style was *fashionable*. Individual details, which took on great significance, could not disturb the generally accepted tone. One's overall appearance had to be immaculate and admirable. His innate good taste meant that Chopin began to be associated with refinement. For the elite, he was a great artist because he was every inch the *fashionable*. In demeanour, as in his gestures. Cyprian Kamil Norwid visited him on rue Caillot, when he was gravely ill.

> ...he was extremely beautiful, just as always in the movements of the most everyday life, possessing something complete, something monumentally drawn... something which the Athenian aristocracy might have regarded as religion in the most beautiful period in Greek civilisation – or that

which the brilliant dramatic artist plays out, for example, on classical French tragedies, which though wholly dissimilar to the ancient world through their theoretical polish, the genius of such as Rachel, for example, can render more natural, more plausible and indeed classical... Chopin had just such a naturally apotheotic perfection of gesture however and wherever I found him.[149]

The 'upper echelons' accepted Chopin because he impressed them. And only his wonderful elegance allowed him to neutralise the two wholly natural feelings that were apt to bring this 'waxen world' into conflict with an artist of that sort: the feeling of superiority over a man who can boast neither high birth nor fortune, and the feeling of inferiority in respect to an artist who towered above them with his genius and celebrity. This conflict with the incomer from those 'espaces imaginaires', the beauty of which could only be guessed at by that elite, listening to his music or... rubbing shoulders with him in a salon, was eliminated by a well-conceived and well-executed 'dress policy'. 'His bearing had so much distinction', wrote Ferenc Liszt, 'and his manners such a cachet of good breeding that one naturally treated him as a prince'.[150]

The effect of this strategy was success, and with it the financial security that ensured Chopin of the possibility of composing and of an appropriate standard of living. He was inundated with pupils. And he was paid more than respectfully for his performances. His fees could no longer be the lowest. However, a substantial proportion of the money he earned had to go on maintaining the elegance that guaranteed his continued success. He had to work in order to remain an elegant man.

---

[149] Cyprian Kamil Norwid, *Czarne kwiaty* [Black flowers], in *Pisma wszystkie* [Complete writings] (Warsaw, 1971), vi:178–179.
[150] Quoted in Zamoyski, *Chopin*, 99.

'Today I have five lessons to give', he wrote in the above-quoted letter to Dominik Dziewanowski. 'Do you think I'm making a fortune? A cabriolet costs more, and white gloves, without which you would not have *bon ton*' (KS i: 223).

Thus Chopin's existence was determined. 'My mill' – that is how he described the lessons he gave at home to rich ladies (KR 151). 'I shall soon have to think about the mill, that is, about my lessons', he wrote in a letter to his family on 11 October 1846 (KR 159). In Polish, the metaphorical mill denotes intensive work, a wearying self-subordination to the mechanism one has set in motion, the revolutions of which grind a man's life into a senseless powder. *Molino vivo.* 'I'm giving lots of lessons', wrote Chopin to his family on 11 February 1848. 'I am much engaged on all sides, besides that I'm doing nothing' (KR 174).

God alone, who looked down from heaven at his elegant attire, knew that this outfit of the spiritual aristocrat, this sign of victory, had been bought at the cost of great anguish. And only God heard the grinding of the millstone of his tormented existence. But – as we shall see – Chopin's God was ruthless and stern.

2. THE FORGE OF MYTHS

A place is sometimes defined by words which the British school of analysis usually calls indices. Thus a thing in space can find itself here, there or somewhere. The word 'somewhere' informs us that it is not known where that thing should be sought; thus it renders the thing mysterious. The situation is different with the first two words, since here and there can be defined. What is more, the moment we begin to fill them with specific content, these words immediately assume a strict relationship to one another. Suffice it to say that each specification of the index 'here' brings a dichotomous division of space. If 'here' means my flat, then 'there' starts beyond its threshold. If by 'here' I mean a house, then 'there' begins on the street, and ends in infinity. If by 'here' I understand my village, town or city, then 'there' can signify my country. If by saying 'here' I am thinking of my country, then 'there' extends to the rest of the planet. If, in turn, 'here' encompasses the Earth, then 'there' can denote the infinite material cosmos. Finally, if the word 'here' denotes the entire material cosmos, then 'there' directs one towards spiritual transcendence in the 'other world'. When Faust came across such a division of space, he understood that he was faced with a fundamental choice. And he chose. Here is what he said to Mephistopheles:

—

> It doesn't worry me, your 'over there';
> If you can manage to destroy

This world, the next can have its turn for all I care.
This world's the source of all my joy.[151]

—

It is generally considered that the Romantic was always dissatisfied with his 'here' and was continually longing for another 'there'. Yet as a social person, he lived in a particular time, which inevitably defined the style of his behaviour. So since I am to speak of Chopin, I must abandon the abstract categories of time and space, and see him in a single, uniform time-space.

Chopin lived in a period when Poles finally grasped what place was. Exile and banishment were a philosophical education on a massive scale. The awareness of a man whose home suddenly stood 'there', whose 'here' was reduced to a hole in a Siberian mine, had to change fundamentally. Poles forced into exile after the defeat of the November Rising suddenly understood the gulf that divided a family home from a room that one inhabits out of necessity. So let us first differentiate between 'home' and 'habitation'.

We will not call a separate building a 'home', since one can occupy a whole palace but possess only a habitation. One can also live in rented rooms and have one's own home. 'Home' denotes a space which is in some sense sacred, something of a 'fixed point', a 'centre of existence'. In our experience of space, it is a privileged place, which contains, mainly thanks to the constant presence and closeness of our family, an invisible axis of the world, organising man's existence into a sensible system, despite all the vagaries of history. In a home understood in this way, a family accumulates or rather 'capitalises' – as Gaston Bachelard would have it – its successive victories over the cruelty of history, and, from that 'capital', each of its members obviously draws

---

[151] Johann Wolfgang von Goethe, *Faust*, tr. John R. Williams (Ware, 1999), 1660–1663.

strength for living.[152] A habitation, meanwhile, is a place along the way, which can be abandoned without feeling that one has lost something essential, with the conviction that one is leaving not a 'fixed point', but a temporary, passing shelter. A habitation, or 'here', which does not have a sacred character is devoid of the power that is accumulated through the generations. From it, one cannot draw strength to combat the horror of existence.

So when Polish emigrants found themselves outside the country, 'here', in France, they could possess only a habitation. Their home remained 'there', in their native land. Their consciousness was forever split. Chopin is a most moving example of this splitting. During the first years of residence among foreigners, such a situation seemed to be the emigrant's irrevocable destiny. But a little later, some exiles attempted to lift this sentence by starting a family, which at once changes every 'here' into a home. Men without a family could have no more than a habitation. The home remained in the realm of their daily recollections. Chopin was aware of this desperate situation and tried to change it by finding a wife: the centre of any home.

A Polish artist in exile who had not started a family had to consider the appearance of his habitation. Even a nomad in the desert adorns his tent in some way. The size and character of this temporary shelter depended primarily on the artist's financial resources. In order to better understand Chopin's decisions in this domain, I will invoke once more the figure of the poet who represented his opposite in this instance, too. Let us dwell a while on Juliusz Słowacki's habitations in exile.

He was not just an exile. He travelled a great deal, and so often abandoned his temporary 'seats'. Chopin changed his habitation because – let's assume – a different part of Paris took his fancy. Słowacki moved because curiosity drove him

---

[152] Gaston Bachelard, *La poétique de l'espace* (Paris, 1958), 50–78.

out into the world. Sometimes he settled in a new city because of the tasks he had set himself. But each time he arranged his habitation according to the same principle, giving it the style of a 'hermit's cell'. He was a poet and philosopher, and so he turned that 'cell' into a workshop. He was not rich; he had to count every penny. Therefore, his 'cell' bore no resemblance to the elegant chambers of Renaissance intellectuals. As one would expect of a poet, he organised the space to be conducive to contemplation. He created an intimacy that enabled him to forget that he was 'on the road'. In 1831, he found himself in Dresden, where he had planned a short stay. Although he had not yet thought about a workshop, he set about ensuring that his habitation would not remind him of that accursed temporality. 'For 6 thalers a month,' he wrote to his mother on 12 April, 'I have a lovely little drawing-room with 5 windows. [...] The drawing-room in its entirety is furnished very nicely, with even an alabaster lamp, like the one at Hersylka's, just a little dusty – in a word, I can light the lamp in the evenings and Byronise.'[153] On arriving in Paris, where he stayed for a longer time, he immediately created a cosy 'hideaway'. 'In Paris,' he informed his mother on 10 September 1831, 'I have as yet few acquaintances, and none from the salons. But I feel fine with that. I have an exquisite little room with mahogany furniture and a marble fireplace – what a pleasure in the winter.'[154] When he settled in Florence, following a journey to the Orient, he rented a two-room flat with a sumptuous view over the church of Santa Maria Novella. He now had a bedroom, a parlour 'with patio and statues', 'and then', he wrote to his mother on 24 November 1837, 'steps lead up to a little belvedere. It is a little square room in a tower, from which through four windows I can see the whole of Florence and its surroundings. [...] I often stay

---

[153] *Korespondencja Juliusza Słowackiego*, i:63.
[154] Ibid, 78.

for a while in that belvedere, and I thank God that in my life he allows me to feast my eyes on ever more beautiful images and thereby draws the bitter sting from my solitude, changing it into sweet melancholy.'[155] The parlour was again lovely, and on the patio 'an exquisite second parlour' could be arranged. Tender souls evidently long for loveliness. And so he once invited to this homely snug six young female acquaintances from an Italian family with which he was on friendly terms. This was not an audience, since he did not, unlike Chopin, have his own audience, his own admirers, and did not have to swathe his doorway in an aura of mystery. 'Wishing to entertain these young ladies,' he wrote in a letter of 22 February 1838, 'I invited them home several times and gave them a little soirée in my parlour: they danced, ate biscuits and were amazed at my elegant furniture, my lamp, which I lit for them, my piano, my carpeted floor.'[156] He himself most probably lit a hookah he had brought from the Orient. On returning to live in Paris, the complex of homelessness immediately enslaved his tastes. 'I needed', he wrote on 12 April 1840, 'something to keep me from continually wandering around the world: so what did I do? – […] I bought myself just furniture and I live like at home, and not in some wayside abode.' This was not furniture, but 'little fittings'. There was an air of modesty and neatness about it. 'But all is in order and to my liking, as my habitation has the greatest effect on my mood. I pay for it 25 ducats a year, which is a very small sum for these parts […] With everything settled, I am a quiet and calm little bird in my little cage: I work, ponder…'[157] A chick that had flown its nest and fallen into a strange cage. Oh, excuse me, into a lovely little cage.

---

[155] Ibid, 378.
[156] Ibid, 386.
[157] Ibid, 435–437.

146

Thus all of Słowacki's habitations in exile fulfilled three basic functions. They eroded the memory of his forced wandering and stifled his constant longing for home. They blunted the dangerous 'sting of solitude'. And they enclosed the loner and the poet in seclusion. Even the furnishings of that little parlour, nonetheless intended for his guests, suggested that this was the pad of a poet. Of course, anyone who found themselves there was the recipient of remarkable favour, but he or she also received a warning not to disturb the peace of the meditating 'hermit' without special permission.

When Słowacki dressed himself, it was the eccentric and *provocateur* in him that took the upper hand. His attire was designed to convey the idea that he was a person who disdained norms and ignored the opinion of the world of waxed floors. However, the acute complex of the wayside dwelling forced him to transform his habitations into 'lovely' poetical retreats. In his habitation, he wished to feel 'like at home'. It was an artificial paradise of the Polish artist in exile. Expressed in his dress was Słowacki's predilection for the grotesque; in the appointment of his habitation, his melancholy lyricism.

Compared to Słowacki, Chopin's policy with regard to his habitation had a completely different aim. But then Chopin was no ordinary outcast. He remained in exile of his own free will. He was a creative artist of Europe-wide renown, and his financial situation was good enough for him to help many of our poor exiles. He set himself specific musical tasks, and his habitation was a crucial part of his artistic strategy. Słowacki's lovely little rooms were an intimate, private refuge. Chopin's elegant habitation was a sign for the social elite. In satisfying his own preferences, at the same time Chopin transmitted information that discharged a very specific function.

The attempt to destroy the accursed antinomy between home and habitation only appeared when, after an unsuccessful attempt to start his own family, Chopin took up with George Sand. Immediately upon his return from Majorca, he found himself at Nohant and entered a home. If I may proffer some well-grounded assumptions on this matter, from that moment on he tried to become a 'card-carrying' member of that home. His status was always peculiar. From the point of view of the lady of the house, for her good friends, Nohant was something of a home in the country. But Chopin, partly unawares, transformed Nohant from a summer residence to his own home. Or, more accurately, into something like a home, since he was not sure whether that family would ever accept him. So at Nohant he had just a room in the home of a hospitable friend – like, say, Delacroix, when he visited. From this point of view, it was only a permanent summer home, albeit with exceptional care. George Sand did not intend him to join her little community. So Chopin's sojourn at Nohant was merely a pleasant, or perhaps also unpleasant, game of 'home', which merely reflected the strength of the dreadful complex of all emigrants.

In Paris, during the winter/spring season, this aspect of his life looked for some time very similar. He kept his own apartment at 5 rue Tronchet, where he gave lessons, received visitors and occasionally gave musical soirées. Yet at the same time, he effectively moved into Mrs Sand's flat at 16 rue Pigalle, where he had his own room. Here he slept and here he was ill. So again he had a room in a home, since Mrs Sand, although she rented apartments in Paris, naturally set up home wherever she went with her children. A similar arrangement arose when Chopin moved into a two-room flat at 9 Square d'Orléans and Mrs Sand rented a spacious first-floor apartment at no. 5. And so he played 'home' in Paris, too. These games ended when Chopin took a stance over the drama that was destroying the community in which he had been living for ten years, and George Sand considered that he had, uninvited and illegitimately, invoked the prerogatives of the 'father of the family'.[158] It was a terrible blow, and one is hardly surprised that he never forgave her for it.

So after leaving Warsaw, Chopin essentially never had anything more than habitations. Although he did manifest a lively interest in the walls between which he spent his life, the family and friends of his Warsaw home were constantly reminding him of it in letters from Poland. Of course, the main concern was that he live in healthy rooms. 'I am very glad', wrote Mikołaj Chopin to Jan Matuszyński, probably in January 1836, 'that he has acquired a fireplace that better heats his flat, because it is most unpleasant to work with numb fingers' (KS i: 272). His solicitude was quite touching, yet on this occasion the parental oversensitivity was unfounded. Chopin always took care over his living space, even when he was still on the road and unaware that he would be settling abroad for good. When Tytus Woyciechowski left Vienna to join the uprising, Chopin had to move into cheaper lodgings. 'I'm standing on the 4th floor', he wrote to Jan Matuszyński on 29 December 1830, 'of what is admittedly not the most beautiful street, but I would have to peer carefully through the window if I wished to see what was going on down there. My room (you'll see it in my new album, when I return to your fold), which the young Hummel is drawing for me, is large, well-shaped, with 3 windows, the bed standing opposite the window, a (wonderful) pantaleon to the right, and a sofa to the left. A mirror between the windows, in the middle a beautiful, large, mahogany, round table; polished floor. Quiet' (KS i. 166). But that first Parisian habitation, when he did not yet know how his life would unfold, modest, as befitted an unknown musician,

---

[158] Compare the ironic term 'le père Chopin' in a letter to Marie de Rozières of November 1846 (KGS ii: 218), and also the quite explicit utterance in a letter to the same addressee of 8 May 1847: 'I cannot make Chopin the head of the family and the family council, the children would not accept it and I would lose my dignity' (KGS ii: 223).

was not a cheap and cosy loft pad. On 18 November 1831, he wrote to Norbert Kumelski:

> Sometimes on my 5th floor (I stand at 27 Boulevard Poissonière, you'll not believe how lovely is my abode, I have a little room beautifully furnished in mahogany, with a balcony over the boulevards, from which I can see from Montmartre to the Pantheon and along the whole beautiful world; many envy me the view, but no one the stairs) (KS i: 187).

Before he became a well-known and acknowledged Parisian composer and pianist, when he was still a migrating bird, the little room in which he lived, like Słowacki's 'cell', was above all lovely. So he craved refuge and cosiness. As soon as he became well known and was earning relatively well, he thought about realising the ideal that clearly held his soul in thrall. He dreamed of interiors that befitted an artist who knows his worth.

Beginning with his move to 5 Chaussée d'Antin, Chopin's habitation always comprised several rooms. Apart from 'facilities', such as a room for his servant, it was divided into 'lair' and 'apartment'. These are terms that the composer himself used (KS ii: 47). Revelatory terms, since Chopin generally chose words that were so astoundingly apt that his linguistic labours resemble the work of a poet. The word 'lair' perfectly conveyed the character and function of his 'inner apartments', as one of the memoirists called them.[159] It denotes a well-protected place in which an animal isolated from a community stays alone by itself. Here, its young are bred. Still today, the sound of this word evokes multiple associations. It bids us think of lying and a breeding-ground.

---

[159] Kornel Michałowski, 'Nieznane wspomnienie o Chopinie – Ignacego Krzyżanowskiego' [Unknown memories of Chopin – Ignacy Krzyżanowski], *Rocznik Chopinowski*, 17 (1985), 208.

It is understandable that in his bedroom Chopin primarily slept, but I am convinced that the word 'lair' came into his head because he very often lay there bed-ridden from another bout of illness. Sometimes, as we know, such a lair was situated in the home of Mrs Sand. His bed was not just a place to sleep, but also the lair of an ailing man. I suspect, and it is only a suspicion, as we have no written evidence to that effect, that it was here that music often flowed down upon him. Of course, a musical idea can occur to a composer at dinner, on a walk, or even amid the dull hubbub of a salon, since it comes unexpectedly and uninvited, albeit summoned. But, like all creative thoughts born within the mysterious depths of one's 'I', it very often appears on the surface of consciousness just before sleep, when one finds oneself on the edge of conscious and unconscious existence. I can picture him then, heeding some irrational injunction, leaping out of bed, sitting down at the little 'practice' piano that stood in his bedroom, and taking up some manuscript paper to write down a musical thought. So the occasionally cursed lair was most likely the breeding ground of his works.

The apartments were stylishly appointed. This was a fundamental principle, which surfaced with each successive move, usually an important event in Chopin's life. Here are his instructions sent from Nohant on 25 September 1839 to Julian Fontana, who was preparing Chopin's flat at 5 rue Tronchet.

> Choose paper like I had at home before, *tourterelle* [pearly colour], but shiny, glossy, for both rooms, and dark green cord for the border. For the vestibule something else, but decent. But if there are some more beautiful and *more fashionable* papers which you like and you know that I'd like as well, then take them. I prefer smooth, the most modest and plain to *common, ordinary, parochial*. That's why I like pearly, since it's neither *gaudy* nor ordinary (KS i: 357).

So no concessions to the shopkeepers' tastes. Nothing gaudy. The walls were to be distinctly modest. As his 'most-splenetic-English-Polish-stuffy beloved friend' (KS i: 365), and on account of his 'elegant tact' (KS i: 360), Fontana also took care of the decor of Mrs Sand's Paris apartment, since Chopin had faith in his English taste, which his old friend had imbibed during his several years on the British Isles.

When a Romantic artist was wealthy, and also liked to surround himself with elegant objects, he would turn his room into something that could be called a gentleman's grotto. Here is the young Zygmunt Krasiński's room in the family seat at Opinogóra, Mazovia. He is looking through the window at the Gothic lodge he has had built, which boasts 'a tower with rosaces and Moorish pillars', and describing his room's interior in a letter to his English friend Henry Reeve: 'The walls are white, unpapered; at the windows, green and white curtains; a superb piano along the wall; near it, on a table, a solid silver washstand: tumblers, mirrors and all the little knick-knacks for cleaning one's nails, teeth, hair, etc., etc., bottles filled with exquisite perfumes; then comes the fireplace, with two little geographic globes; then, next to that, hanging on the wall, three shining double-barrelled guns, two hunting horns mounted on gold and ivory, a sword, silver damascened pistols, gamebags, powder horns, etc.; then comes the door, then a stove; then my bed at an angle to the stove, covered with fine sheets and a cashmere dressing-gown; right by that, an enormous casket, filled with essentials, in which, on my arrival, I found four thousand florins and where I've placed H.'s letters; then comes a desk, where there stands an antique bronze vase with a bouquet of flowers, surrounded by my English books and my music box, and the Coliseum cross, and my dagger, and the things that you know. That's my room.'[160] Chopin could well have

---

[160] Letter of 18 August 1832, in *Correspondance de Sigismond [Zygmunt] Krasiński et de Henry Reeve*, ii (Paris, 1902).

accepted this interior, but the four thousand florins he would have had to place in the casket himself, as he did not have a rich daddy.

When a Romantic artist was wealthy and had an irresistible inclination to flaunt his fantasy and flair, he would sometimes turn his apartment into a display of curiosities or a museum, as Bożena Mądra-Shallcross writes. Here is the apartment of Victor Hugo on rue de la Tour d'Auvergne. The description, which we owe to Théophile Gautier, will be rather long, but most delectable. So let us steal a glance at a room which was the opposite of Chopin's famous 'discretion'.

> The little antechamber, covered in embossed and gilded Cordoba leather, framing two panels of very old gothic tapestry, more ancient even than the tapestry of Bayeux, was lit by a window with German or Swiss panes; a sculpted oak fireplace, a mirror in a terracotta frame where the principal scenes from the novel *Notre-Dame of Paris* unfolded through the arabesques of the ornamentation, a negro bust in touchstone, some fragments of antique wainscoting, a large marquetry clock, in tortoiseshell and in copper, a chaise longue and a Chinese bamboo armchair, such were the furnishings of that little room, the greatest singularity of which consisted in a mobile lectern, turning like a wheel, and designed to bear infolios on its palettes; an old Bible, open […]
> From this little room, one enters the poet's bedroom, somewhat reminiscent of Thisbe's chamber. A bed with Solomonic columns and gilded headboards occupies the back of the room with its ample valances of old damask from the Indies. The walls are decked with Chinese hangings, and the ceiling is adorned with an allegorical painting by Châtillon, representing a recumbent woman, smiling at a figure dressed liked Petrarch who is perusing a large book. Basking in the fireplace, made of joined pieces of gothic bas-reliefs, are two doleful iron

firedogs, doubtless lifted from the colossal hearth of some burg on the Rhine, and on which Job and Magnus perhaps rested their steel-shoed feet.

The shelves are strewn with a whole world of chimerae, oriental vases, sculptures, ivory, reflected by Venetian mirrors in etched copper frames; a handsome oak bench, of the most delicately fenestrated and flowered gothic work, serves there as a sofa. – Hiding in a corner is the little table on which so many beautiful poems, moving plays and imperishable pages were written. An old compass, some seals, an inkpot and an elaborately worked iron casket fill the old tapis that covers it. Hung on the walls are several drawings by masters, some bearing epigraphs.

The drawing-room, hung in blue silk damask, has a large tapestry with themes taken from *Telemachus* stretched across the ceiling; the decoration of this room, the largest of the house, comprises cressets supported by gilded wooden negroes [...] ancient mirrors, paintings by Saint-Evre, Paul Huet, Nanteuil, Boulanger; portraits of the poet, of his wife and children, a monumental bust by David, Japanese lacquer doors, and a large piece of furniture from floral white satin.

The dining room, which precedes it, is hung with old tapestries, decorated with carved oak dressers, cressets and Dutch chandeliers. The shelves and sideboards are piled up with porcelain from Japan, faience from Rouen and Vincennes, glass from Bohemia and Venice, a thousand curiosities accumulated one by one by the patient fancy of the poet while rummaging around the old quarters of the towns he has travelled through.[161]

Chopin travelled little and did not collect souvenirs. Not for all the treasures of the world would he have hung his

---

[161] Gautier, *Histoire du romantisme* (Paris, 1874), 129–132.

life-story on the walls of his own apartment or piled it up on etageres. He was not interested in the gaudy, multi-coloured lavishness of 'artistic things'. No excess. The tone of his apartment was set above all by elegant furniture, on which, of course, he spared no expense. When he was setting up home at 5 Chaussée d'Antin, his very moderate and prudent father, who learned of his son's 'folly', did not omit to admonish him: 'So you have your own flat, a little extravagant, so it seems, but I understand that you could not have done otherwise, since you give lessons at home, and in the present times, as indeed always, everyone is judged by appearances. However, my Friend, one should not overdo it...' (KR 97). His brilliant progeny never overstepped the mark, be it only on account of his good taste, yet he always took exceptional care over furniture. Indeed, the Romantics appreciated a tasteful assemblage of 'old furniture', with which one had contact every day. Suffice it to read a little prose by E. T. A. Hoffmann.

At around the same time, Edgar Allan Poe published the essay *The Philosophy of Furniture*, in which he described his ideal room, cosy and warm, not over-filled with furniture, just pieces conducive to concentration. The walls of this room, he instructs us, should be lined with 'a glossy paper of a silver gray tint', which, incidentally, Chopin liked very much. 'The colours of the curtains and their fringe – the tints of crimson and gold – appear everywhere in profusion, and determine the character of the room.' Generally speaking, at every turn one should see there 'rich giltwork' or 'gold cord'. To Poe's mind, this was a beautiful, but by no means lavish, interior.[162]

Chopin did not adhere to any contrived ideal model of a room's interior. Indeed, he would surely have gone mad in a clamour of crimson and gold. As far as we know, his furniture,

---

[162] *The Philosophy of Furniture* was first published in May 1840. It was then issued in a slightly altered version in 1845.

like his wallpaper and draperies, reflected his particular sensitivity to the 'ordinary' taste of *nouveau riche* townsfolk. In 1910, Ferdynand Hoesick noted down an account given by Antoni Jędrzejewicz, who inherited things left by the composer. At that time, there were still some very valuable souvenirs. 'As you know,' said Chopin's nephew, 'Chopin loved elegant furniture, stylish of course, and since he never counted his pennies he only had to see something he liked to immediately buy it. In this way, over the twenty years he was residing in Paris, he assembled in his apartment a veritable museum of the most exquisite furniture, everything remarkably expensive (such as this shoe cupboard), trinkets, porcelain, pictures, books in magnificent editions, and so on. Apart from this, as an adored artist, he was continually receiving the most diverse gifts, and since people knew of his princely tastes, he was not given just anything.'[163]

His flat gave the impression of being neat to the point of excess.

As we read in the memoirs of Emilia Hoffmanowa, 'Moving almost exclusively among the loftiest social circles, he himself had lordly habits, and, elegant by nature, he loved beautiful furniture, expensive carpets and various knick-knacks and accessories, etc. In his apartment – and he was living at that time on Square d'Orléans – everything was soft, elegant and refined, carpets and curtains everywhere, to such an extent that even the pianos were draped in silk covers, embroidered by *grandes dames* and his admirers. In general terms, he lived like a woman; one might even wish to say – like a cocotte.'[164]

He sometimes bought curios. Perhaps he wanted to amuse his friends with them. 'At the Palais Royal,' he wrote to Julian

[163] Quoted in Czartkowski and Jeżewska, 529.
[164] Ibid, 420. Emilia Porzęcka was the wife of Doctor Aleksander Hoffmann (1805–1865), who was a friend of Chopin's from Warsaw and for two years lived with him in Paris at 5 rue de la Chaussée d'Antin. For a while, she was a pupil of the composer.

Fontana in mid June 1841 from Nohant, 'in the gallery on the theatre side, almost in the middle, there is a big shop with accessories (as they say *chez nous*); it has two windows with displays of various caskets, knick-knacks and trifles, shiny, elegant and dear. You'll enquire there whether they have little ivory hands for scratching one's head. You must have seen such a bibelot more than once: a little hand, usually crooked, white, set on a black stick. I think I've seen one there; ask, and they'll tell you. Anyway, seek out this knick-knack and send it; nb. if it's not dearer than 10, 15, 20 or 30' (KS ii: 20–21). He did not, however, transform his habitation into either an elegant glory-hole or the boudoir of a spoiled young lady. Here is Ferenc Liszt:

> Without approaching the dazzling wealth with which some
> Paris celebrities decorated their apartments at that time, he
> knew how to maintain in this respect, as in his attire, a happy
> medium between too little and too much, the instinctive line
> of *comme il faut*.[165]

This sounds to me a bit like criticism of the taste of Victor Hugo.

Chopin had an exceptional sense of the significance of an interior. He knew that it had to be assimilated. When he rented the apartment of a certain Franck, about whom we still know very little, he did not omit to inform Ferdinand Hiller, in a letter of 20 June 1833: 'I feel perfect within these walls, where we met so often' (KS i: 228). He was convinced that a habitation shaped a man's personality, moulding his spirit through the thoughts that the interior casts upon him. On 8 October 1839, he sent Fontana, who was furnishing the flat at 5 rue Tronchet, the following instructions: 'Also give orders, my Dearest, in the new flat, once

---

[165] F. [Ferenc] Liszt, *F. Chopin*, 4th edn (Leipzig: Breitkopf & Haertel, 1890), 208.

such an able person, that no black thoughts or choking coughs visit me – think, that I would have been good – and sweep away for me, if you can, many episodes from the past' (KS i: 366).[166]

So his habitation was his intimate space, which he defended in a manner as ruthless as it was ingenious. 'My doors never close,' he wrote to his family on 8–9 June 1847, 'on account of the various visitors, whom I cannot always send away empty-handed. – I should have been regarded as impolite long before now, but somehow not yet' (KR 169). That was only because he imposed specific rules on those 'various visitors'. In this case, his justification was very simple and remarkably genuine. He was occupied, busy and ailing. He had plenty of lessons, and could choose his pupils. His time was too valuable to be fouled up by everyone who wished only to meet a famous celebrity. The flat was guarded by a servant, who dismissed most of the 'visitors' with an elegant lie, that his master was not at home or was ill. This ruse, as we know, is respected throughout the civilised world, and in this case worshippers of the truth are transformed into uncouth churls or mindless intruders. Occasionally, the barrier was broken by a visiting card with a recommendation. Such was the case, as we know, with Lenz. Interesting friends were received

---

[166] One must hope that the excerpt quoted here was not deformed in the KS edition, since the form of other parts of this letter raise serious concerns. Sydow suggests that he reproduced this letter from the autograph, because he did not accept Karasowski's version. He gives one of the sentences in the following wording: 'Ale dobrze by było, żeby nie bardzo Ordowskie albo Zimmermanowskie, albo Karsko-Końskie, albo Sowińskie, albo świńskie, albo inno-zwierzęce było' (KS i: 365–366). Karasowski has Orłowskie instead of Ordowskie. Fontana, to whom this letter was addressed, quoted this fragment when writing to Stanisław Koźmian on 6 June 1850. And it turns out that the names concerned read Orłowskie and Kątsko-Końskie, and not Ordowskie and Karsko-Końskie. (Józef Fijałek, 'Wybór listów Juliana Fontany do Stanisława Egberta Koźmiana z lat 1844–1868' [Selected letters written by Julian Fontana to Stanisław Egbert Koźmian in the years 1844–1868], in *Rocznik Biblioteki PAN*, i (Wrocław, 1957), 225–226). All will be resolved by the edition currently being prepared by the leading Chopin scholar and editor Krystyna Kobylańska.

even when he was really ill. In the summer of 1849, when he was very poorly, Cyprian Kamil Norwid came to his apartment on rue Chaillot. '…the French maid tells me he's asleep; I soften my step, leave my card and depart. I've not descended more than a couple of steps when the maid comes back for me, saying that Chopin, on learning who it was, invites me in – that in a word he was not asleep, but does not wish to receive'.[167]

A painstakingly appointed apartment discharged a very particular function in establishing his musical career. The matter is somewhat complex, but clearly visible to the trained eye. So let us take on board the fact that no ordinary musical soirées were held there. Only the initiated gathered there. The famous of Europe. Here again is Liszt:

> The most eminent minds of Paris met on numerous occasions in Chopin's salon […] he possessed that innate grace of the Polish welcome, which not only subjugates one's host to the laws and duties of hospitality, but also makes him forgo all personal consideration, constraining him to attend to the desires and the pleasures of those he is receiving. We liked to visit him, because we were charmed there, and because we felt at ease […][168]

Around his piano, Chopin assembled people of the calibre of Heine, Nourrit, Delacroix, Niemcewicz, George Sand, Mickiewicz and Liszt. At a soirée on 4 December 1836, which was described in detail by Józef Brzowski, the guests were Liszt, Mrs Sand, Nourrit, the marquis Astolphe de Custine, Eugène Sue, Pixis, Wojciech Grzymała and Jan Matuszyński.[169] Chopin's circle, as Liszt noted, 'comprised a group of famous names, and

---

[167] Norwid, *Pisma wszystkie*, vi:178.

[168] Liszt, *F. Chopin*, 143, 144.

[169] Czartkowski and Jeżewska, 210–216.

those names bowed down before him, like the kings of various empires gathered together to fete one of their own. They paid him in full the tribute that he was due'.[170]

But this was no 'artists' den'. That explains why Chopin was so gleefully visited by Eugène Delacroix, who had an aversion to Bohemia. He was impressed only by creative artists who combined the loftiest spiritual culture with the lifestyle of a lord, such as Rubens, who was really very rich, or Chopin, who, though not in possession of a huge fortune, was also a past master of refinement, discretion and tact. In this salon, exhibitionism and ostentatious Bohemians were unimaginable.

The walls were hung with splendid prints, which Chopin liked and collected. Astolphe de Custine sometimes chose them and sent them to him (KS i: 297). The guests would lean against ravishing consoles, glance at themselves in a fabulous mirror that intensified the candlelight, and sit on chairs that once belonged to King Ladislaus IV. After crossing the threshold, a new arrival would receive special signals. The black piano was illumined by yellow candles, flames flickered in the fireplace, drawing the guests into a circle of sympathy. There was a smell of violets, which Chopin particularly liked. They were taken care of by a special flower arranger (KS ii: 20). When he returned, sick and weary, from his tour of Britain, he sent Wojciech Grzymała a request: 'Have a bouquet of violets bought on Friday [24 November 1848], so it might smell in the salon – may I still have a little poetry at home on my return – passing through the living room to the bedroom – where I shall lie down for a long time' (KS ii: 289). He had them arranged in low vases and presented them to his lady guests. 'On one occasion, however,' recalled Emilia Hoffmanowa, 'he had prepared too few, and so when the tardy Mrs Delfina [Potocka] arrived, there were no violets left for her; seeing this, Chopin broke off a camellia from

---

[170] Liszt, *F. Chopin*, 142.

the sumptuous bush standing in the salon and offered it to the beautiful countess'.[171] Anyone who could smell violets could be sure they were standing in Chopin's apartment.

Such gatherings were like feasts of elegant wit. There were splendid jokes, brilliantly worded, which subsequently flew around Paris. In keeping with the tone of the salon, in which the host's profound complex of absolute solitude vanished for a while, no one was so bold as to make any intimate confessions. Of course, those assembled amused themselves and joked, but always with the utmost refinement. Eccentricity was out of the question; dandies were barred. No one here would have taken any interest in such a 'boudoir prop'. And if, by chance, one of their ilk had happened to get in, he would have hastily retreated, embarrassed or enraged.

So musical soirées chez Chopin were attended solely by wonderful artists and selected connoisseurs. No pure-bred aristocrat or purse-rattling plutocrat was allowed. The Marquis de Custine belonged to this company because he was a prose writer with an exceptional mind. This was the scene of mysteries for an artistic elite, about which both the 'upper echelons' and the wealthy townsfolk had heard but little. Hence issued stories of extraordinary elation and heavenly improvisations. Hence hied the news that Chopin's pianistic artistry reached its pinnacle only amid a small group of listeners, among whom this genius felt at ease.

So Chopin turned his Paris habitations into a succession of temples to the aristocracy of mind and spirit. It was here that the legend was born of the indescribable qualities of his music and his playing. Thus in his apartment he took revenge, in some sense, on the 'upper echelons' upon which his fate largely depended. The legend created here was then exploited in his public performances. The Ariel of the piano hid in the

---

[171] Czartkowski and Jeżewska, 422.

mysterious and inaccessible space of his habitation, so that each of his public concerts would be a grand event and an exceptional – and quite expensive – act of grace. From this point of view, elegant rooms were an investment that brought good returns. In the forge of myths, he cast his fame and fortune. And so his clear-headed thinking is just as captivating as the poetic flights of his musical genius.

3. Epiphany of a Musical Idol

Like a poet or a painter, a composer reveals himself to the world in his works. Consequently, his artistic existence is dependent upon his corporeal epiphany. Expressed in English, this notion in somewhat nebulous, but expressed in French, it is as simple as it is precise. *Son être n'est pas son paraître.* It is different for an actor. In a play, so Michel Lemaire writes, he cannot come into being unless he shows himself in person, since he transforms himself into a work, which is then revealed to the public. For an actor, therefore, to come into being artistically equates to revealing himself. *Son être est dans son paraître.*[172]

On arriving in Paris, Chopin, who decided to steer his career himself, realised that a musician like him, and so one who was both composer and pianist, was in some sense split. As a composer, he could have remained in hiding, only revealing himself to the world in his opuses. As a pianist, meanwhile, he had to show himself to the public in person. In this respect, the virtuoso musician is no different to the actor. This truth was very important, as Chopin understood that it would be easier for him to conquer Paris if he first appeared as a master of the piano who happened to present his own compositions.

Not wishing to upset his Warsaw teacher, who saw in him above all a composer of stage music, Chopin calmly explained that he had not yet grown into such responsible work: 'Your letter', he wrote to Józef Elsner on 14 December 1831, 'was further proof of that fatherly solicitude, of those truly sincere wishes, that you have deigned conserve for your most devoted

---

[172] Lemaire, *Le dandysme*, 79.

pupil. In the year 1830, though I knew how much I lacked and how far I was from satisfying any of the models that I had in you, if I had wanted to try, I nonetheless dared to think to myself: I am getting a little bit closer to him, and if not an Elbow-high, then perhaps some Spindleshanks will issue from my brain-box' (KS i: 204). He loved his old teacher very much, and yet Chopin would not have been himself had he not had an elegant dig at him, now clearly irked by his compatriots' constant calling for a national opera. Elsner, who wrote at least three musical works for the stage on themes taken from Polish history, *Leszek the White* (*Leszek Biały*, 1809), *King Elbow-high* (*Król Łokietek*, 1817–1819) and *Jagiellon at Tenczyn* (*Jagiełło w Tenczynie*, 1819), believed that his brilliant pupil would write one more opera, and a better one at that – about, say, Ladislaus Spindleshanks (Władysław Laskonogi).

In those days, Polish theatres were swarming with kings and national heroes, but Chopin had no intention of writing an operatic history of Poland. He resolved once and for all that he would be a composer of piano music, which he would, as far as possible, present on the stage himself. He explained this to Elsner:

> But today, seeing all hopes of this kind thwarted, I am obliged to think about seeking a path for myself in the world as a *pianist*, setting aside for only some time the *loftier artistic perspectives* that you rightly set out for me in your letter. In order to be a *great composer*, one needs enormous experience, which, as you taught me, is acquired not just by listening to others, but more by listening to one's own works. [...] For me, as regards *revealing* oneself in the musical world, happy the man who can be composer and actor in one (KS i: 204–205).

Thus he was aware that as a pianist his situation would be that of an actor, since in order to make his name he had to reveal himself on the concert platform. His artistic existence was identified with his showing himself. *Son être est dans son paraître*. And since a concert is akin to a theatrical performance, it ought to be well directed. On the concert platform, the virtuoso has to play the role that he has devised for himself. His conquering of the audience depends upon the performance of that role. Therefore a pianist's performance is a kind of monodrama.

This awareness of the theatrical character of the virtuoso's performance was somehow linked to Chopin's skills in mimicry and acting, which he had demonstrated since his early youth. He had already played Austrian generals before a group of ladies in Vienna. 'It's a new punchinello, freshly produced by myself, you've not yet seen it,' he wrote to his family, 'but those who see it, burst with laughter' (KR 74). Later, he was quite widely known for such gifts in the artistic circles of Paris. Those great actors of the Romantic era Bocage (Pierre François Touzé) and Marie Dorval spoke of him with recognition. The fame of his skills was so widespread that Balzac mentioned it in *A Man of Business*.[173] Mickiewicz compared him to David Garrick.[174] After a feast of music, so George Sand writes, 'suddenly, as if to cancel this effect and the memory of its pain, he would turn and steal a look in the mirror, arrange his hair and his tie, and all at once mimic a phlegmatic Englishman, an impertinent oldster, a sentimental English lady, or a mercenary Jew.' Many diarists state that those gathered in the salon literally held their sides

---

[173] Ludwik Bronarski, *Szkice Chopinowskie*, tr. Anna Szweykowska (Cracow, 1961), 15.

[174] See Teofil Lenartowicz, *Listy o Adamie Mickiewiczu* [Letters about Adam Mickiewicz] (Paris 1875), repr. in Stanisław Pigoń (ed.), *Adama Mickiewicza wspomnienia i myśli* [Memories and thoughts of Adam Mickiewicz] (Warsaw, 1958), 210.

with laughter. He also willingly took part in domestic farces put on at Nohant.[175]

Such a talented person must have been sensitive to the very essence of the thespian art, which involves a remarkable combination of cold calculation and imagination taken at times to the point of distraction. Although on principle I steer clear of such judgments, it is difficult here not to state that just such a character is also possessed by his music. Aware that the virtuoso is an actor, a Chopin concert, during which he usually revealed himself as a 'composer and actor in one', was a demonstration of harmonious concord between strict reckoning and spontaneous rapture. A work elaborated painstakingly and at length was now performed in a surge of inspiration. A precisely conceived performance was now played out by a gifted actor. Such was his policy regarding his self-revelation on the stage.

He had acquired some experience before arriving in Paris. His Viennese debut, on 11 August 1829, showed Chopin to be a level-headed entrepreneur. The concert was planned as a presentation of the composer and the virtuoso. '…were I to appear solely as executor,' he wrote to his family on 8 August, 'it would mean less, but I am appearing with my works, and so I can certainly be bold' (KR 50). The composer, who could remain hidden and absent, then becomes present and visible in the figure of the pianist. Chopin was assured about the composer, but he was anxious that the pianist might not represent him so well.

Before taking to the concert platform, he made a meticulous reconnaissance of the situation. First he set in motion an impressive array of recommendations and gave a few connoisseurs a taste of his talent. He tamed the journalists. In those days, they

---

[175] Sand, *Story of My Life*, 1105. On the farces at Nohant, see KGS ii: 32, 75, 88, 142. On the theatre at Nohant, see Sand, 'Le théâtre des marionettes de Nohant', in *Œuvres autobiographiques*, ed. Georges Lubin (Paris, 1971), 1240–1276.

were a terrible tribe; as a matter of fact, they are still, as a group, unpleasant today. Following the French Revolution, during the times of romanticism, the press took on huge significance, and its might was swiftly demonised. In the general conviction, a single review was capable of destroying genius or elevating utter mediocrity.[176] So not without reason did Chopin reassure his family in a letter of 12 August: 'Be not anxious about my person and my reputation. The journalists have taken a liking to me; they might have the occasional dig at me, but that is needed to nuance their praise' (KR 51). He also organised his own intelligence, as it was important to him to gather the opinions of the concert-going public that were not yet shaped by the press. 'My friends and colleagues spread themselves around the corners in order to listen to the various opinions and critiques. Celiński can say how little reproof was heard; only Hube heard the greatest. Some lady declared: "Schade um den Jungen, dass er schlechte Turnure hat". If that was the only reprimand I received, and they swear to me that they heard nothing but praise and that they never started the ovations themselves, then I have nothing to be perturbed about' (KR 51–52).[177] He prepared everything. Only the actual decision to perform in front of the Viennese public seemed to him ill-conceived.

> So my first appearance was as happy as it was unexpected. Hube claims that a person will never achieve anything by the customary means and according to the plan he has conceived; something must be left to fate. And so trusting to fortune I allowed myself to be talked into giving a concert. If they are so scathing in the papers that I'll not be able to show myself to the world again, I have decided to paint rooms, as

---

[176] See Honoré de Balzac, *Stracone złudzenia*, tr. Tadeusz Żeleński-Boy (Warsaw, 1950), 86, 87; Eng. tr. as *Lost Illusions*.
[177] 'It is a pity this young man has so little tournure'.

it is easiest to draw a brush across paper, and one is always
a son of Apollo (KR 52).

The effect was so good that for the rest of his life Chopin
'drew across paper' not a brush, but a pen, tracing his notes.

That fight to make a name for himself in the musical world
taught him that a concert was a combination of elements that
could be controlled to some extent and elements that elude all
control. Therefore, on arriving in Paris, he sought to create
a model of performance from which all risk would eventually
be eliminated.

His Warsaw performances were also not without significance, as they taught him the importance of preparing opinion
beforehand. Prior to a public performance, he gave what might
be described as a closed concert, which took place on 19 December 1829 in the old Merchants' Hall. This was followed by
'well-arranged reports' in the press.[178] This was taken care of by
journalists of his acquaintance, who happened to be genuinely
convinced of his exceptional talent, such as Stanisław Egbert
Koźmian. Continually repeated in these articles and notes were
calls for a concert, in which the young musician should allow
the Warsaw public to hear him before leaving the country.[179]
The young artist kindly allowed himself to be heard twice, on
17 and 22 March 1830. There were reviews aplenty.[180] Let us
note that Chopin again learned the significance of well-orches-
trated advance information in the press and of 'news' circling
around the 'upper echelons'. The hall was practically full. Only
an empty auditorium would have been an unmitigated disaster.
Not even the most vitriolic reviews would have been such a great

[178] Czartkowski and Jeżewska, 110.
[179] These articles have been gathered together by Czartkowski and Jeżewska,
111–112.
[180] For Chopin's reaction, see his letter to Tytus of 27 March 1830 (KS i: 114–
121).

blow. As it happens, they were good, and even enthusiastic. He looked through them all most thoroughly, but dispassionately. He still set great stall by the views of his listeners. He rued not being able, as in Vienna, to organise his own intelligence in the hall and the cafés. 'I would like to be at Cinderella's', he wrote to Tytus Woyciechowski on 27 March 1830, 'so as to hear the *debate* that must have been carried on over my person' (KS i: 115).

Before leaving for Paris, Chopin, who was under no illusion that the concert platform was anything other than a battleground, who knew that an audience, that enigmatic, many-headed monster, the Leviathan of performing artists, was highly capricious, learned the importance of scrupulously eliminating the accidental elements. He also paid close attention to the social make-up of the audience. Already in Warsaw, he knew that an audience was composed of various strata and that the expectations of him were different among the 'gallery' and 'town', the 'uppermost classes' and 'first-floor boxes', and musical connoisseurs. He also knew that 'no one has ever been able to reconcile everyone' (KS i: 115–116). Hence in Paris he took pains to unify his audience.

He also knew that under no circumstances could he trivialise the actions that might protect him against that greatest of perils: rows of empty chairs, gaps in the auditorium, the dreadful blackness of empty boxes. This, he could ill afford, even in Warsaw, where he was known, loved and appreciated. Especially in Warsaw, which was in effect to finance his journey abroad.[181] So he arrived in Paris with a well-considered 'policy on public performances'.

During the 1830s, parallel to Chopin, grand concert work was being pursued by the composer and conductor Hector Berlioz. So on Chopin's arrival in Paris, France had the chance to

---

[181] The concert actually brought little revenue. See letter to Tytus of 27 March 1830 (KS i: 116).

admire two musicians who presented two entirely different ways of conquering the 'many-headed monster'. It is of no matter that Berlioz stood on the rostrum, baton in hand, to lead a grand orchestra of up to several hundred musicians whereas Chopin most often sat on the concert platform alone, with just a single instrument. I am not concerned here with the manner of music-making, but with the model of the artist's struggle with his audience. After all, the character of this model was determined not so much by the kind of music being cultivated as by the mind of the artist, dictating to him a very specific concept of public performance. So let us look first at how Berlioz solved this problem.

He is regarded as the ideal embodiment of the Romantic mentality. 'In this renaissance of 1830,' wrote Théophile Gautier, 'he represents the Romantic musical idea: the breaking of old moulds, the substituting of new forms for invariable straightforward rhythms, the complicated and skilful richness of the orchestra, the fidelity of local colour, the unexpected effects of sonority, the tumultuous and Shakespearean depth of passions, the amorous or melancholy reverie, the nostalgia and postulations of the spirit, the undefined and mysterious feelings that speech cannot render, and that something over and above all this which eludes words and which notes allow us to divine [...] Hector Berlioz was a true Romantic, and as such was engaged in the great battle, where he fought with an incredible ferocity and determination.'[182] Gautier forgot about his exaltation, fed on the literary frenzy of the Romantics, about his love of the macabre, his fascination with cruelty, orgies, satanic masses and massacres.[183] 'Under the combined influence of poetry, music and association', we read in Berlioz's *Memoirs*, 'I would work

---

[182] Gautier, *Histoire du romantisme*, 260, 262.
[183] Mario Praz, *Zmysły, śmierć i diabeł w literaturze romantycznej*, tr. Krzysztof Żaboklicki (Warsaw, 1974), 139. On *delectatio morosa*, see p. 123; Eng. tr. as *The Romantic Agony*, tr. Angus Davidson (London, 1933).

myself up into an incredible state of excitement. The triple in-toxication always ended in floods of tears and uncontrollable sobbing. [...] What madness, many will say. Yes, but what happi-ness. Sensible people have no idea what it is to have this intense consciousness simply of being alive. One's heart dilates, one's imagination expands and soars, one exists with a kind of frenzy; under the influence of extreme nervous stimulation, one's very body seems made of iron.'[184]

One fundamental trait of Berlioz's nature was Titanism. 'Although Berlioz was generally regarded as mad,' wrote Théo-phile Gautier, 'he inspired that terror which is spread around him by every being who is known to be invested with a secret power. Through his bizarre, obscure and exaggerated behaviour, one divined an energy that would yield to nothing [...] He felt like a Titan capable of climbing up to heaven and fronting Jupiter, and he had to stay nailed to the Caucasus cross, with diamond nails, by the Force and the Power, like Aeschylus' hero'.[185] This means that every one of his actions was guided by an irresist-ible urge to overstep measure and norm. Everything he did was a challenge.

A man of this sort had no intention of coming to some arrangement with the public. He knew it was a Hydra. As we read in *Evenings in the Orchestra*, 'the public of three-quarters of Europe is today as devoid as the Chinese sailors of all feeling for musical expression. We have no surer means of ascertaining what it finds distasteful and wearisome than to examine what we find beautiful and inspiring, and vice versa. What we worship it blasphemes, it enjoys what we reject.' 'It [the public] only goes to the Opéra or to a concert if it can get there without any trouble or inconvenience, without too much expense, of course, and if

---

[184] Hector Berlioz, *The Memoirs of Hector Berlioz*, tr. and ed. David Cairns (London, 2002), 154–155.
[185] Gautier, *Histoire du romantisme*, 262, 268.

it has strictly nothing better to do. [...] Nobody will sacrifice to music a dinner, a ball, or even a simple walk, still less so a +race-meeting or a sitting of the assizes'.[186] So he was under no illusions as to whom he was dealing with. As a matter of fact, at times the whole hall would react with fury. One evening, at the Salle Vivienne, an impresario somehow managed to force through the now famous *Symphonie fantastique*. Once its final movement had ended, young people in the audience picked up their chairs and started to smash them, screaming, on the floor.

He was aware, therefore, that a performance is essentially a merciless battle.

> In France, my dear fellow, you must train the public just as you train racehorses; it's a special art. There are persuasive artists who will never master it, while others who are dismally second-rate make irresistible trainers. Happy those who possess both these rare qualities.[187]

For the monster to be vanquished, it had to be wowed. Thus a concert could easily turn into an attempt to gain the favours of the monstrous oaf. 'The public, once your slave and now your master, your emperor! Come now, make your bow, you're being applauded... *Moriturus salutat.*'[188] In those days, a musician on stage was a gladiator.

Berlioz knew what a dark force he was challenging, and yet challenge it he did. Since everything he undertook had to be gigantic, he had to have a lot of concerts. At that time, the organising of every performance was torture. 'In France,' he wrote, 'whoever gives a concert is taxed. [...] There are people

---

[186] Berlioz, *Evenings in the Orchestra*, tr. C. R. Fortescue (Harmondsworth, 1963), 226 (twenty-third evening), 64 (second evening).

[187] Ibid, 65 (second evening).

[188] Ibid, 91 (sixth evening).

whose function it is to levy (in other words to take) one eighth of the gross receipts of every concert, and they even have the right to take as much as a quarter if they think fit. So, you come to Paris, you organize at your own risk a musical matinée or evening. You have to pay for the hall, the lighting, the heating, the posters, the score copiers, and the performers. As you are unknown, you must count yourself lucky if you take eight hundred francs. Your expenses amount to at least six hundred francs, so that you should have a profit of two hundred francs; but in actual fact you will be left with nothing. The tax-collector makes do with your two hundred francs which are his by law. He pockets them with a bow, for he is most polite.'[189] In spite of this, he readily organised concerts. A true Titan is fearless, and so his monster could even boast several thousand heads. A true Titan is proud, and so Berlioz challenged the monster to an open fight, aware that capital subordinated art to itself to a truly shameless degree, thrusting it into a bordello erected for the amusement of new barbarians. 'I belong to a nation', he wrote in his *Memoirs*, 'that has ceased to be interested in the higher manifestations of the mind; whose only god is the golden calf. The Parisians have become a barbarian people. In scarcely one rich house in ten will you find a library – I do not say a library of music. [...] We are witnessing the triumph of industrialism in Art, raised to power by the crude popular instincts to which it panders, and trampling with brutish contempt on the values it has dethroned.'[190] He accepted this situation because, despite his exaltation, he was capable of taking account most judiciously of social realities. And he took up the fight. For a Titan, as long as he is fighting, never gives up hope of victory. He either perishes in humiliation or he turns the oaf into an angel.

---

[189] Ibid, 63 (second evening).
[190] Berlioz, *Memoirs*, 510.

The battle-ground were the *concerts-monstres*. Multitudes helped to organise them. Multitudes also performed the compositions, and multitudes listened to them. Berlioz was not afraid of the masses. As the industrial society developed, new forms of concert life appeared, and Berlioz accepted the challenge laid down to musicians by the era of mass culture. An ocean of townsfolk poured into concert halls, and Berlioz hovered over it, baton in hand, like God over the original waters of chaos. Against the great crowds, he pitched a great orchestra. Possibly because his aesthetic ideal was a monumental sound, but also perhaps for a more mundane reason. The mass listener was impressed by loud musical onomatopoeia. This was taken on board by virtuosos of the violin and piano, as well: by Paganini and Liszt. The conductor, who presided over a huge orchestra and several choirs, seemed to the hordes like a holy ruler. In some sense, this was all symptomatic of the Romantic overstepping of the norm. In Berlioz's case, 'social demand' seems to have been merely the impulse, or even the pretext, since this whole musical movement that set out to meet the mass receiver was essentially a manifestation of Romantic Titanism. One lone artist stood facing a human mass, which he had to master, having initially captivated it with beautiful music. Orpheus in front of a host of townsfolk in their Sunday best. When standing on the conductor's rostrum, Berlioz may well have felt that he was waging war with an elemental force.

Let us take a closer look at one such performance. On 1 August 1844, a concert was held to mark the end of the Industrial Exhibition in Paris. The idea came from Izaac Strauss, a professional organiser of carnival amusements, or 'director of society balls'. It was designed as a 'true festival devoted to exhibiting industrialists'. The grand organisational matters were handled by one Senac, secretary to the minister of trade. The original idea was for dances to be held after the concert, and for a buffet with food and drink, but it was rejected by the prefect of the Paris police, Gabriel Delesset, who was worried that it was an ideal opportunity for political agitation. The concert was to be enormous, and so Berlioz, who was entrusted with the musical side of things, engaged virtually all the choristers and instrumentalists of Paris. He also began to practise with particular groups of instruments and choirs.

Meanwhile, a gigantic hall was prepared. It was a huge pavilion, previously used for an exhibition of industrial equipment. 'Yet on the eve of this crucial trial [reference to the dress rehearsal], while the carpenters were constructing the platform, the hall had yet to be vacated. A large number of heavy iron machines lay encamped on the space intended for the audience. No arrangements had been made to have these monsters removed.'[191] He had to kick up a fuss about everything, because he had difficulties with everything. Berlioz was a man of extraordinary energy and great inner discipline, and so capitulation did not enter the equation.

The start of the concert resembled a flood. At 1 p.m., when he raised his baton, 'the crowd, which had burst through the wooden barrier […], armed with tickets just purchased at the box office, now surged into the hall with shouts of satisfaction'.[192] In the hall, the Hydra was heaving with thousands of heads, and then suddenly an unexpected influx surged in. Eventually, it all calmed down, and more than one thousand artists were waiting to take their bows. Of course, the dimensions of the hall and its acoustics justified the large numbers of musicians and singers. For example, in the Scherzo from Beethoven's Fifth Symphony, there were thirty-six double basses alone. Berlioz was assisted by two leaders and five choirmasters, who were positioned so as to be able to transmit his movements to the singers, since

---

[191] Ibid, 379.
[192] Ibid, 380.

the latter stood with their backs to him. He conducted with the help of seven 'beaters'. A woodcut published in the Parisian *L'Illustration* in 1844 shows this huge pavilion in the form of a gigantic rectangle crammed full of listeners.[193] Singled out in the middle is a circular stronghold of human bodies. This is the sacred circle of musicians, arranged in several concentric circles around a central point at which Berlioz stands, raised above the performers. So he is standing on the summit of a musical island, with an unfathomed ocean of listeners all around. With every movement, his famous blond mane shakes. Now everyone can discern this 'beautiful head of an angry eagle, eager for space',[194] carved out by the troubles and the heroism of the artist.

Amadé Mereaux's 'Chant des industriels', to words by Adolphe Dumas, was poorly received, but there was enthusiastic applause for a song from Halévy's opera *Charles VI*, as it aroused, as Berlioz noted, 'the brute instincts of opposition that always lurk in the breast of the Parisian populace'[195]. After the concert, problems arose with the Home Secretary and the prefect of the Parisian police. But the real rows only erupted when the revenue was being divided. Berlioz, of course, suffered a nervous breakdown. The Titan trampled the hordes like fields of grass, but he was driven to the brink of a heart-attack by the state skinflints. A physician friend bled him, to save him from apoplexy, and prescribed a trip to Nice, to the southern sea, to calm his nerves. The conductor's entire income went on the treatment.

So Berlioz resolved the eternal conflict between musician and audience on the concert platform itself. Nothing he did

[193] This woodcut is reproduced in Heinrich W. Schwab's album *Konzert. Öffentliche Musikdarbietung vom 17. bis 19. Jahrhundert* (Leipzig, 1980), Abbildung 72. *Grosskonzerte unter Hektor Berlioz*, 102–103. A similar impression is made by illustrations from a concert at the Olympic Circus, held in 1845, and from a performance at the Palace of Industrial Products in 1855.

[194] Gautier, *Histoire du romantisme*, 270.

[195] Ibid, 382.

before the concert was intended to ensure his triumph. The only difference between an ordinary concert in a music society hall and the *concert-monstre* was that in the latter case the press could summon greater crowds, augmenting the monster with hundreds more heads. And yet in every hall sat the same city-dweller who had to be won over – or aesthetically educated, to wit. So the concert platform was a place of uncertainty and battle. The musical Titan raged and fulminated, but essentially he had what he wanted.

In Chopin's case, this sort of stance was inconceivable. From the documents at our disposal, it emerges that both artists quite quickly understood that they occupied opposite aesthetic positions. The differences concerned not just the relations between the 'musical idea' and the sound, but also the question of the listener's status, and so the relationship between artist and audience. For this reason, I would plead once again for the opposition orchestra/piano not to be exaggerated. As Adam Zamoyski writes:

> Through Liszt [...] Chopin met Heinrich Heine, and at the end of 1832 Hector Berlioz, just back from his Italian trip. Chopin now found himself in the kitchen of the Romantic movement [...] They would meet for dinner in a restaurant; for an evening of music at Chopin's, where the light of one candle cast great shadows in which, as Liszt put it, some of the greatest names of the next decade listened in silence; for a picnic lunch at Berlioz's; or at Liszt's for 'hours of smoky discussions' as they puffed at Turkish pipes.[196]

Zamoyski presumes, and not without good reason, that serious aesthetic differences emerged already during these discussions. In any case, Chopin learned then that his ideals, Bach

---

[196] Zamoyski, *Chopin*, 92.

and Mozart, were not appreciated by the 'rabid Romantics'. As the years passed, the differences grew, until eventually Chopin and Berlioz were divided by the question of 'harmoniousness'.

This was a very serious problem. Here is Delacroix:

> My dear little Chopin was strongly opposed to the school that ascribes an important part of music's effect to the sonorities peculiar to particular instruments. There is no denying that some men, Berlioz among them, are that way inclined, and I think that Chopin, who hated him, was all the more averse to music that is nothing without the aid of trombones opposed to flutes and oboes or concordant with them.[197]

So Chopin could not abide works in which the sound replaced a 'musical idea', clearly identified with the theme, or rather with the melody. This means that he was critically disposed to every composer who muddied the depths of inventiveness with effects of orchestration. In Chopin's circle, Berlioz was not highly regarded, as the mysterious wisdom of music was considered to lie in that 'musical idea', and not in the sound, which was seen as 'decoration'. Delacroix, although aware that 'there is in some sonorities, irrespective of their expression for the soul, a pleasure for the senses', professed that Berlioz's noise was murderous, and that his music as a whole was a 'heroic mess'. In fact, Delacroix was irritated by all exaggerated transgression – if one may put it like that – of the forms

---

[197] Delacroix, *Journal*, ed. Michèle Hannoosh (Paris, 2009), 1345; unfortunately, neither of the English-language editions, containing translations by Norton and by Pach, is complete, hence the recourse here to the most recent integral French edition (tr.). Similar observations appear on pp. 1108 (13 April 1857) and 1768 (16 May 1857, 'Carnet d'Augerville (Grenoble), 1854–1859') of Hannoosh's French edition. See also Delacroix's criticism of Berlioz on p. 579 (Hannoosh), from 15 February 1852.

of expression.[198] George Sand held it against herself that when she was a 'child in the sensing of art', she had delighted in Berlioz's 'brass symphonies'.[199] Chopin's piano music laid bare the extraordinary power of melody, and many of his admirers could no longer be seduced by the sonoric effects of Berlioz's orchestra. To the immortal question 'what is music in music?' in Chopin's circle the answer was 'the musical phrase', because music was 'wordless speech'. Here, they were communing with the very mystery of music, and so no one was drawn to 'colourful sound'. Keen wisdom vs noisy effect. Lucid depth vs needless clamour. That was most probably how this controversy looked to the participants in Parisian Chopiniadas.

The divergent aesthetic ideals meant that in actual fact Chopin split with Berlioz, who in turn was repelled from Chopin by his entirely different model of public performance. Berlioz was a friend of the Czech violinist and composer Heinrich Wilhelm Ernst. While on tour, he met Ernst in various parts of Europe and always had a sincere admiration for him. As it happens, Chopin also held Ernst in high regard and performed with him several times. Berlioz knew that Ernst was readily compared to Chopin, and so he provided one further comparison of his own.

> Chopin, again, was strictly the virtuoso of the elegant salon, the intimate gathering. For Ernst, vast halls, crowded theatres, the great pulsating public, hold no terrors. On the contrary, he loves them and, like Liszt, is never more potent than when there is an audience of two thousand to subjugate.[200]

---

[198] Ibid, 488 (19 February 1850), 443 (23 April 1849).
[199] Letter written by George Sand to Eugène Delacroix of 26 January 1846; quoted in Juliusz Starzyński, *O romantycznej syntezie sztuk. Delacroix. Chopin. Baudelaire* [On the Romantic synthesis of the arts. Delacroix, Chopin and Baudelaire] (Warsaw, 1965), 83. See also Thérèse Merix-Spire, *George Sand et la musique* (Paris, 1955), 551, 59.
[200] Berlioz, *Memoirs*, 477.

Berlioz was impressed by hardy spirits who challenged the crowd and overcame it. Chopin was not among them. Consequently, of pianists, Berlioz admired Liszt above all, who in his concert performances employed a pianistic variant of the concert model adopted by Berlioz.

The role of the pianist in those days was not an easy one. 'One day', recalled Berlioz, 'I met one of our leading pianist-composers who was returning, disappointed, from a seaport where he had counted on making an appearance. "There was not the faintest possibility of giving a concert," he told me in all seriousness; "the herring had just come in, and the whole town could think of nothing but this precious food!" However can a man compete against a shoal of herring?'[201] In order to gain the favour of their terrible tyrant, pianists began to display dextrous and showy technique. For the purposes of publicity, they often transformed their performances into something resembling a public rivalry. Liszt and Thalberg competed with one another in an overt, even ostentatious, manner, holding public duels. Liszt abused his rival in the press before making a public display of apology and adoration, only to abuse him even more. Unsurprisingly, Thalberg paid him back in his own coin, and Chopin had to moralise with the sulky and bemused Liszt: 'Why come out with such a strong affront and then belittle oneself before the affronted...'[202]

The performances of some pianists resembled a circus act. Mendelssohn called them acrobats of the piano. 'But why on earth should I be forced to listen for the thirtieth time to all sorts of variations by Herz? They give me less pleasure than rope-dancers or acrobats, for with these there is at least the wicked thrill of always fearing that they may break their necks, and of seeing that after all they don't. But piano-acrobats [*Clavier-*

---

[201] Berlioz, *Evenings*, 66.
[202] Quoted in Czartkowski and Jeżewska, 219.

springer] don't even endanger their lives, merely our ears...'[203]
In their pursuit of success and money, they travelled the length
and breadth of our continent. Liszt, who possessed regal gestures
and a great sense of humour, could speak with irony about his
'triumphant-fairground' concert travels. He knew his listeners
and played the role imposed upon him like a lord. On one occasion, in a city in the north of Europe, where he was performing
with the famous singer Rubini, he found an audience of barely
fifty, instead of two thousand. As Berlioz relates, on taking the
stage, he addressed the auditorium with the following words:
'"Lady [there was only one] and gentlemen, I think you have had
enough music; now may I venture to ask if you will kindly come
and have supper with us?" There was a moment's hesitation
among the fifty potential guests, but since, all things considered,
this unusual suggestion was attractive, they made a point of not
refusing it. The supper cost Liszt twelve hundred francs.'[204]

From Alfred de Musset's parody in *Les Humanitaires*, we
learn that Liszt, while playing, behaved immoderately, to put it
mildly. He would turn a concert into a somewhat kitsch performance. 'Inspiration descends, the eye of the God [Liszt] lights
up, his hair shudders, his fingers arch and pound the keys with
fury. He plays with his hands, his elbows, his chin, his nose.
Everything that can strike hammers away... "Sublime!" they
exclaim. "That'll cost me twenty francs in repairs!" moans the
Divinity of the House [Marie d'Agoult].'[205] There was little exaggeration in this parody. 'He, with his windswept hair,' we read in
the memoirs of Charles Duvernet, 'his gaze fixed on the ceiling
as if seeking inspiration, nonchalantly let his two hands fall onto
the keyboard, which issued forth some dissonant chords, and
seeking a motif for some prelude, when all of a sudden he gets

---

[203] Quoted in Wilfrid Blunt, *On Wings of Song* (New York, 1974), 150.
[204] Berlioz, *Evenings*, 65–66.
[205] Quoted in Zamoyski, *Chopin*, 133.

up, slams the piano shut with a bang and declares that the bear will not be able to dance that evening.' 'Liszt is a poser,' added Duvernet, 'he needs a numerous audience and has no regard for the quality'.[206] He clearly had a complex of the artist as minion, and as a dandy he ostentatiously insulted those around him. Yet he was capable of laughing at himself when parodied. During one private concert at the Mendelssohns', he played a few manic variations on a Hungarian folk song. The assembled guests asked the host to sit at the piano as well, but he demurred as much as he could. 'But Liszt would not take No for an answer, and after some parrying Mendelssohn said, "Well, I will play; but you mustn't get angry with me." With that he sat down at the piano and played – what? First the Hungarian folk song and then all the variations, reproducing them so accurately that only Liszt himself might have discerned a difference. We were all afraid lest Liszt might feel rather put out, because Mendelssohn, like a regular tease, couldn't prevent himself from imitating Liszt's grandiose movements and extravagant gestures. But Liszt laughed, applauded enthusiastically, and admitted that nobody else, not even he himself, could have managed such a piece of bravura.'[207] From this it emerges that Liszt had a repertoire of ready gestures and facial expressions tailored to a popular audience.

Current musicology does not regard expressive gestures while playing an instrument as superfluous. Michelle Biget even assures us that it contributes to the sound of the music and can be interpreted as an element of the musical discourse. The gesticulations of a pianist are particularly eloquent. Broad movements of the shoulders undoubtedly influence the character of the sound.[208] Hence Bertrand Ott states that in the case of Liszt,

---

[206] Quoted in Merix-Spire, 555.
[207] Quoted in Blunt, *On Wings*, 211.
[208] Michelle Biget, 'Étude comparée du geste pianistique chez Liszt et chez Debussy', in *Franz Liszt*, Actes du colloque international (Paris, 1987), 155.

violent physical movements were essential for him to make manifest the musical motion that was most important to that music. He produced music not just from his fingers, but also from his shoulders, and even from his breast. Liszt's movement at the piano was not without its use. It created energy. In this way, the physical was subordinated to the spirit. As Liszt himself once declared, 'My piano is for me what a frigate is for a sailor, a horse for an Arab. Or perhaps even something more, since thus far it has been *my word*, my life…'[209] It is a beautiful confession, but a pianist's performance does not have to be a ballet show.

Chopin could not abide violent movements and buffoonish gestures. We learn from the research of Irena Poniatowska that the principle of 'singing' at the piano imposed restraint on the pianist, and Chopin, in accordance with his rule of 'sing when you play', did not even think of expressive movements.[210] Liszt,

---

[209] Bertrand Ott, 'Le pianisme Lisztien ou le dépassement créatif. Une réalité singulière à révérifier une pianistique universelle à expliciter', in *Franz Liszt* (see above, n. 208), 139–153.

[210] Irena Poniatowska, 'Artykulacja jako środek ekspresji ẇ grze fortepianowej w pierwszej połowie XIX wieku (między metodyką gry a praktyką wykonawczą epoki)' [Articulation as a means of expression in piano playing during the first half of the nineteenth century (between the playing methods and performance practice of the day)], *Rocznik Chopinowski*, 17 (1986), 135–146. So Paul Emil Johns was an impertinent liar. Chopin met him in 1832 through Pleyel. He was a pupil of Chopin, who dedicated to him the 5 Mazurkas, Op. 7. A native Austrian, he lived and worked in the United States. There is no doubt that he was responsible for the false image of Chopin in America. As Henri Kowalski wrote in 1872, 'It was especially the spasmatic mannerisms, nervous tics, rocking body and teary eyes that seemed to audiences particularly original in Chopin's pupil. The dilettantes never doubted for a moment that such exuberance was the proper way to perform that music, and they strove more to imitate that St Vitus' Dance than to seek its emotional essence. With time, that tradition spread to the edges of America, hence Chopin in an interpretation devoid of those whimsical gestures, of that gymnastic fancy, could not have been understood by the American public.' See Aleksander Janta, 'Niejaki Johns z Nowego Orleanu' [A certain Johns from New Orleans], in his book *Nic własnego nikomu* [Nothing of my own to anyone] (Warsaw, 1977), 148.

indeed, was his opposite in every respect. In 1842, our friend Lenz, a German musician resident in St Petersburg, presented himself before Chopin with a recommendation from Liszt. In order to confirm his protector's positive opinion, he immediately sat down at the instrument. Chopin 'smiled,' Lenz wrote later, 'leaned wearily against the piano, and his keen eyes looked me directly in the face'. And after Lenz's rendition, he 'whispered engagingly: "That *trait* is not your own, is it? *He* showed you that! *He* must have his hand in everything; well! he may dare – he plays to *thousands*, I seldom to *one*!"'[211] So Chopin knew that Liszt had made concessions to the thousand-headed monster. In this situation, showmanship was a weapon in the battle for the favours of the crowd. Chopin understood this, although he did not commend it. This controversy between great artists was aptly expressed by Adam Mickiewicz: 'Chopin talks with spirit, and gives us the Ariel view of the universe. Liszt is the eloquent tribune to the world of men, a little vulgar and showy certainly, but I like the tribune best'.[212]

The Ariel of the piano hated crowds. And so George Sand was right that the masses did not know him. He did not wish to tame the masses. He cultivated music for individuals, and not for crowds. One can admire Liszt's solution, taking into account the changes to the structure of music reception in the modern-day industrial society, yet one should not forget that a crowd of listeners by no means constitutes a sum of individuals. In a crowd, every listener loses something of his own personality, and as a result his contact with music takes on different values. Chopin wanted to maintain a personalistic model of musical communication. And I repeat once again that it was not a ques-

[211] Lenz, *Great Piano Virtuosos*, 49.
[212] From a letter sent by the American writer and journalist Margaret Fuller to Elizabeth Hoar, January 1847, repr. in *Memoirs of Margaret Fuller Ossoli* (Boston, 1857), vol. ii.

tion of a single chamber instrument, since Liszt, the tribune of the piano, also sat at that same sole instrument in grand halls. When the form of the public concert arose, the possibility of an intimate understanding between musician and listener disappeared. Perhaps that explains why today we sometimes prefer compact discs to concert halls, individual sensitivity to collective frenzy, quiet experience to philharmonic circus. Chopin did not like crowds by the platform, as he rued the slighted intimacy. 'I do not like publicity,' he confessed to Lenz, 'but it is a duty I owe my position'.[213]

In the nineteenth century, Chopin's ideal of music-making was a utopia that could be realised in a private salon. But the highly intelligent Chopin allowed that utopia to become manifest also on the public concert platform. He was helped in this undertaking by many factors, among which I would number a remarkably sober exploitation of his own frustrations.

Chopin was afflicted by a lasting aversion to public concerts. As Jean-Jacques Eigeldinger writes, the reason for this dislike lay 'partly in Chopin's aristocratic conception of music, referring to eighteenth-century tendencies. On the pianistic level, this conception was made manifest in the art of almost legendary nuance, in the art of "the ephemeral shades of the microscopic playing of Mr Chopin", as one of the critics of the day maliciously put it'.

Hence he came across poorly when he played with an orchestra, and one is not surprised that in 1840 he stated: 'Concerts are never true music; they are music that one must renounce, in order to hear that which is most beautiful in art'. On 22 February 1835, Chopin performed at Erard's with Ferdinand Hiller. Afterwards, the critic of *Le Pianiste* wrote:

---

[213] Lenz, *Great Piano Virtuosos*, 52.

Chopin's talent, quite exquisite as it happens, is so delicate, so full of unfathomed nuances which only a sensitive and trained ear can pick up, that it is disadvantageous to listen to it with others. Chopin should play alone, to be appreciated as he deserves.

Eigeldinger clearly suggests that Chopin heeded this advice. On 5 April that same year he performed at the Théâtre des Italiens in the first movement of one of his concertos 'with the accompaniment of an orchestra, which happened for the first and only time in his Parisian career'. 'The Parisian audience', wrote Wojciech Sowiński, after François Joseph Fétis, 'received him coolly, although the hall was filled with connoisseurs. The event so discouraged Chopin that he did not perform in public for a long time after'. Eigeldinger ends his exposition with the observation that 'the unsuccessful concert at the Théâtre des Italiens unquestionably marks the beginning of his departure from the concert platform'. Henceforth, he definitively rejected the concert in favour of the recital.[214]

Yet the very thought of performing in public continued to torment him. 'I am not fit to give concerts,' he confessed to Liszt, 'the crowd intimidates me and I feel asphyxiated by its eager breath, paralysed by its inquisitive stare, silenced by its alien faces; but you, you are made for it, for when you cannot captivate your audience, you at least have the power to stun it.'[215] Liszt and Chopin were capable of employing refined causticity most beautifully. As Adam Zamoyski rightly points out, the French word *assommer* means not only 'to beat, crush or deafen', but also 'to weary or bore'.

---

[214] Jean-Jacques Eigeldinger, 'Koncerty Chopina w Paryżu w latach 1832–1838' [Chopin's concerts in Paris in the years 1832–1838], *Rocznik Chopinowski*, 17, pp. 147–148, 165–166.
[215] Quoted in Zamoyski, *Chopin*, 89.

This fear of the crowd, this fondness for musical intimacy, was turned by Chopin into an implement in the most refined method of taming an audience known to music history.

New forms of particular phenomena, although understandable and necessary, very often violate their essence. Chopin must have known this or he would not have been such an ardent supporter of music-making within a close group of friends. The public performance theatralised musical reception, depriving the 'wordless speech' of its character of intimate personal experience. In those times, an urge to make music in the home was, apart from anything else, an expression of opposition to the despiritualisation of feelings that arose with mass music concerts. Had Chopin not realised this, he would not have played with such relish for a small, select group. The Romantic artist distinguished the 'chosen few', whose opinion was of crucial significance for him, from the 'wide audience', for which even Liszt held a low regard, and which was incapable of peering deep into the essence of a work of art.[216] The opinion of the 'chosen few' about Chopin's private concerts was most telling. Let us listen to the perceptive Berlioz. 'Only a small circle of chosen listeners, in whom he could confidently anticipate a genuine desire to listen to him, could induce him to approach the piano. What emotions he could then summon up! In what ardent and melancholy reveries he liked to pour out his soul! It was usually around midnight that he rendered himself up with the greatest abandon; when the flighty spirits of the salon had departed, when the political question of the day had been treated at length, when the scandalmongers had all run out of anecdotes, when all the traps had been set, all the perfidy committed, when the company was heartily weary of prose, then, in answer to the silent prayers of some beautiful, intelligent eyes, he became a poet and sang the

[216] Delacroix, *Correspondance générale*, ii:214. Quoted in Juliusz Starzyński, *O romantycznej syntezie sztuk*, 73.

Ossianic loves of the heroes of his dreams, their chivalrous joys, and the suffering of his absent homeland, his dear Poland…'[217] So he played not for the 'salon', but for the 'select'. As George Sand wrote to Eugène Delacroix in mid May 1838, 'To incite you to come this evening, I shall tell you only that Chopin will be playing in a small group, with elbows on the keyboard, and at such times he can be really exalted. Please come at midnight, if you are not too great a lie-abed; if you meet some acquaintances of mine, please tell them nothing about it, as Chopin is terribly afraid of *Welches*' (KGS ii: 10).[218] Playing for a casual Frenchman might have seemed to him senseless; similarly, the audience in a concert hall is a crowd of casual strangers.

The small group of Chopin's listeners felt they were experiencing some supernatural phenomenon. Adam Zamoyski writes, with profound understanding, that Chopin 'held people spellbound, not merely by the beauty of the music, but also by the consciousness of something extraordinary taking place.'[219] It was a phenomenon that sat at the piano. Chopin did not 'play'

---

[217] Berlioz, column in *Le Journal des débats* of 27 October 1849.

[218] In Germany, the word *Welsch* was hurled with contempt and ire at the French. It was well known west of the Rhine. Voltaire explained to Empress Catherine that he was no *Velche*.

[219] Zamoyski, 99. In the second half of the twentieth century, the idea of the epiphany of a mysterious genius became degraded. One example of that is the way in which productions were organised in the theatre of Jerzy Grotowski, which adhered to the principle of the drastic restriction of the audience, justified by a theory that overused the notion of mystic meditation and the supernatural character of the connection between viewer and actor. A spectacle was turned into a kind of black mass for a handful of viewers, distinguished as 'co-participants'. Thus contempt for the audience went hand in hand with the flattering of a small group of crazed fanatics. These devices were intended to gag the critics. If you weren't at the mass, you can't express an opinion. What went on within that theatre was related by the organisers themselves, availing themselves of a form not yet known during the Romantic era: the interview. The theatre's reputation was moulded by a handful of fans and journalists let into performances, from Copenhagen to New York. Thus Grotowski's theatre employed the epiphany of a Romantic deity, but primarily for the purposes of publicity.

with his face, did not furrow his brow or throw himself about. He was just incredibly focussed. Everyone sensed that they were in the presence of a man deep in thought; that in playing, Chopin transmitted his thoughts. Hence his playing produced the impression of 'wordless speech'. Here is Félicien Mallefille:

> Barely had the genius of melancholy spellbound in his instrument acquainted itself with the only hands that possess the power to make it speak and begun to express its hidden suffering, when we were already submerged in deep reverie. [...] So what were all of us together dreaming about and what thoughts did the melodious voice of his piano stir within our souls? That I cannot answer, since in music, like in the clouds, everyone sees something different (KS i: 326).

And so, when he was playing, Chopin radiated an idea expressed by means of the sound of the piano, as he put it himself. And that is just what we see on the brilliant portrait of Chopin painted by Eugène Delacroix.

Although Chopin did not roll his eyes or sigh, some of his listeners sensed that they were in the presence of an unearthly being. That was understandable during the Romantic era, when manifestations of divinity were feverishly sought not just in history, but also in art, and even in everyday life. On hearing Chopin improvise, the pianist Charles Hallé noted: 'There is nothing to remind one that it is a human being who produces this music. It seems to descend from heaven – so pure, and clear, and spiritual.' During Romantic times, it was widely believed that an improviser, in his spontaneous act of creation, made contact with the supernatural realm. One is hardly surprised, therefore, that these improvisations also opened up the heavens for the poet Hyacinthe de Latouche. That explains how Chopin stirred within his listeners the desire to idolise him. 'It was perfection in every sense', wrote Hallé, '[…] I could have dropped on my knees to worship him'.[220]

The distinguished listeners to those concerts for the 'select few' forged the wonderful Romantic myth that first circulated in Paris and then engulfed the whole of cultural Europe. That myth told of the unearthly character of Chopin's music and compared his renditions of his own compositions to revelations, of an almost religiously ecstatic character. And it was that myth which enabled Chopin to captivate concert hall audiences.

And so somewhere in the exclusive salons of the intellectual elite hid not the *moi monstreux* of the concert platform, as Liszt said of Paganini, but the ethereal Ariel of music. So it sufficed to announce that on a particular day, most probably just once, he would show himself to a 'wider audience' for the music lovers of Paris to fall into a feverish whirl. All were overcome by an irresistible desire to hear the mysterious Idol. It was generally known that he performed only rarely, and so acquiring a ticket for his concert was treated like a stroke of luck, although that good fortune also cost quite a hefty sum. '…one tells all one's acquaintances', wrote Astolphe de Custine to Chopin, 'to go to Chopin's concert, and everyone says: we've had our tickets for a week, and we've been vainly asking for more for our friends – they're all gone already!' (KS i: 311). Each public appearance strengthened the myth, since reviewers wrote that they had been fortunate enough to attend an extraordinary event. A concert by Liszt promised only a fantastic virtuoso. A concert by Chopin promised an epiphany of the God of Music. One expected of Liszt above all dazzling technique, whereas the music of Chopin was seen as 'speech from elsewhere', as

---

[220] Quoted in Jean-Jacques Eigeldinger, *Chopin: pianist and teacher as seen by his pupils*, tr. Naomi Shohet with Krysia Osostowicz and Roy Howat, ed. Roy Howat (Cambridge, 1986), 271.

absolute, revealed wisdom, all the more fascinating for being mysterious and indeterminate, beyond all earthly speculation. So from the point of view of the relationship between the artist and his audience, the situation was clear. Liszt could enslave the many-headed monster only during a concert. Chopin slew it before he even appeared.

Commentators on Chopin's public concerts very shrewdly fathomed the essence of his concert tactics. They were, as a rule, quite exceptional individuals. In a review of Chopin's performance in Rouen on 2 March 1838, where he was playing in a benefit for his Warsaw friend Antoni Orłowski, the well--known writer and critic Ernest Legouvé wrote the following in the *Revue et Gazette musicale de Paris*: 'Here is an event that is not without importance in the musical world. Chopin, who has not been heard in public for several years; Chopin, who imprisons his charming genius within an auditorium of five of six people; Chopin, who resembles those enchanted islands reached by barely a handful of voyagers, and about which they tell so many marvels that they are accused of lying; Chopin, whom one cannot forget once one has heard him; Chopin has just given, in Rouen, a grand concert, in front of five hundred people, to the benefit of a Polish teacher. A good deed to be done and the memory of his country were necessary for him to conquer his loathing of playing in public. And well! the success was immense! immense!'[221] Thus Legouvé identified all the underlying causes of that triumphant effect. He had not been heard for several years, since he revealed his genius to only a handful of listeners. It was music from a mysterious magical island, inaccessible to ordinary mortals. Then suddenly this denizen of other realms reveals himself to the crowd. How can one ignore the favour of this deity? Yet Legouvé was unable to grasp why Chopin did not take part in the pianistic tournaments that were

---

[221] *Revue et Gazette musicale de Paris*, 5/12 (25 March 1838), 135.

so exciting music lovers at that time. 'Go on, Chopin, go on!' he cried, 'let this triumph sway you! Don't remain an egoist, give your beautiful talent to everyone; let everyone know you for what you are; resolve the great debate among artists; and when the question falls as to who is the foremost pianist in Europe, Liszt or Thalberg, may everyone be able to reply, like those who have heard you…: it is Chopin!'[222] Had Chopin joined the 'pianistic circus', he would have destroyed the Romantic myth of the inaccessible god that underpinned his 'policy on public appearances'.

One man who did grasp the profound sense of this tactic was, of course, the magnificent Liszt. On 18 April 1841, the famous singer Pauline Viardot received the following news from George Sand. 'Great, *grandissime* news, little Chip Chip is giving a huuuuge concert. His friends hammered it into his head for so long that he finally allowed himself to be persuaded. He continually maintained that it was too difficult to organise and would have to be abandoned. Matters proceeded quicker than he could have supposed. Barely had he uttered that fatal *yes* when everything was done as if at the waving of a magic wand; three-quarters of the tickets were sold before the concert had even been announced. He then awoke as if from slumber, and it would be hard to find anything more amusing, more fearful and more indecisive than a Chip Chip who can no longer change his mind. […] Chopin's nightmare will take place at the Salle Pleyel on the 26th. He wants no posters, no programmes and no large audience; he wants nothing to be said about it. So many things terrify him that I suggested he play without candles and without an audience, on a mute piano' (KGS ii: 70–71).

Eventually the designated day of the performance arrived, and of course the 'nightmare' was a success. Describing the

---

[222] Ibid.

event in the *Revue et Gazette musicale de Paris*, Liszt pointed out that the triumph, the like of which other contemporary musicians dreamed of in vain, was due to the fact that Chopin's appearance bore the hallmarks of a one-off epiphany. For that reason, every one of his concerts set him essentially beyond criticism, made him untouchable.

> [...] it is but rarely, at very large intervals, that Chopin has allowed himself to be heard in public; but it is precisely that which for any other would have been an almost certain cause of oblivion and obscurity that has ensured him of a reputation loftier than the caprices of fashion and protected him from rivalry, jealousy and injustice. Chopin, remaining outside the excessive movement that for several years has pushed performing artists from all parts of the universe onto one another and against one another, has been constantly surrounded by faithful followers, enthusiastic pupils and warm friends, who, protecting him from unpleasant clashes and painful blows, at the same time have unstintingly promoted his works, and with them admiration for his genius and respect for his name. As a result, this exquisite celebrity, residing on high, exceedingly aristocratic, has remained unsullied by any attack. The critical voices have already fallen entirely silent, as if posterity had come [...][223]

That is the most penetrating description of Chopin's concert-giving tactic, and only Liszt could have made it, thanks to

---

[223] *Revue et Gazette musicale de Paris*, 8/31 (2 May 1841), 245. Chopin's tactic is perfectly understood by Krystian Zimerman. In April 1987, following a performance given by Zimerman in New York, the reviewer of the *New York Times* wrote that he adhered to the following principle: to be sufficiently unknown to live quietly in seclusion, and sufficiently famous to fill a hall with every appearance. I am merely transmitting here an idea I heard on Radio Free Europe, jammed at that time in Poland.

his wonderful intelligence, sharpened a little by his most charming jealousy. But after all Liszt was describing his anti-'I', by
whom he was in some way fascinated.

This sort of tactic arose as a result of the skilful, and at the
same time spontaneous, functionalising of his own preferences.
It was based on a respect for his own identity, disregarding the
demands of the music market. In reality, Chopin did not like performing in public, and that was the main reason for him limiting
the number of his public concerts. He did not like coming out of
his hiding, which – as George Sand rightly emphasised – was
full of glory (KGS ii: 74). Whilst remaining himself, at the same
time he defined the shape and style of his performances. The rest
was achieved by the myth of the mysterious genius. Before he
even took to the stage, the many-headed monster was grateful
to him for deigning to appear. When he touched the keyboard,
he did not have to show off. There was no question of affected
expressions or gestures, because the audience wanted to hear and
see Chopin as he really was: the Chopin of the myth propagated
by the spiritual aristocracy. On the concert platform, Chopin was
to be himself and himself alone.

So Chopin's concert style involved, on one hand, eliminating the theatrical character of the musician's public performance
and, on the other, returning to the personal listening to music,
in spite of the crowd in the hall. As Astolphe de Custine wrote
to Chopin following one of his concerts, '…the listener is alone
with you, even among the crowd… only art as you feel it can
unite people divided by the real side of life; people love and
understand one another through Chopin. You turned the audience into a group of friends; ultimately, you matched yourself;
that says enough' (KS i: 297–298). And so beholding Chopin as
he played, the crowd became a sacred circle of people united in
a Dionysian elation of cognising the wordless wisdom of music.
It was a collective initiation, during which, without losing their

personal character, individuals began to form a community. But a community is not a crowd.

One is not surprised, therefore, that he baulked at fame on the level of the masses, at the fatuous adoration of the crowd. In August 1845, he wrote to his family: 'Liszt bids himself cry *er lebe!* in Bonn, where they erect a monument to Beethoven and expect crowned heads. In Bonn, they sell *véritables cigares à la Beethoven*, who most probably smoked only Viennese pipes; and they have sold so much furniture, old desks and old shelves left by Beethoven that the poor composer *de la Symphonie Pastorale* would probably have had a huge furniture business. It reminds one of that *concierge* in Ferney, who was forever selling Voltairean walking sticks' (KR 147). 'Chopin is very modest', wrote Charles Gavard in a letter of recommendation to Hallé in London, in April 1848, 'he is anxious that people not attempt to gain profit out of his name (at least that is my impression); advertising fills him with dread' (KS ii: 240).

Chopin's last public performance in Paris took place at the Salle Pleyel on 16 February 1848, and it was the crowning moment in his concert strategy. The Idol had 'flu', but around 10 February he already felt sufficiently recovered to discuss a very weighty problem. Here is what he wrote to his family on the subject.

> My friends came one morning and told me that I had to give a concert, that I was to bother myself about nothing, just sit down and play. – There have been no tickets left for a week, and the tickets all cost 20 fr. apiece. The public is signing up for another – (which I am not even thinking about). The court demanded 40 tickets, and in the papers it was written only that I *may* give a concert, and people wrote to my editor from Brest and from Nantes to order

seats. I am surprised at ssuch *empressement* and must play today, be it only for my own conscience, for I have the impression that I am playing worse than before. I will be playing (as a point of interest) a *Mozart* trio with Franchomme and Allard. There will be no posters or free tickets. The room, comfortably arranged, can seat 300 people. Pleyel is always laughing at my stupidity and is dressing the steps with flowers to encourage me to play. I will feel quite at home and almost solely familiar faces will meet my eyes (KR 173–174).

Compare that to Berlioz's 'industrial concert'.

On this occasion, the reviewer of the *Revue et Gazette musicale de Paris* transformed the Salle Pleyel, which Chopin graced with his presence, into the Temple of Jerusalem, or more accurately into its most sacred part, its Sanctissimum or Sanctum Sanctorum. As we know, the high priest entered there once a year, in order to commune with the Transcendent Presence. So everyone descended upon the Salle Pleyel to commune with the God of Music. 'A concert by the Ariel of pianists is a thing too rare to be given, like other concerts, by opening both wings of the doors to whomsoever wishes to enter. For this one a list had been drawn up: everyone inscribed thereon his name: but everyone was not sure of obtaining the precious ticket: patronage was required to be admitted into the holy of holies, to obtain the favour of depositing one's offering, and yet this offering amounted to a louis; but who has not a louis to spare when Chopin may be heard? The outcome of all this naturally was that the fine flower of the aristocracy of the most distinguished women, the most elegant toilettes, filled on Wednesday Pleyel's rooms. There was also the aristocracy of artists and amateurs, happy to seize in his flight this musical sylph who had promised to let himself once more and for a few hours be approached, seen and heard.'[224] And so that concert was on one hand a miracle that happens only in a magical Shakespearean forest, and on the other a temple liturgy.

Like at the entrance to a temple, a material sacrifice was naturally made. Pleyel had to make a profit, and the sylph did not live in the cups of woodland flowers. Following his performance on 26 April 1841, George Sand wrote to her half-brother, Hippolyte Chatiron: 'Chopin has given a concert that will allow him now to idle the whole summer long. In two hours of two-handed tapping he pocketed six thousand and several hundred francs, amidst the cheering, encores and stamping of the most beautiful women of Paris' (KGS ii: 73). 'Monday last', wrote Stefan Witwicki to Bohdan Zaleski after that same event, 'Chopin gave a concert that went most successfully; I was there with Adam [Mickiewicz]. The audience was magnificent and received little Chopin in the best manner possible, leaving him apparently six thousand francs. Declaim your verse for three quarters of an hour, for he surely played no longer, and may they hand you 6000 francs for it.'[225] The concert that took place on 26 February 1842 also brought a fabulous revenue. 'Mon vieux', wrote Sand again to Chatiron, 'the great Chopin's concert was equally beautiful, dazzling and lucrative as last year's (more than 5000 fr. income, something wholly exceptional in Paris, which proves how much the public craves to hear the most excellent and most splendid of musicians)' (KGS ii: 100–101). It also proves that the concert style, representing the apotheosis of an artist's identity, brought Chopin quite a sum of money, which – in turn – assured him of that identity.

---

[224] *Revue et Gazette musicale de Paris*, 20 February 1848; quoted in Frederick Niecks, *Frederick Chopin as a Man and Musician*, 2nd edn (London, 1890), ii:206.

[225] Stefan Witwicki, *Listy do J. B. Zaleskiego* [Letters to J. B. Zaleski] (Lviv, 1911), 69.

Some of the listeners gasped with delight that they had been singled out: that they belonged to the select few. Well read in the latest Romantic literature, they knew that they were watching a Platonic 'divine frenzy' of a genius 'shrouded in mystery', as Astolphe de Custine would say of Chopin. Some, meanwhile, were not so much listening as watching the God of Music's triumphant descent from the clouds. But the emotion of at least several of the audience was of an almost religious character. '…listening to you', wrote de Custine to Chopin, 'I always feel alone with you, perhaps even with something better than you, or at least with that which is best in you' (KS i: 311). He did not exclude the possibility, therefore, that Chopin was a medium of supernatural values. On 30 May 1842, Eugène Delacroix wrote to George Sand:

> Please tell my dear Chopin that for me the most pleasant
> diversion is to talk about music while wandering around the
> garden, and in the evening to listen to it in the corner of the
> drawing-room, when God himself descends through music
> onto his fingers. And literally so, My Dear (KS ii: 63).

Although he did not like performing in public, Chopin sensed that his fate was fulfilled not so much in the salons as in the concert halls, among a large circle of the 'initiated'. In a musical 'conversation', 'heart to heart' with each individual listener. For somehow he must have appreciated those performances, despite the fear they inspired in him, given that he took his final journey in his concert dress. 'Chopin', wrote Ferenc Liszt, 'who of all the foremost contemporary artists gave the fewest concerts, wished nevertheless to be laid to rest in the clothes that he wore there.'[226] That was his final sign, sent from the grave. He knew the value of signs. He gave his heart to Warsaw, so that it be

---

[226] Liszt, *F. Chopin*, 200.

known where his identity was formed. He took his concert tails with him to Mother Earth, so that they would turn to dust with his body. After all, it was merely the overall of a labourer who ruined his health on the 'mill of life'.

Chapter III

THE CONDITIONS OF HIS TALENT

In Chopin's letters, there are really no lengthy and illuminating utterances about music, and yet the regrets that are occasionally expressed on that account would appear to be unjustified. Among the crumbs of his thoughts, one finds several astonishing judgments – casually dropped and concealed within information about everyday affairs – that concern a certain crucial aesthetic problem. Reference here to the relationship between music and existence. This problem – as we will recall – was troubling Chopin already during his second stay in Vienna. In the Romantic era, it was frequently discussed, on account of the stark contrast between the historical experiences of the artist and the sort of aesthetic abstraction that the musical work undoubtedly constitutes. If we consider that art as a form-generative element in life was intriguing at that time both to creative artists and to the recipients of their art; if we remember that romanticism was far from treating music as mere amusement rendering man's life more pleasant; if we strive to not forget that it was regarded then as a wisdom greater than the deepest philosophy (which happens to be true), then an analysis of at least a few of Chopin's passing utterances appears to be more sensible than any futile regrets. Chopin did not leave us any systematic outline of his views on music. He did, however, make a number of comments here and there that are worth dwelling on, since they attest some serious reflection. So let us enter another trail of the shadow of a swallow that, once soaring above the vault of human affairs, also tormented itself with its own twittering.

1. Espaces imaginaires

At the age of barely twenty, Chopin began to depart the world – into dreams.

In Chopin's day, Calderón's wonderful theme 'life is a dream' was interpreted in two ways. Some Romantics were interested chiefly in eliminating the opposition between knowledge gained during sleep and waking cognition. So for them, a dream was no ordinary nocturnal apparition, but rather the revelation of an unseen reality. It freed man from his material finiteness. And it heralded Plato's Really Existing Reality, since what today is still a dream will one day become our 'total awareness', and then we will not have to formulate the results of cognition in abstract terms. We will dream the world, and our cognition will be freed from the limitations and falsities connected with the sensory nature of perception. We find an ideal example of this view in Novalis' *Henry von Ofterdingen*.[227] A very similar, if not so presumptuous, theory of dreams was expounded by the protagonist of the third part of Adam Mickiewicz's *Forefathers' Eve*.[228] But there were also Romantics interested in the oneiric character of cognition. For them, quite simply, the very experi-

---

[227] Albert Béguin, *L'Âme romantique et le rêve* (Paris, 1956), 195.

[228] Following a critique of the sensualist theory of dreams as reminders of everyday life and the playing of an unbridled imagination, he voiced the opinion that dreaming was 'a silent, deep-lying, mysterious world', in which the 'true life of the soul' was lived out, entirely different from the waking world. Manifest in dreams was that which took place 'deep within the heart', in the subconscious, in the deep 'self'. Dreams pull the soul out of the chthonic abyss and allow us to contact a higher, unseen and immaterial world, enabling us to transcend our finiteness. The protagonist assures us that he has already visited such a space. See Mickiewicz, *Dzieła*, iii:130.

encing of the world resembled dreaming. Waking cognition was no less nebulous, vague and indefinite than the images of dreams. So our diurnal knowledge of the world was just as fragmentary as a dream and just as contrary to the principles of logic.

Two short, but telling, declarations of Chopin appear to link his thinking to the views of the latter group of Romantics. The sensualist theory of dreams, prominent at the end of the eighteenth century, stated that a dream was a reminder of waking life. Chopin, by contrast, clearly held waking recollection to be a variant of dream-time vision. On 18 November 1831, he wrote from Paris to Alfons Kumelski: 'At times, in the evening, when I am looking through letters or writing something into that album and glancing at the litany, I have the impression that all those recollections are a dream; I give no credence to that which actually occurred...' (KS i: 187). So to remember meant to enter the realm of dreams. Maurycy Mochnacki, a friend from the Warsaw years of his youth, had similar impressions, as he wrote to his father on 25 July 1834, also from Paris: 'Now, when I remind myself that I had so many brothers and sisters, so much family, that I lived in the home of my dear parents, it seems to me that it was only a dream, and every thought of that kind rends my soul with deep sorrow...'[229] In both cases, then, the images conjured from the past were just as incredible as the visions of dreams.

Did Chopin perceive the present in a similar way? Did the material reality he beheld 'with his own eyes' also possess such a character? Here he is sitting in his Vienna apartment on New Year's Day 1831 among a merry group of friends, as he related in a letter to Jan Matuszyński which he did not take to the post office because he would produce another, more succinct version: '...in my room, your old colleagues Rostkowski,

---

[229] *Listy Maurycego Mochnackiego...* [The letters of Maurycy Mochnacki...] (Poznań, 1863), 251.

Schuch, Freyer, Kijewski, Hube et al are holding forth. And I laugh, I laugh, but in my soul, just as I write this, some terrible presentiment befalls me. It seems to me a dream, a daze, that I am with you and dreaming what I hear. Voices to which my soul is not accustomed make no other impression upon me than that clattering of carriages along the street or some other indifferent noise' (KS i: 167–168). So what he had before his eyes, what he heard, that very corporeal, tangible reality, quite noisy and virile, seemed to him like a dream, since at that moment his 'I' was in Warsaw. Here, in Vienna, he dreamed the world even when awake. So he ceased to identify existence with what was actually taking place.

In this way, for some Romantics, moments in time, threaded on the temporal continuum, supposedly experienced in reality, but in essence as if dreamt, comprised one great dream. 'Life is a dream'. 'All is a sorrowful dream', pronounced the Shaman to Anhelli, the protagonist of Juliusz Słowacki's epic poem. Thus when Anhelli is dying, he asks himself: 'What did I do on the Earth? Was it all a dream?'[230]

Declarations of this sort made by Chopin attest that current waking reality, like the remembered past, took on an oneiric character whenever his awareness fled from 'here' to another corner of the material world. The blurring of the boundaries between dream and reality also occurred during the return of his awareness from the 'land of imagination', from the phantasmal realm. During the sojourn on Majorca, after a walk around Palma, where she had gone with her son, Mrs Sand observed that Chopin was in some curious state. 'On seeing us come in, he rose, uttered a loud cry, then said with a wild expression and in a strange tone of voice, "Ah, just as I imagined, you have died!" When he had gotten back his bearings and saw the state we were in, he was sick at the retrospective display of our

---

[230] Słowacki, *Dzieła wszystkie*, iii:45 and 56.

dangers. He confessed to me later that, while waiting for us, he had seen all that in a dream and, no longer able to distinguish dream from reality, he had calmed himself and played the piano drowsily, persuaded that he had died himself.'[231] Let us note that when sinking into 'some dream', Chopin again, as in Stuttgart, turned into a 'living corpse'.

All these facts suggest a split personality, and so let us now try to consider another, equally interesting, record of his thoughts.

In May 1834, Chopin travelled to Aachen, accompanied by the German composer and pianist Ferdinand Hiller, whom he had befriended soon after his arrival in Paris. As we read in Victor Hugo's *The Rhine* (1842), 'As regards invalids, Aix-la-Chapelle [Aachen] is a hot, cold, mineral, ferruginous, sulphurous bathing place; as regards the pleasure-seeker, it is a region of balls and concerts'.[232] The purpose of our travellers was not the waters, but the famous Lower Rhine Music Festival, with a performance of Handel's oratorio *Deborah* on the programme. That is how it once was: one undertook a long journey to hear a masterpiece by an old master. And that had to suffice for one's whole life.

After the concert, they were taken home by Felix Mendelssohn. In Düsseldorf, our Parisians walked, visited cafés, played skittles and of course made music. Then they boarded a steam ship for Koblenz. Mendelssohn saw them off as far as Cologne, where the three men visited together the Church of the Twelve Apostles. And when they found themselves on a bridge over the Rhine, as Hiller later recalled, 'we parted in a rather comic way. I was staring down at the river, making some extravagant remark or other, when Mendelssohn suddenly cried: "Hiller getting sentimental; heaven help us! Adieu, farewell!" – and was gone'.[233]

[231] Sand, *Story of My Life*, 1091–1092.
[232] Victor Hugo, *The Rhine*, tr. D. M. Aird (London, 1848), 55; Fr. orig. *Le Rhin* (Paris, 1842).
[233] Blunt, *On Wings of Song*, 171.

And it was perhaps while they were still approaching Cologne, although most probably following Mendelssohn's sudden departure, in any case on board the steamship, that Chopin's companion wrote a letter to his mother, Regina Hiller. Chopin decided to add a note from himself and sought an idea for a well-wrought missive to a lady.

It is hard for us today to conceive, but in those days the steamship was genuinely admired. Europe was gripped by a paroxysm of delight over inventions, which were beginning to alter the landscape of our continent. Even the spiritual Romantics succumbed to a collective fascination with the power of steam. Several years later, George Sand's dramatic poem *The Seven Strings of the Lyre* (1839) featured a Spirit which seems to have journeyed to France from the forests of Germany and Lithuania. In an exalted paean to the human mind and the civilisation forged by man, the Spirit draws particular attention to the force propelling the 'chariot[s] of Vulcan' that were already moving through the fields of Europe, 'rolled by the formidable hand of invisible cyclopses'. And right alongside the railway, he mentions the steamship, on account of the fact that in this instance the 'motive power' had overcome not just space, but also an element: 'See also on the waters the power of this vapor that furrows the surface of the sea by means of fiery paddle wheels and makes it docile, like the plain to the slicing of the plow'.[234] A decade or so later, Mickiewicz made steam, which contained a mighty, although elusive, power, a representation of the soul. 'What is divine in the soul constitutes a propulsive force that is comparable to steam: that force performs all the works of humanity'.[235]

---

[234] Sand, *The Seven Strings of the Lyre*, tr. George A. Kennedy (London, 1989), 145; Fr. orig. Les sept cordes de la lyre (Paris, 1839).
[235] Mickiewicz, *Dzieła*, x:237.

So the steam that trailed above the ship heading for Koblenz was one of the phenomena currently arousing interest for its newness and unusualness. At that time, it was a Big Sign, impossible to ignore. Hence Chopin, on seeing clouds of steam above him, realised that he had finally found an idea for his note. So he went to his cabin, or perhaps to the mess, and wrote in German a few sentences in which he placed as much menace as elegance. To my ears, at least, this little note sounds like one of Mozart's piano fantasias.

> Dear Madam,
> I am today like the steam on our steamship – I break up in the air and feel as if one part of myself was travelling to my homeland, to my nearest and dearest, and the other part to Paris, to you. It journeys full of respect, finds you in your study and makes a beautiful bow (KS i: 239).

The salon-style levity of this utterance failed to obscure Chopin's insightful idea about his 'self'. 'Ich bin heute…'; 'I am today…' The 'self' is always in some specific time, a particular 'today' – if, of course, it is at all. Yesterday is past, and tomorrow has not yet come. I can sense and know how my 'self' is only today, only here and now, *hic et nunc*. So the beginning of the note informs the reader that awareness of the 'self' is like a blink. Moreover, when the word 'today' is uttered, particularly in a letter in which the 'speech' is ultimately of a spontaneous character, the semantic horizon of the word is very unclear, since it is given a specific sense by the particular situation and context of the utterance. So I have no intention of losing sight of Chopin's situation at that time.

'I am today like the steam on our steamship…' Free, in an unenclosed space, steam does not remain immobile and is not focussed, but like a thing indeterminate and amorphous it

is diffused in the world. It is, but is constantly disappearing. '...
Ich löse mich in der Luft...' 'Sich auflösen' does not mean to
dissolve. It is not a gentle word. Inflected with menace, it means
to disintegrate, to undergo disintegration. Used as a noun, 'das
Auflösen' means simply death. I would not even wish to mention
how we associate it today.

So Chopin's 'self', his 'I', like that steam in the air, disinte-
grates and disperses. Essentially, it goes to its death. This disintegration takes on a very specific form of splitting: '...and I feel as if
one part of myself was travelling to my homeland, to my nearest
and dearest, and the other part to Paris, to you'. In the Romantic
era, such a splitting of personality was nothing out of the ordinary.
The Romantic, especially the Polish Romantic, was by nature a
dual man.[236] Maurycy Mochnacki understood this as 'dispers-
ing into two'. At the root of this phenomenon, or perhaps rather
illness, lay a painful splitting of awareness between 'here' and
'there'. This is what Helmuth Plessner has to say on the subject:

> Initially, I am always 'here', namely in such a way that 'here'
> can be replaced by 'I', although the two words have different
> meaning. 'There' denotes the area that is occupied by other
> people and things.[237]

I am here because my body is here, but in spirit I can be
there, where my body once was – 'in the land of childhood',

---

[236] On dual personalities in Polish romanticism, see J. M. Rymkiewicz,
'Ludzie dwoiści. Barokowa struktura postaci Słowackiego' [Dual persons.
The Baroque structure of Słowacki's character], in Maria Żmigrodzka (ed.),
Problemy polskiego romantyzmu [Questions of Polish romanticism], 3rd series
(Wrocław, 1981), 65–107. Also discussed there is the functioning of the Calde-
ronian motif of 'life is a dream' in Polish romanticism.
[237] Helmuth Plessner, 'Aspołeczna towarzyskość. Uwagi do pewnego pojęcia
Kanta' [Asocial sociability. Remarks on a certain notion of Kant], in *Pytanie
o conditio humana. Wybór pism* [The question of the human condition. Selected
writings], tr. and selected by Zdzisław Krasnodębski (Warsaw, 1988), 288.

as Adam Mickiewicz wrote, or in the 'cradle of thought', in a mental reality consisting of everything remembered and loved, everything imagined and created in the mind.

So staring at the splitting plume of steam, Chopin understood that here, on board the ship, was only his body; in other words, to stick with the Mickiewiczian terminology, 'amid' the steamship's passengers 'sat' only his 'corpse'. His 'I' was fleeing, splitting into two, since it possessed not one, but two 'theres'; the lost native land and Paris, in which he had begun to live and work. The 'I' heads both there to Warsaw and there to Paris. Here, meanwhile, remained just an empty cage, from which his soul, the white steam, had flown. Therefore, on board that steamship sailing to Koblenz was a consciousness without a 'self', something like a 'living corpse'. In the Stuttgart hotel, as we recall, Chopin experienced the annihilation of his identity whilst retaining an awareness of his 'I'. Now, on the Rhine, his person appeared to him as a 'corpse', from which his 'I' was taking flight. As Georges Poulet writes about such cases, he thus experienced the absence of being sensed by being.[238] So when gazing at those almost imperceptible traces of the swallow's flight, I am astonished and alarmed by a peculiar fear encountered at every step and expressed in various ways: a fear of the phantomisation – constantly threatening him – of his own person. A fear of becoming disinherited of his own identity, of its disintegration, something that would appear to torment creative individuals in particular.

The dramatic splitting of one's thoughts between 'here' and 'there' besets exiles and emigrants of all kinds, although disconnection, if the title of a famous poem by Juliusz Słowacki may be used as an anthropological term, is a structural feature of human existence, since thought is continuously pulling away

---

[238] Georges Poulet, *La pensée indéterminée*, i:*De la Renaissance au Romantisme* (Paris, 1985), 280.

from the body, from the Platonic cage, into infinity. Polish exiles, even those who entered exile of their own free will, understood this very quickly. As Zygmunt Krasiński wrote on 15 March 1840, 'Division, death and illness are the three great nothingnesses or tortures; the three evil things that walk this Earth with a face accursed, unknown to God, visible to people; and those three curses can be encompassed under a single name: death and illness are nothing other than *division*. The only evil of this world is *division*! [...] Wherever there is no concord or harmony, there is dissonance, fighting, pain, distress, deterioration, unhappiness; in a word – *splitting*. In nature and in man, therefore, the only evil always and everywhere is *division*.[239]

Chopin had already found himself split between life itself and thinking about life when, at news of the outbreak of the uprising in Warsaw, he wrote from Vienna to Jan Matuszyński: 'I'm living with you' (KS i: 169). His entire life outside Poland was one great experience of the threat of disintegration and division. It was this that so deeply distressed George Sand, that keen observer of Chopin; the latter, although he tried so very hard, could not conceal everything from her eagle eye. Sand wrote the following to Ludwika Jędrzejewicz when inviting her to Nohant in 1844:

> I have no need of enjoining you to strengthen his fortitude, constantly tried by the enduring separation from everything he loves. [...] He has long since been preoccupied solely by the happiness of those whom he loves – since he cannot share it with them. As for me, I have done everything to lessen that cruel privation... (KGS i: 384).

---

[239] Zygmunt Krasiński, *Listy do Delfiny Potockiej* [Letters to Delfina Potocka], ed. Zbigniew Sudolski (Warsaw, 1975), i:174–175. Emphasis Z. K.

The cruel absence of his nearest and dearest, *cette cruelle absence*, made that 'division' a particularly insidious torture. At first, Chopin was convinced that the temporary presence of those he loved would allay the sadness of his dual existence. 'It would seem', he wrote to Marie de Rozières on 2 October 1848, 'to be without significance, and yet it is the greatest consolation for us in a foreign country when someone carries us home whenever we look upon them, whenever we speak with them or listen to them' (KGS ii: 301–302). And yet such a presence of his loved ones left behind it very painful traces. He wrote to his sister Ludwika after her departure from Nohant: 'the Lady of the House is living with her pupil, as I wrote to you to Vien[na], in your room; often, when I go in, I look to see if you left something behind, and I see only that same place by the sofa where we drank chocolate – and those drawings that Kalasanty [his sister's husband] copied. – More is left of you in my room – lying on the table is your embroidery of that slipper, wrapped in English crepe – and on the piano the little pencil that you had in your pocket-book and which serves me splendidly' (KR 138). These traces could only direct his thoughts once again from 'here' to 'there'.[240]

The 'I' that is forever fleeing from its one-off 'here' of today heads clearly towards imaginary spaces. Chopin was perfectly aware of this. In July 1845, he admitted to his family:

> I am always one foot with you, the other in the next room – where the Lady of the House is working – and not at all in myself at that moment – just, as usual, in some curious space. They are doubtless those *espaces imaginaires* (KR 141).

If he was 'there' 'as usual', then Chopin must have regarded that 'curious space' as his normal state. And so he 'dwelt' not here, where his body was, not 'in himself', but, after

---

[240] So this splitting is a structural feature of his existence.

splitting, seemingly habitually in those *espaces imaginaires*, which Bronisław Edward Sydow and Krystyna Kobylańska defined as imaginary worlds, and Julia Hartwig as the space of the imagination. In Chopin's circle, this expression was probably used quite frequently. 'Voyez moi', wrote Solange Clésinger to Chopin on 30 September 1847, 'avec mes goûts de luxe qui aurais trouvé un carrosse à six chevaux à peine digne de me porter, moi qui comptais vivre dans des espaces imaginaires avec des rêves de poésie au milieu des nuages et des fleurs...' ('Take me, who with my taste for luxury would have found a six-horse carriage barely fit to carry me, I who was counting on living in those imaginary spaces with dreams of poetry midst clouds and flowers...') (KGS i: 190, 192). In this case, to dwell in the space of the imagination meant to float in the clouds, to give oneself over to naive dreams. Ferenc Liszt, meanwhile, considered that such imagined climes, or *régions imaginées*, were the natural dwelling-place of Chopin's thoughts, and only when he was playing his own works did he take his listeners there with him.

The dictionaries state that this metaphor was often used in phrases like 'voyager dans les espaces imaginaires' ('to travel in an imaginary world'), which sounded objective, as it were, or 'se perdre dans les espaces imaginaires' ('to lose oneself in imaginary worlds'), which already indicated that they were dangerous realms. Incidentally, this expression was used by Descartes, but in a very special sense.[241] The Romantics, understandably, fell in love with these spaces. When Victor Hugo wrote that the mind was tossing around an 'imaginary space', he understood

---

[241] See *Le monde ou traité de la lumière* V and VI (1633), in Ferdinand Alquié, *Kartezjusz*, tr. Stanisław Cichowicz (Warsaw, 1989), 193–194; Fr. orig. *Descartes, l'homme et l'œuvre* (Paris, 1956). See also Kartezjusz [Descartes], *Zasady filozofii*, tr. Izydora Dąmbska (Warsaw, 1960), 65–66; Lat. orig. *Principia philosophiae* (1644). In the former translation, they are described as imaginary worlds; in the latter, as imaginable worlds.

it to mean that the mind was lost in impenetrable darkness, in oblivion.[242] On one hand, this was the 'mind's night'; on the other, it was the 'world of the ideal', the sphere of artistic truth. It is a pity that Chopin was not familiar with the expression that Adam Mickiewicz used:

—

Jest u mnie kraj, ojczyzna myśli mojej,
I liczne mam serca mego rodzeństwo;
Piękniejszy kraj, niż ten co w oczach stoi;
Rodzina milsza niż całe pokrewieństwo.[243]
(There is in me a land, the homeland of my thoughts,
And many are the siblings of my heart;
A lovelier land than that which stands before mine eyes;
A family dearer than all my relations.)

—

It is a pity that he could not have read Juliusz Słowacki's description of the 'land of thoughts':

—

I godzinami myśli w nieruchomość wbite,
Tonąc w otchłań marzenia, szły prostemi loty,
Za okresy widzenia, za wzroku przedmioty.
Gdy patrzał w niewidziane oczyma obrazy.[244]
(And his thoughts fixed for hours in immobility,
Drowning in the depths of dreams, flew straight,
Beyond the bounds of vision, beyond the things we see.
When he looked upon images invisible to the eye.)

—

Jean-Paul Sartre pointed out that those 'imaginary spaces', the work of a consciousness forever fleeing from 'here', are something like an anti-world. Imagining itself absent, conscious-

---

[242] Hugo, *Notre Dame de Paris* (Paris, 1831), vol. ii, ch. 7.
[243] Mickiewicz, *Dzieła*, i:377.
[244] Słowacki, *Dzieła wszystkie*, ii:80

ness surrounds itself with 'a cortège of phantom-objects. These objects,' we read in *The Imaginary*, 'although having at first sight a sensible aspect, are not the same as those of perception. [...] As soon as we fix our look on one of them, we find ourselves confronted by strange beings that escape the laws of the world. [...] Ambiguous, poor and dry at the same time, appearing and disappearing in jerks, they are given as a perpetual "elsewhere", as a perpetual evasion. But the evasion to which they invite us is not only that which would make us flee our current condition, our concerns, our boredoms; they offer us an escape from all the constraints of the *world*, they seem to be presented as a negation of the condition of *being in the world*, as an anti-world.'[245] Sartre goes on to write that even the wildest phantasmagorias must nevertheless form 'against the background of the world'. This means that they are constituted from images remembered while perceiving the world of corporeal presence. So the imagination of Chopin, who 'as usual' found himself forever 'somewhere else', created for itself a reality 'escaping the laws of the world': *espaces imaginaires*.

George Sand noted that those 'imaginary spaces' were also teeming with delusions, or phantasms. The word 'phantasm', *le phantasme*, is used to define a variety of phantoms of a stimulated imagination, which make up a fantastical world. They are undoubtedly 'phantom-objects', but of a particular kind. The Romantics – as Maria Janion writes – played an important role in the spread of that word. They linked it to a theory of a creating imagination, of imagination as a cosmic spiritual force that rendered the reality produced through the procedures of dreaming more valuable, more authentic than the world of material presence. Occasionally, a phantasm reinforced an artist's conviction that to truly exist was to be

---

[245] Jean-Paul Sartre, *The Imaginary*, tr. Jonathan Webber (Abingdon, 2010), 135–136; Fr. orig. *L'imaginaire* (Paris, 1940).

someone else and to be somewhere else.[246] Thus Chopin's *espaces imaginaires* were a mental reality that he himself, in spite of everything, did not confuse with material reality. That imaginary space was filled with the phantasms of his inner life. Almost every person surrounds himself with such 'phantom-objects', which are not subject to the laws of the world of material objects. They enable us to move into the creative domain of fantasy and to free ourselves from the laws of the empirical world.[247] That is because the imaginary space is not a product of a sick mind, although it has long been dealt with by doctors in clinics.[248] It is – as Maria Janion writes – an inner theatre of the soul, which incidentally is not necessarily a conscious artistic organisation. It often arises during an unfeigned improvisation. Thus Chopin's anti-world was created by the imagination of a man who often 'dreamt until morning', especially during sleepless nights (KS ii: 178), who, bustling about during the day, just as often, particularly when feeling out of sorts, had 'frayed nerves' (KS ii: 253).

The vaudevillist, rhymester and political activist Emanuel Arago, an indubitably reasonable man befriended of George Sand, irritated by the Romantic cult of the imagination, once posed a question that is actually entirely justified: 'When one has imagination, one takes up literature, and when one does not go in for literature, what is the use of imagination?'

---

[246] Maria Janion, 'Projekt krytyki fantazmatycznej' [Plan for a phantasmal critique], typescript (1985), 1–2. See also 'Fantazmat jako „forma bytu"' [The phantasm as a 'form of being'], in Maria Janion and Remigiusz Forycki, 'Fantazmat ściętej głowy' [The phantasm of the severed head], *Twórczość*, 7 (1989), 49–51.

[247] See Sigmund Freud, *Wstęp do psychoanalizy*, tr. Stefania Kempnerówna and Witold Zaganiewski (Warsaw, 1982), 464; Ger. orig. Vorlesungen zur Einführung in die Psychoanalyse (Vienna, 1917).

[248] A typically 'medicalised' take on the notion of the phantasm was presented by Sami-Ali in his book significantly titled *L'éspace imaginaire* (Paris, 1974), 23.

(KGS i: 299). One might reply that it serves to compose music, to paint pictures, to make scientific discoveries, penetrate myths and cognise the symbolic signs that surround us. But of course that was not what he was getting at. Arago hated imagination, accusing it of continually falsifying one's picture of the world. In those times, many Frenchmen harboured such an obsession. Clearly, in 1839, the indignation of the Classics had not been entirely forgotten.

The Romantics' view of the functioning of the imagination was sober and discerning. It can be encapsulated in the simple, albeit terrifying, statement that the essence of the phenomena and mysteries of existence can only be cognised thanks to the imagination; that that same imagination is also the source of all kinds of phantasms and the cause of the psyche's destruction. In a word, the Romantics linked the dual character of cognition to imagination. That confirmed their conviction that everything was dual and antinomic, above all cognition. The protagonist of Part IV of Mickiewicz's *Forefathers' Eve*, on which Chopin was brought up, expounded on this at length. What Juliusz Słowacki wrote on the subject, in a letter of 27 October 1833, sent from Geneva, was also most eloquent. 'Mama, it is odd that my imagination is the sole source of all my unhappiness – and of all happiness on the Earth… for truly, I am often happy at that creative power of imaginary events – I am happy each evening when I write – each morning when I walk over dry leaves in the garden'.[249] According to the Romantics, imagination quite simply was the constant companion of thought. Academically speaking, it is the epiphenomenon of thought. 'I repel all ill thoughts,' wrote Słowacki in another letter to his mother, sailing from Beirut to Livorno on 14 June 1837, 'but the monotony of the sea spawns delusions and shows strange images to the eyes of the soul… One must think,

---

[249] *Korespondencja Juliusza Słowackiego*, i: 217–218.

but while thinking one cannot control one's imagination…'[250]
I fear that this is the most veritable truth, as terrifying as it is
blessed. In Chopin's case, the main cause of the hypertrophy
of his imagination was that intense and aggressive idea that
manifested itself to him as 'frayed nerves'.

Chopin was aware that a rampant imagination brings unhappiness upon a man, especially when he finds himself in the
'mire'; that is, when he starts colluding with passion, hysteria
and false pride, when he turns life into a theatre of appearances.
At Christmas 1847, he wrote to his sister Ludwika: 'For me, Mrs
S[and] cannot have only good memories in her soul when she
looks back one day. In the meantime, she is in the most curious
paroxysm of a mother *playing the role* of a better and fairer
mother than she really is; and that is a fever for which there is
no remedy in heads with such an imagination, when they venture
onto swampland' (KR 171).

Mrs Sand gave as good as she got and described what
happened with Chopin's imagination when he ventured into
the 'swampland' of thought. At such times, he was cursed by
phantasms, brutally shoving his consciousness into the anti-
world. George Sand was of the opinion that Chopin owed it all
to his acute oversensitivity. 'His sensitivity was flayed alive',
she wrote later in *Story of My Life*: 'a crushed rose petal, the
shadow of a fly made him bleed.' It goes without saying that
this was due in part to his constantly 'frayed nerves'. 'Where
his deplorable health was concerned, he accepted its real dangers heroically, but he tormented himself to wretchedness over
insignificant changes. This is the story of all creatures whose
nervous system is excessively developed.' Already during their
time on Majorca, Mrs Sand noticed that Chopin's imagination
was full of delusions:

---

[250] Ibid, i:358–359.

What I had feared – but not sufficiently, unfortunately – happened. He allowed himself to become completely demoralized. He could endure suffering with courage enough, but he could not conquer the anxieties of his imagination. For him, the cloister was full of terrors and phantoms, even when he felt well. [...] When I would return from my nocturnal explorations in the ruins with my children, I would find him, at ten in the evening, pale at his piano, his eyes haggard, his hair standing almost on end. It would take him several moments to recognize us. He would then make an effort to laugh, and he would play us the sublime pieces he had just composed, or, to be more accurate, the terrible and harrowing music which had come to him unawares in that lonely hour of sorrow and fright.[251]

Seeking the reasons for the appearance of these phantasms, Mrs Sand unwaveringly pointed to Polish cultural habits. 'The death of his friend Dr Matuszynski and, then, that of his own father were two terrible blows for him. Catholic dogma endows death with an awful dread. Chopin, instead of dreaming of a better world for those departed souls, had only terrifying visions, and I was obliged to spend many nights in the room next to his, always prepared to get up from my work a hundred times a night to chase the phantoms from his sleep or his insomnia. The image of his own death appeared to him, escorted by all the superstititions of Slavic fantasy. As a Pole, he lived in a nightmare of legends. Specters called to him, clutched him, and instead of glimpsing his father and his friend smiling at him through beams of holy light, he found himself shoving away their fleshless visages, and struggling against their icy grasps.'[252]

---

[251] Sand, *Story of My Life*, 1093, 1091.
[252] Ibid, 1108.

Mrs Sand's utterances have at times been treated as the product of the exuberant fancy of an exalted woman of letters. Yet her testimony should not be trivialised, given that it is confirmed by the utterances of Chopin himself, who did indeed experience hallucinations of that kind. On 9 September 1848, he wrote to Solange Clésinger from Scotland: 'When I was playing my Sonata in B flat minor amidst a circle of English friends, an unusual experience befell me. I executed the Allegro and Scherzo more or less correctly and was just about to start the March, when suddenly I saw emerging from the half-opened case of the piano the accursed apparitions that had appeared to me one evening in the Charterhouse. I had to go out for a moment to collect myself, after which, without a word, I played on' (KGS i: 225–226).[253] So this was a persistent spectre, resembling somewhat our Slavic 'duch powrotnik', but there is nothing strange about that, given that it was born in a Carthusian monastery cell in Valldemosa, which Chopin's imagination transformed into a coffin (KS i: 332). This occurrence showed that Chopin was both often and easily ruled by his vexed imagination. Only a man with an imagination capable of transforming psychic activity into reality; only a man creating what the psychologists call 'beings not really existing, although real', could penetrate our Anti-world, the Anti-Earth, the musical presentiment of which – to my mind – is the fourth movement of the Sonata in B flat minor, Op. 35.[254]

---

[253] Bernard Gavoty, who published this letter, is of the opinion that this incident occurred in a salon in Manchester on 29 August 1848. Krystyna Kobylańska draws attention to a particularly significant confirmation of this unusual fact: 'The invited critic of the *Manchester Guardian* asks in the issue of the following day [30 August 1848], bewildered by the sudden break in the performance: "Did Chopin feel unwell?"' (KGS i: 226).

[254] Please forgive my unlawful incursion into foreign territory, but on this occasion I find it difficult to refrain from a few remarks. My interpretation of the B flat minor Sonata is strongly influenced by the opinion of Robert Schumann. (See reprint of his review in Robert Schumann, *Ein Quellenwerk über sein*

Like George Sand, Chopin also considered that the exuberance of his imagination derived from his Polish mentality. He expressed this briefly and simply, albeit in a quite unusual way. Thus we read in the above-quoted letter to his family: 'They are doubtless those *espaces imaginaires*, but I'm not ashamed of that; after all, we're the ones with the proverb that "through imagination he went to the coronation"' (KR 141).

In order to understand this original commentary to the psychoanalysis of his own mind, I must now deal with the say-

---

Leben und Schaffen (Leipzig, 1956), ii:100–101.) This opinion was criticised in Poland first by Ludwik Bronarski, in his essay 'Stosunek Schumanna do twórczości Chopina' [Schumann's attitude to Chopin's work] (1929) (reprinted in his *Szkice chopinowskie* [Chopin sketches] (Cracow, 1961)), and then by Karol Szymanowski, in his essay 'Fryderyk Chopin i muzyka współczesna' [Fryderyk Chopin and contemporary music] (1930) (reprint in Szymanowski's *Pisma* [Writings], i: *Pisma muzyczne* [Writings on music] (Cracow, 1984), 297–298). In both instances, the authors took issue with the idea that Chopin's sonata sounds like a derision of music, and that its 'strangeness' and 'morbid eccentricity' derived from its Polish spirit. It seems, however, that Schumann's error involved primarily a disturbance of the hierarchy between form and essence. Schumann was attached to the familiar, coherent and fixed structure of the sonata. For him, such a structure was the audible and phenomenal sign of ideal form. He interpreted Chopin's work as derision because it did not for him resemble the generally accepted sign. It is clear from the German Romantic's review that he still considered Presto from the point of view of the ideal sonata model. The shock must have been massive, since the finale of that form had never contained mystery or wisdom from beyond. Schumann was captivated by Chopin's genius, but he knew only that this was a terrifying spirit, *ein eigener grausiger Geist*, and he understood that Chopin had composed that movement without a melody, *ein melodielosen Satz*, in order to deride sonata form, and so the 'lofty originality of the Sarmatian' was reduced to Romantic irony, about which the Germans had been talking since the times of the Schlegels and Jean Paul. Schumann admired the 'sarcastic smile of the Sphinx' in places where he ought to have heard music from the Anti-world. Since he failed to comprehend that movement, he also did not understand the work as a whole. After all, what could have concluded a sonata about human existence, particularly after the third movement, which was not a Beethovenian *Marcia funebre*, but an 'image' of life in the shadow of death? Schumann did not grasp the new meaning of old musical names, such as *Marche funèbre* and Finale. And he did not understand that in the Presto, Chopin wrote that which Schumann himself would hear when nothingness stood beside him.

ing quoted by Chopin, which alleviated him of the feeling of embarrassment at the madness of his imagination. Only then will we understand that Chopin treated an oversensitive imagination, which can sometimes be the source of false suppositions about oneself, with characteristic irony.

The saying he quoted derived from events that took place in 1669, during the election of King Michał Korybut. Their protagonist was Aleksander Polanowski, one of the most illustrious officers of the crown army.[255] His military career was glittering, and so he was widely admired. Although the electoral records are silent on these events, they are described in the journal of Jan Pasek, a masterpiece of Polish prose which was often quoted in Chopin's day. It turns out that the petty gentry, offended at the scheming of the magnates, who were imposing some foreign prince upon them, decided to choose a king from among their own number. And so when 'Vivat Piast!' began to ring out, representatives of the Łęczyce and Brześć Kujawski voivodeships – so we read in Pasek – launched the propaganda that 'we do not need a rich sire, because he will be rich on becoming the Polish king. […] If we had had Czarniecki, then he would most probably have taken to the throne; since God has taken him from us, let us choose his pupil, let us elect Polanowski'.[256] Of course, there was a great commotion. Pasek states that the representatives of Sandomierz immediately put forward the candidature of the son of the famous

---

[255] For a biography of Aleksander Polanowski, see E. Jonas, *Polski Słownik Biograficzny* [Polish biographical dictionary], xxvii:377–379. Like almost every educated Polish nobleman during the seventeenth century, he had a perfect command of prose. See his letter to Jerzy Lubomirski, Polish Crown Hetman, of 9 February 1664, in W. S. de Broel-Plater (ed.), *Zbiór pamiętników do dziejów polskich* [Anthology of memoirs for Polish history] (Warsaw, 1859), iv:146–148.

[256] Jan Pasek, *Pamiętniki* [Journal] (Warsaw, 1955), 302. The publication of Pasek's prose became a great literary sensation of the Romantic era in Poland. Like everyone, Chopin most probably read this notable work.

warrior Jeremi Wiśniowiecki, Michał Korybut. The nobility was enraged, and perhaps out of alarm that a lieutenant of the hussars, albeit officially titled 'colonel', might become king, after brief resistance, Primate Mikołaj Prażmowski announced the election of the magnate's son, Michał Wiśniowiecki, and intoned *Te Deum laudamus*. Thus the news got about that the king was an elect of the 'nation's blood', and a huge cry of 'Vivat Piast!' again went up. Pasek relates that the Łęczyce and Brześć delegates cried out just as loudly, as they thought that their candidate had been chosen. Further events are not so clear, since we do not know whether Andrzej Polanowski, believing he had been elected king, did indeed travel to Cracow for the coronation, set for the 29 September, or whether his enemies spread such news in order to humiliate him. Pasek was not yet familiar with the saying quoted by Chopin. In any case, possibly already in 1669, perhaps during Polanowski's lifetime or after his death, it began to be told in the Commonwealth of Poland-Lithuania that there was a nobleman who imagined he had been chosen as king and skipped along to Wawel Hill for the coronation. Over the course of time, the name faded away, and there remained the saying: 'through imagination he went to the coronation'.

It was first written down by the great historian of the Romantic era, Joachim Lelewel, in his treatise *Korona Polski i jej królewskość* [The Polish crown and its majesty], first published in French (Paris, 1840). Lelewel quoted this 'old Polish proverb' against the party of Prince Adam Czartoryski, which saw in its leader a future king of Poland. 'There are such people ill of mind who in their mania proclaim Polish sovereignty and in their imagination picture that they will go to behold its future splendour'. So the quoted saying was a taunt aimed at Polish monarchists, who 'themselves take the title of king and then give it to others, having earlier handed out nominations for high positions'.[257] If Chopin read that treatise, as is highly likely, then he appreciated the acerbity of that *proverbium* like no one else.

Having taken all this on board, let us now set about defining the function of this proverb in Chopin's declaration, which was actually an excuse. The best way to proceed will be to attempt to reconstruct the deep meaning of Chopin's idea.

So I usually dwell in 'some curious space', in *espaces imaginaires*, in an anti-world, 'but I'm not ashamed of that; after all, we're the ones with the proverb that...' The term 'after all' often precedes some justification. So I am not ashamed at dwelling in the realm of phantasms, because I come from a country which has a proverb about the power of imagination. Linde's dictionary notes that in Polish at that time 'imaginacja' meant not only imagination, not only fancy, those two creative powers of the mind, not only delusion, which today we call phantasm, but also something completely made up and somewhat ridiculous, nonsensical. The man from the proverb was not so much deluding himself that he had been chosen king as getting into his head the crazy notion that an ordinary nobleman could adorn his brow with a crown (although the laws of the Commonwealth of Poland-Lithuania did in fact allow for such a thing).[258] So I have no shame about dwelling in the realm of phantasms – I am still

---

[257] Joachim Lelewel, *Porównanie dwu powstań narodu polskiego 1794 i 1830–1831* [A comparison of the two uprisings of the Polish nation of 1794 and 1830–1831], tr. W. Zwierkowski (Paris, 1840), 105. Books of proverbs published during the nineteenth century give a whole range of variants of this expression. In one of them, it was a peasant, not a nobleman, who went to the coronation, deluding himself that a peasant could indeed become king. In Józef Dzierzkowski's novel *Wieniec cierniowy* [A wreath of thorns] (1855), it is indeed a nobleman who sets off, but in his imagination he travelled not to a coronation, but to a confederation, which turned out to be not such a crazy claim (Józef Dzierzkowski, *Powieści* [novels], vii:147).
[258] Adam Kersten, *Hieronim Radziejowski. Studium władzy i opozycji* [Hieronim Radziejowski. A study of power and opposition] (Warsaw, 1988), 17–18.

reconstructing Chopin's deep thought – because 'back home' it has long been known that imagination can sometimes make a plain fool out of someone. It can lead him into the pure 'land of thought', but it can also set him up for public ridicule. I know this, and yet I still flee into my anti-world. I can pay any price for it, since that is simply the way 'back home', and I am a cast-iron Pole: '…after all, we're the ones with the proverb that "through imagination, he went to the coronation"; and I'm a true blind Mazovian' (KR 141).

He was indeed born in Mazovia, a province incorporated into the kingdom quite late, during the reign of King Sigismund I the Old, in 1529. Provinces with an older culture and cultivated tradition were rather ill-disposed towards the Mazovians. The custom of ridiculing or even maligning them spread quite quickly throughout the Commonwealth and prevailed for at least two hundred years. Linde quotes Jan Innocenty Petrycy: 'The Mazovian land has something inelegant and coarse about it, such that we have come to make fun of their speech and behaviour'. One Kargowski irritated Pasek, 'because he was continually jibing the Mazovians that they are born blind and are of a villainous nature'. When 'a calf's head was brought to the table, he said it was a Mazovian pope. On seeing the yellow batter placed under the veal, he said that it was Mazovian hosts'. At first, Pasek, who considered himself merely a neighbour of the Mazovians, as his native province of Rawa was incorporated into the kingdom in 1642, was continually appeasing him, but when Kargowski sang him the following ditty he could not contain himself.

—

Mazurowie nasi
Po jaglanej kaszy,
Słone wąsy mają,
W piwie je maczają,

(Our Mazovians
After millet groats,
Have salty whiskers,
So they dip them in beer.)

—

He grabbed a squab with both hands and rammed him into
the singer's chest. Kargowski, falling, whacked his head against
the edge of a bench and fell unconscious.[259]

So they were maligned, and called blind Mazovians. 'Ma-
zury ślepaki niezdarne jak raki' [Blind Mazovians clumsy as
crabs]. 'What a blind Mazovian!' was once uttered about someone, actually in admiration.[260] There was a persistent rumour that
Mazovians were born blind. They were also regarded as blind
of mind; in other words, ignorant and uneducated. Sometimes,
a blind Mazovian was understood to be a person who was head-
strong and stubborn. During the Romantic era, this tendency
continued to grow. While still a student, the 'philaret' Tomasz
Zan, a friend of Mickiewicz, said admiringly of the outstanding
scholar and philosopher Jan Śniadecki, enumerating his qualities: 'Blind Mazovian'.[261] And in Chopin's day, the animosity
between Mazovia and Lithuania was far from extinguished, giv-
en that Mickiewicz, in his *Księgi narodu i pielgrzymstwa* [The
books of the Polish nation and of the Polish pilgrims] (1832),
warned: 'The Lithuanian and the Mazovian are brothers: do
brothers quarrel over one being called Władysław and the other
Witowt? Their surname is one: the surname of the Poles'.[262]

---

[259] Pasek, *Pamiętniki*, 296–297.
[260] See Julian Krzyżanowski et al (eds.), *Nowa księga przysłów i wyrażeń
przysłowiowych polskich* [New book of Polish proverbs and proverbial ex-
pressions] (Warsaw, 1970), ii:418–420.
[261] Tomasz Zan, 'Notatki pamiętnikarskie' [Diary notes], in Henryk Mościcki
(ed.), *Z filareckiego świata. Zbiór wspomnień z lat 1816–1824* [From the world
of the philarets. A collection of memoirs form the years 1816–1824] (Warsaw,
1924), 186.
[262] Mickiewicz, *Dzieła*, vi:36.

Unsurprisingly, therefore, a note of pride sounds in Chopin's statement:

'…after all, we're the ones with the proverb that "through imagination, he went to the coronation"; and I'm a true blind Mazovian.' He then added, with characteristic wit: 'And so not seeing very far I have written 3 new mazurkas…' (KR 141). They were published as opus 59.

This is what Cyprian Norwid wrote about the mazur(ka) in his essay *Tańce polskie* [Polish dances] (1852?): 'The mazur – a creation aesthetically superior to the krakowiak, as it is not connected, through an elementary, identical way of dancing, with the improvisation of a song, but is entirely expressed in the dance itself; hence it has gained the right of citizenship in Europe and is not the property of the province alone. Chopin could even raise it to symphonic distinction, and enclose it within a musical creation alone, even without the dance (he was a born Mazovian himself and opened up broad vistas on the world for his province's creation). In respect to such a creation that can be expressed through a single organ of art, one may conclude that as an element of similar aesthetic status to, for example, the Dorian or Ionian element, it is more than provincial, but part of the integral national harmony.'[263] Thus in his 'imaginary spaces', this 'blind Mazovian' transformed his mazurness into an 'aesthetic element' that was not the property 'of the province alone', but belonged to the whole of humanity, like the architectural styles of ancient Greece.

Every creative act placed Chopin in a particularly sharp conflict with empirical reality, since in writing music he departed this world, even though by nature he was of the earth, immersed in historical existence. As we learn from George Sand, who I would still advise against trivialising:

---

[263] Norwid, *Pisma wszystkie*, vi:386–387. Norwid dedicated this piece to Wojciech Grzymała.

He was devoured by dreams of an ideal and fortified by none of the customary worldly tolerance afforded by philosophy or compassion. He was never willing to compromise with human nature. He in no way accepted things as they were. Therein lay his vice and his virtue, his greatness and his misery. Unforgiving of the slightest flaw, he had enormous enthusiasm for the least spark of talent, his impassioned imagination doing everything possible to see it as the full blaze of genius.[264]

He was here. He ate the dust of time, was affected by the cry of the tormented, was afraid of death, breathed in the smell of cut grass, enjoyed the taste of aromatic cocoa. And he was there. In his music. In the thicket of abstract 'musical elements' that ultimately, paradoxically – and so as is usual in life – proved more earthly than transient everyday reality. So he began to depart the world when composing his very first work. He departed, of course, that he might, in those 'imaginary spaces' of music, stay with us forever.

---

[264] Sand, *Story of My Life*, 1107.

2. Talent and the tone of life

Given that Chopin knew he would not free himself from the dictates and whims of his imagination, how did he take being condemned to the fate of an artist? How did he assume the weighty yoke of his talent?

After his separation from Sand, in a letter to his sister, Ludwika Jędrzejewicz, of 10 February 1848, he worded a highly original view on the relationship between an artist's talent and his way of experiencing the world. 'Meanwhile, mother [George Sand] is writing a most beautiful column in [*Le journal des débats*]. She is play-acting in the country, in the room of her connubial daughter, forgetting herself, intoxicating herself as much as she can, and will not wake up until her heart, which is now oppressed by her head, begins to really hurt. I did my stint. May the Lord God love her, if she cannot distinguish true attachment from flattery. Or perhaps others only appear to be flatterers to me, and perhaps her happiness is indeed there, where I cannot see it. For a long time, her friends and neighbours could understand nothing of what was happening there in recent times, but perhaps now they have become accustomed to it. Moreover, no one will ever be able to follow the trail of the caprices of such a soul. Eight years of some kind of order was too much. The Lord God granted that those were the years in which her children were growing, and were it not for me, I don't know how long the children would already have been with their father, and not with her. [...] But', Chopin concludes these reflections, 'perhaps those are the conditions of her life, her talent for writing, her happiness?' (KR 172–173).

229

In order to avoid mistakes in our further considerations, let us first concern ourselves with the meaning of the word 'kondycja'. In the Poland of old, it most often meant property, assets, fortune, estate, and so substance.[265] In his immortal dictionary, Samuel Bogumił Linde enumerated several other meanings, such as social estate, situation and fate. It was said, for example, that one person was of the noble 'condition', and another of the peasant 'condition', and instead of human fate, one spoke of the human condition. A seventeenth-century Polish preacher would say that 'Christ quashed Lazarus' human condition'. But the Polish intelligentsia educated during the times of the Congress Kingdom associated 'kondycja' above all with 'condition'. In that same letter to his sister Ludwika, Chopin went on to write that: '...I could not go there, bound as I was by the condition of silence about the daughter' (KR 173). This meant that he was allowed to show up at Nohant provided he did not start any conversations about Solange. Interestingly, for Maurycy Mochnacki, whose linguistic habits, like those of Chopin, were formed in 'congress' Warsaw, two meanings harmoniously coexisted in the word 'kondycja': fate and condition. On 2 September 1834, he wrote from Paris to his parents that the Russian embassy in the French capital was setting Polish exiles the following conditions: 'Anyone who applied at the embassy for an amnesty should be told that if he is an army soldier, he will have to serve 15 years in the Perm or Yaroslav province. Can you believe it, papa?' Mochnacki expressed his indescribable astonishment. 'And two hundred immediately accepted that condition'.[266] In this case, therefore, to fulfil a condition meant to determine one's fate. And that whole terrible truth about the

---

[265] e.g. letter from Aleksander Polanowski to Jerzy Lubomirski, Grand Marshal and Crown Field Hetman, of 9 February 1664: '...having received in their absence banishment at the tribunal, my cousins turned up on my estate'; in de Broel-Plater (ed.), *Zbiór pamiętników*, iv:148.
[266] Mochnacki, *Dzieła* [Works] (Poznań, 1863), i:256.

existence of many people boiled down to a single word: 'kon-dycja'. So in the letter to his sister, Chopin was expressing the opinion that it was a specific style of experiencing life that was most probably a condition of both Mrs Sand's happiness and also her talent. Consequently, as Chopin understood it, talent was not some mysterious daimon that subjugates an artist in an unfathomable act of his 'I', but a disposition, clearly dependent on his lifestyle.

Chopin lived in an era that was particularly fond of using the word 'genius'. It was ever-present on the pages of periodicals and novels; it was overused in poetry, in particular, and resounded in literary salons. It was admittedly sometimes employed by the staid and the scholarly. Chopin knew the verdict of the examinations committee from the Central School of Music in Warsaw, which through its vice-chancellor Józef Elsner was worded as follows: 'Third-year Szopen Friderik. Special ability, musical genius'.[267] Over the course of the hundred years preceding the school's declaration, the word 'genius' had already succeeded in taking on a most specific meaning, and so Elsner, brought up in the culture of the eighteenth century, knew what the Polish musical public was being told by that dazzling report.[268] Polish society was prepared for understanding this word

---

[267] Krystyna Kobylańska, *Chopin w Kraju* [Chopin in Poland] (Cracow, 1955), 125.

[268] In 1752, Christoph Willibald von Gluck arrived in Italy. Hector Berlioz recorded an anecdote that was still circulating during the Romantic era '... one day, in Naples, there was a performance of *La Clemenza di Tito* [...] The students of a conservatoire who, as poor musicians, naturally loathed Gluck, were delighted to find this series of supposedly defective harmonies in his aria. They promptly took the *asino tedesco*'s score to their maestro Durante, and gave it to him for condemnation without naming the author.' The long-serving director of the Conservatorio di S. Onofrio a Capuana was a very highly regarded pedagogue, who had trained many illustrious musicians, but I doubt that either Pergolesi or Paisiello was among the pupils who jeered at Gluck's score. Francesco Durante, as Berlioz goes on to relate, 'studied the passage carefully, then gave the simple verdict: "No rule, it's true, justi-

both by authorities, such as Jan Śniadecki,[269] and by handbooks, such as *Prawidła wymowy i poezji* [The rules of oratory and poetry] by Euzebiusz Słowacki, Juliusz's father.[270]

Chopin's family was well familiar with Elsner's opinion, which was expounded to them during a pow-wow called in Warsaw when they received the news that the famous Kalkbrenner had agreed to teach Fryderyk for three years. In a letter of 27 November 1831, the composer's sister, Ludwika, passed Elsner's opinion on to her brother: '...Mrs Szyma[nowska] ventured to say about Kalkbrenner *que c'est un filout*, and so it is some kind of speculation on Fryderyk – the lesser if it is only to call him his pupil – but there is some such that despite a love

---

fies this combination of sounds; but if it is an error I admit that only a man of rare genius can have been guilty of it".' (Berlioz, *Evenings*, 227). During the eighteenth century, it was considered that a genius had the right to break rules. Talent was understood as an artist's innate ability, given to him 'directly from the hand of nature'. Genius, meanwhile, was 'an innate disposition of the mind for originality', or 'an ability to create that for which no specific rule can be given.' Immanuel Kant, who codified this difference in his *Critique of Judgment*, considered that a genius could not describe or indicate how his work had been created. '[an author] himself does not know how he came by the ideas for [the product of his genius]; nor is it in his power [*Gewalt*] to devise such products at his pleasure, or by following a plan, and to communicate [his procedure] to others in precepts that would enable them to bring about like products.' (Immanuel Kant, *Critique of Judgment*, tr. Werner S. Pluhar (Indianapolis, 1987), 175). Genius is thus truly creative, but unpredictable. Its achievements cannot be reproduced. It owes its originality to its mysterious 'I'. This was understood by Elsner, when writing his verdict into the Conservatory documents; at the same time he noted in his diary that Chopin had 'opened a new era in music, with both his astonishing playing and his compositions'. (Józef Reiss, *Ślązak Józef Elsner – nauczyciel Chopina* [The Silesian Józef Elsner, Chopin's teacher] (Katowice, 1936), 33). Talent was not capable of this. For this, genius was needed.

[269] Jan Śniadecki, 'O pismach klasycznych i romantycznych' [On Classical and Romantic writings] (1819), in *Pisma filozoficzne* [Philosophical writings] (Warsaw, 1958), ii:117.

[270] Euzebiusz Słowacki, *Prawidła wymowy i poezji* [The rules of oration and poetry] (Vilnius, 1826), 213: 'The principles of poetic genius should be sought in a great sensitivity of the heart combined with an extraordinary vivid imagination'.

of the art is designed to cramp your genius. […] Your ideas can be better than those essayed hitherto; you have innate genius and your works are fresher and superior. […] Your genius is not to sit at the piano and in concerts, you are to immortalise yourself in operas. He says that as well formed as you are, in which superior to perhaps all those once of your age and today famous composers, with such genius you should aim there, where your genius drives you, and not follow anyone. […] he insists in maintaining that sensing today what is good and what is better, you should forge a path for yourself; your genius will guide you.' (KR 78–79)

In spite of Elsner's unequivocal judgment, Chopin's family avoided the grand word as best it could, possibly because the Romantic era had transformed the genius into a tragic demi-god.[271] Condemned to suffering, misunderstanding and solitude, the Romantic genius was oppressed by a hostile society, which found it difficult to tolerate the revelation of this 'denizen of higher worlds'. He was persecuted, like every prophet to whom the Creator has ever entrusted a mission, raising him up above the norms of behaviour. And yet the Chopins' family genius should have been understood, accepted and rewarded. So it was better not to overuse the word. When addressing his son, Mikołaj Chopin most often wrote: 'Your talent' (KR 82, 84). That is also how his sister, Izabela, proceeded (KR 77). Chopin himself was similarly modest. He did not like grand words, particularly in

---

[271] See Gretchen R. Besser, 'The Romantic Tradition of Genius', in *Balzac's Concept of Genius. The Theme of Superiority in the "Comedie Humaine"* (Geneva, 1969), 15–80. Robert Schumann's views on this matter were clearly inspired by Kant. 'Talent labors, genius creates. […] It is the curse of talent that, although it labors with greater steadiness and perseverance than genius, it does not reach its goal, while genius, already on the summit of the ideal, gazes laughingly about' (Robert Schumann, *On Music and Musicians*, tr. Paul Rosenfeld, ed. Konrad Wolff (London, 1947), 44, 40; Ger. orig. *Gesammelte Schriften über Musik und Musiker* (Leipzig, J. Jensen, 1891), i:33, 29).

respect to a mystery, which is why he banished from his language that grandiloquent term abused for a hundred years by aestheticians, poets and journalists. He contented himself with speaking of talent, which was sufficiently incomprehensible and sufficiently problematic.

So let us now try to acquaint ourselves a little more closely with what he thought about the relationship between talent and the artist's lifestyle.

From the above-quoted letter to his sister, Ludwika, we learn that he saw the life of George Sand as a constant whirl of passions, which for a few years only was to some extent reined in. The moment her children matured and serious problems began to arise, the novelist again fell into a succession of conflicts, which she attempted to mollify with rather infelicitous ideas. She created a clamorous turmoil, intended to drown out her constant anxiety. These were unsuccessful attempts to ignore the irritating situation in her life, which she actually continued to worsen. '…she forgets herself, stupefies herself as best she can…' The word 'szołomić się' that he uses here, beautiful and ghastly like the swish of a knife being sharpened by a suicide, means to bewilder oneself, to bring oneself into a state of semi-consciousness, a state of intoxication or obfuscation. Chopin was well aware what that word signified: Vienna had once 'bewildered, dazed and beguiled' him (KS i: 103). So this woman transformed her own soul into a wild abyss. Not even an attempt to theatralise her inner turmoil could help. Chopin was under no illusions that the awakening would be painful and would bring with it a series of self-mystifications. '[She] will not wake up until her heart, which is now oppressed by her head, begins to really hurt.' For this was a torrent so mighty that her mind could no longer hear anything other than its continual murmur. In other letters, Chopin described Mrs Sand's behaviour as frenzy, paroxysm and fever (KR 170–171). He even went so far as to call 'the ugliest row, which the whole of Paris knows about today', 'a great mire' (KR 181).

According to Chopin, this disorderly lifestyle determined the conditions of her talent. Perhaps because a novelist needs knowledge of the contradictions of existence. Perhaps because a life in turmoil constituted the essential experience on which her prose lived. Indeed, in order to become a prose writer, one must experience first-hand the antinomies that tear human existence apart, and at times spatter oneself with triviality. Mrs Sand knew this very well herself. Right at the beginning of her career, Henri de Latouche, whom she approached with her first belletristic effort and a request for its appraisal, said to her: 'The novel is life, told with art. You have an artist's nature, but you don't know reality. You're too much of a dreamer. Wait patiently for time and experience; rest assured, those two sad counselors will come soon enough. Let life be your teacher, and try to remain a poet. You need do nothing else.' Just so she would harbour no doubts, he expounded this truth to her several times. 'Use your own fund of knowledge; read in your own life, in your own feelings; render your impressions'. So George Sand amassed that 'fund' for all she was worth. Thus she removed all control over that which Chopin called her 'caprices'. As far as we know, she diligently gathered experiences, but she seems not to have preserved the soul of a poet. A novel does indeed demand 'characters and situations that are true to life', fed on 'all the sorrow' experienced by the author.[272] Therefore, in some instances, Mrs Sand triggered situations from which she drew new experiences. In any case, she needed the clamour of time. When she met Chopin, it seemed to her that she had met the person who would pull her out of that ferment. As she wrote to Eugène Delacroix in September 1838: 'I am beginning to believe that there exist angels disguised as

---

[272] Sand, *Story of My Life*, 916, 921, 922.

men, which dwell some time upon the Earth, in order to console poor, weary and troubled souls, close to ruin, and pull them up towards heaven' (KGS ii: 11). She regarded her life as being steeped in distress. 'That is just how we artists are, nervous and bilious' (KGS ii: 12). So how could it end – that romantic mystification, which allowed her to get excited about her own spiritual chaos and at the same time turn a musician immersed in earthly existence into a 'cloud in trousers'?

Besides Mrs Sand, Chopin also observed Eugène Delacroix, a truly great artist, whose life, although not devoid of great anxieties, proceeded without the histrionic extravagances that were so characteristic of some Romantics. His inner peace of mind could be disturbed by neither politics nor history. He was characterised by moderation and self-control, at times even taken to monastical rigour. His lifestyle was the exact opposite of the model adopted by Mrs Sand. Chopin, who had a very keen eye, must have noticed, therefore, that the 'conditions of the talent' of Delacroix were completely different to the conditions shaping the personality of his extraordinary companion.

On 29 January 1849, when his state of health had made it impossible for him to work, Chopin spent a whole evening with the great painter in quite intimate conversation. The subject of their discussion was the character of Mrs Sand. The composer did not consider that the whirl of life had prematurely burned out her soul, since he held her to be indestructible. This was a sober remark, albeit rather trenchant, but that is not what aroused my interest. As Delacroix noted in his journal, 'As for Chopin, his suffering prevents his taking an interest in anything, least of all in his work. I said that what with age and the unrest of the present day, it would not be long before I, too, began to lose my enthusiasm. He said he thought that I had strength enough to resist: "You will have the enjoyment of your talent", he said, "in a kind of serenity that is a rare privilege, and no less valuable than the feverish search after fame."'[273] To Chopin's mind, the talent of Delacroix was conditioned by his inner balance, which clearly radiated from the artist to those closest to him. This calm was the fruit of an innate ability to take pleasure in the very existence of things. Thus a remarkable sensitivity to things gifted the artist with a harmony that the adventures garnered on his way through life could not alloy. Even highly dramatic events, such as murder, extermination and fighting were observed by Delacroix with a curious composure, which incidentally allowed him to see into the essence of the tragic tensions of existence. Delacroix is an example of how one need not wait for old age to achieve serenity.

So Chopin was aware that the way in which an artist experienced existence set the tone for his life. Were it not for the clamorous sound of that tone, smacking at times of triviality, George Sand would most probably not have written any one of her novels. Were it not for the harmonious tone that enveloped the life of Delacroix, he would not have discovered the mysteries of the reflections of light and the laws of the functioning of objects in space. Chopin did not fix any eternal rules governing the talent of the prosaist and the artist. He simply noted certain facts that emerged around him. He understood that the style of an artist's behaviour affected the kind of his talent. In the art of his friends, he discerned the tone of their life, which proved to be a form-generative element. Mrs Sand could not live without the vociferation of political mundanities and embroiled herself in public and domestic quarrels, causing uneasiness all around her. Delacroix calmly arranged a blue cushion on a red carpet and watched attentively as the two colours began to impinge on one another, as 'red becomes tinged with blue, blue is lined with red and in the middle violet forms'.[274] The nervousness of agitated passions and the calm of perspicacious observation.

---

[273] Delacroix, entry of 29 January 1849, *Journal* (London, 2006), 90–91.
[274] Quoted in Starzyński, *O romantycznej syntezie sztuk*, 188.

During a stay in London, Chopin met the American philosopher Ralph Waldo Emerson, whose acquaintance he had previously made in Paris. They would see one another at musical soirées. Once they probably dined together.[275] And interestingly, in the essays of this charming thinker, whom, incidentally, Adam Mickiewicz so sagely analysed, one comes across an opinion that encapsulates the Romantic view of existence in an exceptionally accurate and succinct way. As Emerson asserted, there was but one wise policy in life: to concentrate; and one bad thing: to be distracted. Concentration and distraction. That was one of the fundamental antinomies of the era. Whilst Chopin did not treat its components as moral categories, he understood that they were the two causes determining two kinds of talent. In order to become an artist, one individual had to focus, and another to dissipate, his 'I'.

[275] On Chopin's relations with Emerson, see KS ii: 200.

3. Aerumnarum plenus

So what was the tone of Chopin's own life? Did he allow himself an exhilarating life in caprice, or did he enjoy inner harmony? Or perhaps everything in his life looked completely different? What element dominated his existence to such an extent that it eventually shaped his talent as well?

In order to arrive at a sensible answer to that question, I am obliged at first to bring in the notion of the existential code. This was formulated by Milan Kundera and defined as follows: 'To apprehend the self in my novels means to grasp the essence of its existential problem. To grasp its *existential code*.' Every such code comprises several key words, which Kundera calls the themes of existence.[276] These are characteristic for every character in a novel, but to my mind every person also possesses such a personal existential code composed of the words defining the tone of his life.

From Chopin's letters, it emerges that in his reflections on his own life the most frequently used are such words as orphanhood, longing, worry, misery and regret, and so the tone of his life is best defined by the Latin word *aerumna*. This signifies care, worry and anguish, and it has the advantage that its semantic field encompasses all the significant words that assail us when we read what Chopin says about himself.

At the same time, this was a magic word of the Polish Romantics. It defined most aptly the character of the existence of a Polish artist during the first half of the nineteenth cen-

---

[276] Milan Kundera, *The Art of the Novel*, tr. Linda Asher (London, 1988), 29; Fr. orig. *L'Art du roman* (Paris, 1986), 46.

tury. It was circulated, so to speak, by Zygmunt Krasiński. On 12 April 1843, he wrote from Rome to Juliusz Słowacki: 'But again, in order to understand my personality, it is essential to know to what extent it has been for a year now tormented by a constant and worsening illness – and how many battles threaten it from all around – and how many cups of bitterness are continually served – death, if it would only listen to its egoism, death would be its only relief, and a plea for it would rise from its lips to God every day – but a sacrifice is needed, and so it prays not for rest or some other less unbearable form to its fortunes and vicissitudes – for e'en in the grave rest cannot be found – it remains and lives, and will continue to live its allotted time! – and it believes, and it loves – but in vain – in itself *aerumnarum plena est! Aerumna* is a delicious Latin word – used by Caesar when, wishing to save the supporters of Catiline, he explained to the merciless senators of Rome that a life full of *cares* was a worse punishment than death'.[277] Słowacki reacted to this with a letter of 3–4 July 1843, from Paris. 'As for me, the first line [of Krasiński's poem *Przedświt* [The dawn]: 'Za dni Cezara…' ('In the days of Caesar')] struck a familiar tone – for the spiritual connection between the author and myself has long since been open… for me this author has no need to write long notes – I already understand his magical words – issuing from Caesar's lips and my own – rhyming with coffin – how sonorous the echo of coffins'. During the Romantic era, rhyme enabled a poet to reveal the deep meanings of words. The difference between languages and civilisations is of no significance here. Irrespective of time and race, the musical consonance of words has freed the essence they contain: *aerumna – trumna* [coffin]. Three years later, Słowacki noted in his *Raptularz* [Jotter]: 'The philosophical aspect of language, the sad soul seeking similar words, quivering at similar words – Caesar's *aerumna-*

---

[277] *Korespondencja Juliusza Słowackiego*, ii:307.

rum plena anima – in a Slavic tongue *trumnica dusza moja*'.[278]
So Słowacki considered that a life full of cares shut a soul still
living in the world inside a coffin. Or rather that it turned the
soul into a coffin for the 'I'. In this way, immersing himself in
his times and living with his times, the Polish Romantic became
a 'living corpse'.

This horror was most suggestively expressed in Cyprian
Norwid's poem 'Aerumnarum plenus' (1850):

—

Więc to mi smutno – aż do kości smutno.

I to – że nie wiem, czy ten ludzki stek

Ma już tak zostać komedią okrutną,

I spać, i nucić, śpiąc: „To – taki wiek!"

Więc to mi smutno, i tak coraz gorzej,

Aż od-człowiecza się i pierś, i byt,

I nie wiem, czy już w akord się ułoży,

I nie wiem, czy już kiedy będę syt![279]…

(So I am sad – sad to the core.

And the fact – that I know not whether this human steak

Is to become now a cruel comedy,

And to sleep, and to murmur, sleeping: 'It's – such an age!'

So I am sad, and thus ever worse,

To the point where breast and being de-humanise,

And I know not whether it will form a chord,

And I know not whether I will ever be assuaged!)

—

Aerumna blighted poets mainly with the sense of an im-
poverishment of their existence. The reduction of life to 'painful
things', to use Słowacki's term, usually ended with the dehu-
manisation of the soul, or at least gave a person a complex

---

[278] Ibid, ii:9. Quotation from *Raptularz* in *Dzieła wszystkie*, xvi (Wrocław,
1954), 461.
[279] Norwid, *Pisma wszystkie*, ii:380, i:133–134.

of dissatisfaction, as expressed most consummately in Polish culture, in the twentieth century, in Stanisław Ignacy Witkiewicz's poem about being unsated. Chopin experienced all this in Stuttgart, and so he knew that enclosing oneself in worries and cares inevitably ends with one turning into a 'living corpse'.

So let us now try to grasp what the words forming that semantic field of despair essentially meant for him. Was it a golden field of corn animated by sadness? Or a black fallow field charred with bitterness? Let us begin with the word 'orphanhood'.

As we know, this feeling serves a specific function in connection with the 'self'. It deprives it of the warmth that spreads over a person from his nearest and dearest. The Polish Romantics knew that their orphanhood was the work of history. They owed their new place on the Earth to a cataclysm of war and a great national defeat. People who had loved one another and lived together were suddenly banished to distant corners of the world and shut inside an idle circle of solitude. They became orphans of their mother, their father, their siblings and their friends, even though their parents, brothers, sisters and sweethearts were still alive. Thrown from the nest, they themselves orphaned their nearest and dearest. Separated from each other, they became a source of mutual worry, albeit sacred and loved. This despair could be soothed only by great love and great pride, as Adam Mickiewicz was well aware, when he found himself banished to Russia. This is how the protagonist of one of his poems, Konrad Wallenrod, consoled his beloved at the moment of their final farewell:

—

Bywaj zdrowa, zapomij; zapłacz niekiedy nade mną; (…)
I niech dumy uczucie będzie pociechą sieroctwa.[280]
(Fare thee well, forget; weep for me from time to time; […]
And may a sense of pride console your orphanhood.)

—

[280] Mickiewicz, *Dzieła*, ii:113.

242

Hence, wishing to cheer his mother, whom, following the November Rising, he had left for the big wide world, Juliusz Słowacki reminded her of this astonishing line from Mickiewicz's poem: 'Dearest Mama!' he wrote from Paris on 30 July 1832, 'It is hard, hard, for me to describe the joy I derived from your last letter – so read my little books! You! mother, perhaps you sometimes have such a moment in which "a sense of pride consoles your orphanhood". That is the truest of Mickiewicz's poems'.[281]

Maurycy Mochnacki saw the positive aspects of this misery – for misery it was. 'The fatherland's state of bewidowment, this state of national orphanhood, is oddly beneficial to the interests of the future Poland and will prevent the deep wounds that the latest uprising renewed and bloodied from healing; every exile keeps the others in hope, in expectation, in anxiety. And that is just what the tsar does not want, and his plenipotentiary does everything he can to make Poles' residence in France increasingly unbearable'.[282] So in this conception, orphanhood was a blessed wound that brought pain and kept Poles in readiness for revolt and struggle.

Zygmunt Krasiński perceived this matter completely differently. Irrespective of all possible vicissitudes of history, the real cause of orphanhood remains the passing of time. During his time on Earth, *homo viator* is an orphan of God.

—
Nie mogłeś umrzeć – odetchnąć – tam zostać,
Gdzie śmierć ci życiem – życie, co ci zgonem,
Rwie się już dalej w inną świata postać –
I tyś jak dzieckiem znów osieroconem![283]

---
[281] *Korespondencja Juliusza Słowackiego*, i:125–126.
[282] Mochnacki, *Dzieła*, i:109.
[283] Krasiński, *Dzieła literackie* [Literary works], ed. Paweł Hertz (Warsaw, 1973), i:98.

(You could not die – take respite – remain there,
Where death is your life – life, which is your death,
Is already pulling off into another form of the world –
And you, like a child, are orphaned once again!)
—

Chopin felt the nation's orphanhood along with his fellow countrymen. However, since he was an exile by choice, in his case this feeling gained unusual hues. As we recall, he first experienced it shortly after leaving the country, on Christmas Eve 1830, when he went to St Stephen's cathedral while staying in Vienna. In respect to the events documented in his letters, orphanhood befell him for a second time towards the end of his life, when he felt a sense of community not only with political émigrés, but also with various vagabonds spending their life outside Poland, where it was impossible to live normally. This declaration occurs in a letter to Julian Fontana, who at the time was seeking work on the New Continent and happened to be in New York, most probably on business, as he was representing the interests of Pleyel's firm across America. Chopin recommended to him his friend Herbaut, who had been his 'first acquaintance in Paris'.[284] He must have been quite attached to Herbaut, as he asked Fontana to receive him like a father or older brother, and even invoked the name of the Warsaw Lyceum to entreat his friend to help. And then, in this short letter, written in Paris on 4 April 1848, among friendly reproaches, he suddenly let fall the following admission: 'You're a curmudgeon, a beast, you've not given me a single honest word in any of your letters; but no matter, somewhere in your soul, you love me, just as I love you. And perhaps now even more, since we are both greater Polish orphans, both Wodziński

---

[284] Both Chopin and Delacroix also spelled this name Herbault. On one occasion, Chopin even wrote Herbeault (KS ii: 77, 357), which is also how Wojciech Grzymała spelled the name.

and Witwicki, the Platers and Sobański have left us. You are my good old Julian, full stop' (KS ii: 239).

As in many cases, more often than is generally thought, here again ordinary and seemingly simple words are with Chopin hard to understand. Not because he wrote obscurely and tortuously, but because he used words in senses known only to himself. In this instance, it is relatively easy for us to comprehend the expression 'Polish orphans'. Those are Poles who for one reason or another are wandering around the world. Children without the mother of their Homeland. But why 'greater Polish orphans'? If they are greater, then there must also have been lesser orphans.

If my understanding of this phrase is correct, then Chopin held all his countrymen in exile to be siblings of a sort. The more death there was in that 'family', the greater was the orphanhood of the others. Several years previously, Chopin and Fontana had been 'lesser Polish orphans', since their beloved friends were still scattered around the world. Now, after their death, they had become 'greater orphans'. But Chopin was alive to a most curious paradox. A wanderer's death increased the love between those who remained alive. And that is what he was trying to convey to Fontana, scrupulously enumerating all the friends who had passed away in recent years. The greater the orphanhood, the stronger the ties between the living. This ostensibly straightforward observation, expressed as if in passing – which actually looks like bantering with his friend about feelings – actually grew out of Chopin's sober heroism. Orphanhood gathers together those who remain in a community; a person surrounded by death draws strength from love. Chopin even drops here a phrase that escapes him whenever something unpleasant afflicts him: 'but that matters not'. We shall come across this expression in a moment, when discussing Chopin's reaction to the strong wave of sadness that engulfs him, since with every wound, with every misfortune, sober thinking bade him seek values that would protect him against the vicissitudes of fate. George Sand reasoned in a similar way, and so one should never lose sight of the deep affinity between those two souls. On 21 May 1839, Dr Marcel Gaubert died. Informing Wojciech Grzymała of the sad event, she sent him the following reflection: 'So you will now be loved twice over and must also love for two. [...] we, who continue our pilgrimage have need of one another' (KGS i: 290).

By contrast to 'orphanhood', the meaning of the word 'yearning' is lost in a semantic mist.

During Chopin's formative years, Warsaw was reading above all poets and writers of the Stanislavian period. The Lyceum vice-chancellor Samuel Linde himself was an ardent admirer of the poetry of Adam Naruszewicz and Franciszek Karpiński. He recited it in the amusing Polish of a Polonised German who did not distinguish voiced from voiceless consonants. His declamation caused much mirth among his pupils, barely masked by their respect for him.[285] As one memoirist recalled, 'At contests and reviews, the youngsters were tickled most by the vice-chancellor's fondness for Karpiński's elegy 'Powrót do domu' [Homecoming] [actually titled 'Powrót z Warszawy do wieś' [From Warsaw back to the country]] and Naruszewicz's idyll 'Pacierz staruszka' [An old man's prayers]. Whenever the opportunity arose, he would immediately enquire: "And does any one of you know these poems?" and would ask to have them declaimed. And if he failed to discern sufficient eagerness in the recitation, then he himself would declaim them, in the most comical way, with a strong Kashubian accent: "Heeyer is my

---

[285] Adam Mickiewicz added to a farce by Tomasz Zan a little fragment entitled 'Dodatek do "Cwibaka"', which features the German Bartłomiej Cwibak ('Zwieback' is German for 'rusk'), who amused young people with his curious Polish. Both Mickiewicz and Chopin long retained a schoolboy sense of humour.

pooer hoe-um'".[286] Chopin, who *heard* every word, must have been particularly amused, and all the more eagerly set about producing his caricatures and parodies, already admired at that time. So Karpiński was a poet of his youth. No surprise, then, that the youthful *Fantasy on Polish Airs* (Op. 13) contains one of the four popular songs of that time written to the words of Karpiński's well-known idyll 'Laura i Filon' [Laura and Philo]. Chopin grew up among words whose meaning was ultimately fixed by the poetry of Karpiński. This applies in particular to words denoting feelings, since sentimentalism painted pictures of subtle, elusive and rather melancholic experiences, such as sadness, grief and yearning.

So Karpiński was capable of missing someone or yearning for someone. It could have been the homeland, as in the poem 'Tęskność do kraju' [Yearning for home], written in 1771, in Vienna – that same Vienna where Chopin would later experience very similar feelings.[287] In this case, the longing had a specific object. A person who felt bad *here* knew exactly to where his heart was tugging, since *there*, about which he feverishly thought, was inexpressibly real. Yet occasionally Karpiński employed the word 'tęsknota' to denote an unspecified, and somehow ambivalent, feeling. Typical in this respect is the poem 'Do Justyny. Tęskność na wiosnę' [For Justine. Ruing the spring].[288] Here, it was a feeling in which a vague sense of losing something essential was accompanied by the awareness of not fulfilling some hopes. And the whole thing

---

[286] Eugeniusz Skrodzki (Wielisław), *Wieczory piątkowe i inne gawędy* [Friday evenings and other tales] (Warsaw, 1968), 321.

[287] Karpiński's stay in Vienna did actually help him to overcome his deep-seated national prejudices. See Roman Sobol, *Franciszek Karpiński* (Warsaw, 1979), 38. Chopin was far from the Sarmatian way of thinking, but he was equally as sensitive as Karpiński to the imperialistic vagaries of the Austrians.

[288] *Poezja polskiego Oświecenia* [Poetry of the Polish Enlightenment], anthology, ed. Jan Kott (Warsaw, 1954), 287.

was shrouded in melancholic dissatisfaction. A person feels bad here, but he does not long for someone or something. He longs in himself. He is tormented by the feeling which Carl Gustav Jung called 'active emptiness'.[289] He feels bad here, but wishes to remain. I have no wish to dissect this expression too finely, since I know that its meaning is elusive, flitting between the words 'hurt', 'unfulfilment' and 'dissatisfaction'. But it never smacks of despair.

Such a longing befell Chopin at an early age, and it also visited him towards the end of his life. Polish Romantics idealised it to the utmost. Anyone wishing to acquaint himself with all of its shades should read Antoni Malczewski's *Maria* (1825), where longing means now sadness, now emptiness. Słowacki clearly linked it to a person's rising above his chthonic existence.

—

Tu Malczewskiego trzeba mięć tęsknotę,
Tęsknotę, co jest w ludziach pół-aniołach...[290]
(Here one needs Malczewski's longing,
The longing that lingers in half-angel men...)

—

Chopin's longing arose out of his historical, earthly and everyday existence. It cannot be identified with a dreaming of contact with Transcendence, since Chopin was far from the metaphysics that so characterised German Romantic musicians.[291]

---

[289] Carl Gustav Jung, 'Psychologia analityczna a światopogląd', in Jerzy Prokopiuk, (ed.), *Rebis, czyli kamień filozofów* [Rebis, or The philosophers' stone] (Warsaw, 1989), 198; Ger. orig. 'Analytische Psychologie und Weltanschauung', in Seelenprobleme der Gegenwart (Zurich, 1931).

[290] Słowacki, *Dzieła*, v:134.

[291] On German musical metaphysics, see Carl Dahlhaus, 'O genezie romantycznej interpretacji Bacha', in *Idea muzyki absolutnej i inne studia* [The idea of absolute music and other studies], tr. Antoni Buchner (Cracow, 1988), 167–168; Ger. orig. 'Zur Entstehung der romantischen Bach-Deutung', in Klassische und romantische Musikästhetik (Laaber, 1988).

In his longing there was plenty of 'active emptiness'. In his early youth, he liked to submerge himself in it. Here he writes to Tytus Woyciechowski from Warsaw on 17 April 1830: 'My dearest life! What a relief I feel in unbearable longing, as soon as I receive a letter from you; today that is just what I needed, as I was more bored than before' (KS i: 121). At times, he felt distinctly that this indefinite feeling could only be expressed in music. Here is a passage from a letter to Jan Matuszyński, written in Vienna on 26 December 1830:

> Dearest Jasiu, I was just returning from Slavik's (a celebrated violinist whom I have befriended; after Paganini, I've heard nothing like it – he takes 96 notes *staccato* in a single stroke, etc. incredible), and at his place the idea occurred to me, upon returning home, of longing over the piano and lamenting the *adagio* to the *Variations* on a theme of Beethoven that we are writing together... (KS i: 161–162).

Sometimes, longing augured spiritual lethargy. It prepared Chopin for metamorphosing into a 'living corpse' (KS i: 184). He must have tormented his friends with attacks of longing, since Stefan Witwicki, writing from Warsaw on 6 July 1831, decided to reprimand him.

> Yet it is to be wished that in future you might remember, dear friend, that you left not to pine, but to hone your art and become a source of consolement and glory for your family and your country. I make bold as to send you this counsel with the permission of your honourable mother. Verily, in order to work to good effect, one must have a free mind, not longing and not worrying (KS i: 180).

Witwicki did not understand that longing could appear unexpectedly, uninvited and accursed; that historical circumstances could nourish it to splendid effect; that it was a secret of particularly sensitive artistic natures that feel existence in a very intense way. In such cases, longing is brought about by anything – the colour of the sunset, the singing of a bird at dawn, the smell of cut grass. 'The Wodzińskis are expecting you here', wrote Chopin from Paris to Tytus Woyciechowski on 12 December 1831, 'I would like you only occasionally, as I fair go mad with longing, especially when it rains' (KS i: 203). It appeared most often in moments of disquiet, when he felt ill and began to fear for his health. Towards the end of his earthly journey, he sincerely loathed it. 'I cannot end this letter,' he confessed to Wojciech Grzymała in July 1848, 'so frayed are my nerves; I am suffering from some stupid longing and despite all my resignation I don't know, but am anxious, what I shall do with myself' (KS ii: 253). He called everything that irritated him 'stupid'.[292] The spiritual chaos that arose during his second stay in Vienna was a 'stupid madness' (KS i: 163). Thus also the longing that appeared in moments of breakdown eventually became stupid. Occasionally, he was doubtless just a step away from a stupid life. Even creative genius does not protect an artist from the dwindling of the sense of existence.

So longing drags a mind into a state of uncertainty, bordering on a fear of the absurdity of existence. Worry, meanwhile, bids us think of the havoc wrought in a person's consciousness by 'painful things'. In worry, one's 'I' begins to gnaw away at itself. The Polish word 'zgryzota' is related to the verb 'gryźć się, zagryzać się', and it means to torment oneself with misery. Zgryzota encloses one's awareness within a circle of cares,

---

[292] Thus there was 'stupid news' (KGS i: 202), his own style could be 'stupid' (KGS i: 223–224), and he himself became increasingly 'stupid' (KGS i: 231–232).

from which it is difficult to extricate oneself. At such times, an *anima aerumnarum plena* collapses beneath the weight of a defeat that is endlessly experienced. The above-mentioned Antoni Malczewski suggested that such *zgryzota* is inherent to human existence. It is true that many Romantics linked it to a specific situation in life, such as exile. Here is Lambro, the hero of a Greek epic poem by Juliusz Słowacki:

—

> Kto on? do tureckiego podobny derwisza;
> Owe siedem lichtarzy jest to siedem grodów,
> Stoi śród siedmiu złotem nalanych narodów
> Wygnaniec. – A włos czarny w siwość mu zamienia
> Nie wiek, ale zgryzota…[293]
> (Who he? resembling a Turkish dervish;
> Those seven candlesticks are seven cities,
> He stands amid seven nations steeped in gold
> The exile. – And his black hair is turning grey
> Not from age, but worry…)

—

Chopin called his experiences connected with the unfulfilled betrothal to Maria Wodzińska the pinnacle of his worries. As we know, his hopes for a steadfast love and stability in his life met with complete failure, bordering on humiliation. At the same time, Julian Fontana also had troubles with his fiancée, whom he left behind in France. That was a misfortune of a different kind, but its effects were very similar, since the two friends found themselves in the same situation: without a wife. Both were filled with bitterness. Yet their matrimonial plans should not be identified with an ordinary marriage. Had they made a home, then the cosmic axis would have passed through their nest. Marriage would have allowed them to sit beneath the Tree of Life. It was an attempt to inscribe themselves in the

---

[293] Słowacki, *Dzieła wszystkie*, ii:109.

order of the world. Its failure drove Fontana to frustration. He started to fret. When fretting reaches the heart, turning life into a hopeless dwelling on one's misfortune, then we say that such a person becomes soured or embittered. Fontana must have poured out his troubles to Chopin, who had clearly stopped worrying about it. Hence the wise reproach: 'Don't sour: the pinnacle of your worries, like the pinnacle of mine, must have passed. We've got over 30 years. Your miss Młokosiewicz, so my sister writes (who asked after her), suffered some misfortune. She fell ill. Some said that it was a swelling of the liver, dropsy; but they pumped out the water or whatever it was, and she's as healthy, thin and shapely as before. No one knows the truth. Our Nowakowski, who was to travel here, is in Warsaw. Content. Some young lady from the Governesses' Institute fell in love with him and he lost his place at the Institute. Remember that he's *bald* and a far greater *oaf* than us, and he's still making conquests! It augurs well for us' (KS ii: 41). And indeed, Chopin did make something of a conquest. Mrs Sand appeared, and on very insecure foundations he began to build his quasi-home and that curious quasi-marriage. Perhaps because he knew that fretting can destroy a man.

The word 'żal' appears in Chopin's letters, as far as I am aware, just once. However, there is documented evidence that he used this word to define the feeling that 'underlay his heart', and so set the tone for his entire existence. This testimony comes from Ferenc Liszt, and so we will consider it with due attention.

The brilliant Jerzy Popiel asserts that only one tenth of the Hungarian composer's book about his Polish friend was written or actually dictated by its author. The other nine tenths were produced by Princess Caroline Sayn-Wittgenstein, née Iwanowska, who for some time ruled his affections. Her overwrought and exalted verbosity irritated even indulgent readers of the Romantic era. Sainte-Beuve tellingly wriggled out of editing it.[294] I myself have found some interesting outpourings shaped by a Romantic mythology of language, but that is an entirely different matter. In general, she did indeed drivel on quite awfully, but when she began to discuss at length the content of Polish words (Liszt, after all, was not equipped to do so), she showed remarkable perspicacity. I would not underestimate her. After all, none other than Charles Baudelaire regarded it as a charming book.[295]

The fact transmitted by Liszt is beyond question. And here is his description. 'Once after dinner, we were but three. Chopin had played for quite some time; one of the most distinguished ladies of Paris [Princess Caroline perhaps?] felt herself increasingly overcome by pious contemplation, similar to that which would seize a startled traveller at the sight of the gravestones that litter those fields of Turkey, the shade and flower-beds of which promise from afar a joyful garden. She asked him whence the involuntary respect that bade his heart bow down before monuments whose appearance presented to the eye merely objects graceful and sweet. What name would he give to the extraordinary sentiment that he placed in his compositions, like unknown ashes in superb urns of finely wrought alabaster… Vanquished by the beautiful tears that moistened such beautiful eyelids, with a sincerity rare in this artist so touchy about anything concerning the intimate relics that he buried in the brillant shrines of his works, he replied that her heart had not deceived her in its melancholy sadness, since regardless of any fleeting moments of good cheer, he could never rid himself of a feeling that formed, in a way, the ground of his heart, for which he could find an expression in his own language alone, since no other possessed

---

[294] Jerzy Popiel, Foreword to Franz [Ferenc] Liszt, *Fryderyk Chopin* (Cracow, 1960).

[295] Charles Baudelaire, *L'Œuvre et la vie de Delacroix*, in *Œuvres complètes* (Paris, 1954), 872.

an equivalent for the Polish word *Żal*! And indeed, he repeated it frequently, as if his ear was avid for that sound which for him contained the gamut of feelings that are produced by an intense complaint, from repentance to hate, the blessed or poisoned fruits of that bitter root.'[296]

Indeed, the sound of that word creates an almost magical impression. Moreover, the consonant 'ż'[297] is an exceptionally aggressive and piercing sound. When it appears between vowels, it sounds like a voice from the depths of a summer meadow. 'I wish you, dear mother', wrote Juliusz Słowacki on 18 December 1834 – 'a good year. And who knows? *może* [perhaps]?... that odd word *może* has the magical sound of Aeolus' harp. Even the slightest breeze plays this word *może* on our thoughts, and always only może... This word must have existed before the creation of the world'.[298] The word 'żal' must have arisen after the first parents were banished from paradise. Its charm lies in the fact that while it is short, like the striking of a key, it ends with a lateral approximant that sounds a little longer, only slightly muffled by a dark tone. Consequently, it does not fade straight away, even when it is set deep within a sentence, among other words. The final 'l' means that it lasts a moment longer, especially after the lovely open 'a'. This word inevitably sends us spinning. In it, we hear the murmur that sounds between being and nothingness. That is precisely how a depressed piano pedal lengthens the sound of the string that has been struck by a hard hammer. There are words that 'belong' to the violin or the oboe. 'Żal' is a word of the piano. And that most probably explains why Chopin repeated it aloud several times. Perhaps he liked a sound that does not want to die.

---

[296] Liszt, *F. Chopin*, 23–24.
[297] Spoken as in the French name 'Jacques'.
[298] *Korespondencja Juliusza Słowackiego*, i:275.

The after-dinner conversation that Liszt noted down proceeded in French. This means that for a long time, Chopin, when speaking, was thinking in the language of Victor Hugo. This process continued unhindered until Chopin was faced with the need to describe the 'feeling that formed, in a way, the ground of his heart'. At that moment, the French language proved inadequate. The Polish word 'żal' invaded his thoughts. It matters little who came up with the French expression 'le sol de coeur', Chopin himself, Liszt or Princess Sayn-Wittgenstein, since we know for certain that it was used in respect to the feeling that nourished his heart, and so – as he saw it himself – the deepest essence of his 'I', constitutive of his identity.

Liszt understandably asked him at once what the word meant. And Chopin gave him an answer. It was very matter-of-fact, although, crucially, Princess Caroline may have added her pennyworth. But it cannot be excluded that the text relates the opinion of our composer, who was singularly aware of the weight of Polish words.

> *Żal!* A curious substantive, of a curious diversity and an even more curious philosophy! Susceptible of different grammatical forms, it embraces all the shades of tenderness and humility of a resigned and murmurless regret, as long as its direct object applies to facts and to things. Bending softly, so to speak, to the law of a providential fate, it can then be translated as 'inconsolable regret following an irrevocable loss'. But, as soon as it concerns a person, and its object becomes indirect, in modifying a preposition that directs it towards him or her, it changes its aspect and no longer has any synonym in either the group of Latin idioms or in that of Germanic idioms. – Whilst of a more elevated, more noble, broader sentiment than the word 'grief', it nevertheless signifies the ferment of rancour, the revolt of reproach,

the premeditation of vengeance and the implacable menace
that rumbles deep in the heart, espying revenge or imbibing
a sterile bitterness![299]

So it is a word denoting both contrition and the threat of
protest, breast-beating and waxing rancour. In *żal* one might cry,
but out of *żal* one can plot one's revenge. In it, one can reconcile
oneself to a deserved defeat, but it can also give rise to anger
over an unmerited insult or injury. A person immersed in *żal* can
fairly judge a transgression against himself. And that is exactly
what Chopin once did: 'When I consider myself, I feel *żal* that
somehow awareness often leaves me' (KS i: 142). But at the
same time, out of *żal* one can also be indignant at the unjust
behaviour of another. We arouse *żal* in ourselves for our own
deeds, but we have *żal* at someone else for his or her actions.
This word is linked to the fundamental relationship of one's 'I'
to oneself and to another. In *żal*, resignation allows one to come
to terms with humiliation; out of *żal*, resentment can bring about
conflict. *Żal* splits a person. It sets him at a crossroads between
noble resignation and treacherous anger. One is not surprised,
therefore, that in Linde's dictionary this word signifies 'pain
of the mind' or 'pain of the heart'. In seeking to give a precise
description of its remarkable content, Linde defined the word
żal by means of the familiar Latin noun *aerumna*.

During the times of the Duchy of Warsaw, somewhere
around the year 1808, a few years before Fryderyk's birth,
within the circle of sentimental novelists centred on the salon
of Princess Maria Wirtemberg, a great literary game of synonym
writing was commenced; it actually lasted quite a long time, up
to the beginning of Chopin's youth. It arose out of a solicitude
for the Polish language, threatened by the administrations of
the partitioning powers. Hence, the writing of synonyms be-

---

[299] Liszt, *F. Chopin*, 24–25.

came fashionable, and even – as Alina Aleksandrowicz writes – something of a patriotic duty. Ludwik Kropiński, author of the famous novel *Julia and Adolph* (*Julia i Adolf*) (1824), defined the word 'żal' at that time as follows: 'Żal arises out of a great loss, especially of persons dear to us... In the first instance, the thunderbolt of distress that strikes the heart freezes all man's faculties. At that moment, the voice of friendship becomes impotent, the voice of pity unbearable, and they both even augment still further the streams of bitter tears'.[300] There is no question here of the ambiguity that allowed resignation to be linked in *żal* to rage, and made it possible to move from despairing calm to unpredictable fury, or to cover fury with calm. From Liszt's account, we learn that Chopin had drifted far from a sentimental understanding of this word.

The tone of Chopin's life arose amidst a fixed set of worries. And this tone determined the character of his talent. On the well-known portrait painted by Eugène Delacroix, it still emanates today through the matt white gleam that envelops our composer's face. And were someone to ask me what we really see on that face lost in thought, I would answer that we see the source of Chopin's music: the *aerumna* of his existence.

[300] Alina Aleksandrowicz (ed.), *Z kręgu Marii Wirtemberskiej* [From the circle of Maria Wirtemberg], anthology (Warsaw, 1978), i:219. See Aleksandrowicz's discussion and comments on pp. 36–53.

4. MUSIC AND EXISTENCE

I hope we still remember that in the period of the November Rising, during his second stay in Vienna, Chopin was dogged by the idea of the uselessness of music. At that time, his art, which in the face of a Pole's moral obligations had proved to be redundant, in respect to the problems engendered by man's historical existence seemed to him to be powerless. *Cur musica?* What is the point of music, if it cannot help a person in times of danger? And here, eight years later, in March 1839, during his sojourn in Marseilles, or actually near Marseilles, where he was restoring his health, so strained on Majorca,[301] he received from Julian Fontana a letter in which the sender, after describing some personal problems, clearly asked him for advice, or at the very least for a response. Judging by Chopin's reply, the matter most probably concerned Poland. Perhaps Fontana was beset by such grave doubts as frequently knock us off our feet, when the Polish question sticks hopelessly in some deadlock and there is no prospect of an imminent solution. In any case, Chopin, without addressing his friend's mysterious anguish in any exact way, informed him briefly and to the point that he would not abandon him in loneliness and hopelessness.

'To your sincere and genuine letter,' he wrote on 7 March 1839, 'you have a reply in the second Polonaise...' (KS i: 337). That was the Polonaise in C minor from opus 40, the whole of which Chopin dedicated to Fontana.

---

[301] On the circumstances surrounding this sojourn, see Franciszek Ziejka, 'Chopin w Marsylii' [Chopin in Marseilles], in *Studia polsko-prowansalskie* [Polish-provençal studies] (Wrocław, 1977), 47–63.

In this little note, Chopin defined the essence of his own musical aesthetic, since it gives rise to the unequivocal conclusion that music, or at least the music of Chopin, is a non-verbal judgment of existence, a wordless wisdom, an answer to man's spiritual dramas. So it is apparently not useless after all. Yet Chopin could be utterly ruthless in respect to himself and his art. His cruel sobriety was often quite frightful. This most crucial statement was followed in the letter by a sort of excuse, Chopin asking Fontana's forgiveness for sending him in response only music, only a work composed by himself. This explanation conceals the idea that in transferring human existential dramas into the domain of music, an artist can do little to help his fellow man:

> … it is not my fault that I resemble that mushroom-like fungus that poisons you when you pull it out of the ground and taste it, mistaking it for something else – I know that I've never been any use to anyone – but also of little use to myself (KS i: 337).

Whence this dreadful self-accusation: ostensibly useful, but essentially injurious? Whence that cruel comparison of himself to a poisonous mushroom?

The Romantics – as we read in Carl Dahlhaus – moved away from sentimental descriptions of instrumental music as 'language of the heart': 'there was a tendency […] to reinterpret the tangible affects as ephemeral, abstract feelings divorced from the world.'[302] No psychological specifics. Only 'abstract internals', as Hegel would have put it. A 'tonal generality' as P. F. Strawson would have said. A 'notionless feeling', which – incidentally – so irritated Ferenc Liszt. As Stefan Münch writes, 'E. T. A. Hoffmann and the young Wagner admitted

---

[302] Dahlhaus, 'Absolute Music as an Esthetic Paradigm', in *The Idea of Absolute Music*, tr. Roger Lustig (Chicago, 1989), 6.

that the emotionality with which music is replete is abstract in two senses: freed from any connection with reality and at the same time supra-individual, just like joy or sadness. Instrumental music was filled not with the composer's private passions, but with symbols of feelings. A. W. Schlegel called this the "rejection of mortal shells". In music without words, a person separates himself from the objective reality of specific feelings and desires, in order to immerse himself in ineffable yearning (Hoffmann)'.[303] While Chopin was still alive, such musical abstraction was treated like an 'inexpressible longing' for cognition of 'the metaphysical essence of the world', although – it should be stressed – such a conviction only became common in the second half of the nineteenth century. One way or another, music is always – as Henri Michaux termed it – 'an endless ascent into abstraction'.[304]

Chopin's assertion that he himself, as both a man and a musician, had 'never been any use to anyone' cannot be interpreted unambiguously. It would appear, however, that this utterance exudes a regret that music, transferring man's existential drama into the realm of suprahistorical aesthetic abstraction, in

---

[303] Stefan Münch, 'Raj utracony i odnaleziony. Rzecz o poglądach romantyków niemieckich na muzykę' [Paradise lost and found. Of the German Romantics' views on music], in *Annales Universitatis Mariae Curie-Skłodowska* (Lublin, 1984), 179. He was writing about a complete break with notions derived from direct sensory perception. In this respect, as A. N. Whitehead states, music is preceded only by mathematics (*Science and the Modern World* (1926; London, 1938), 32).

[304] Henri Michaux, 'Zjawisko zwane muzyką' [The phenomenon called music], *Res Facta*, 2 (1968), 33. See also another significant utterance: 'The destruction of notions in order to create, with unlimited freedom, their new shadows, modifications and nonentities, the freedom to create or not, is a privilege. Some arts avail themselves of it. Among them is music. Its functions are different to the functions of a practical code, to a natural language'. Krystyna Pisarkowa, 'Muzyka jako język' [Music as language], in *Zeszyty Naukowe Uniwersytetu Jagiellońskiego, Prace językoznawcze*, 97 (Cracow, 1988), 38.

a concrete situation becomes quite simply useless. I am only a musician. Everything I could offer you is poisoned, although it may outwardly look like consolement. Don't eat the fruits of my talent. They are poisonous. I can respond to your difficulties in life with my music, but it will be of no use to you whatsoever. Contrary to the Romantic aesthetic, Chopin did not treat music as an initiation in metaphysical secrets. Such speculation was clearly alien to him. Chopin was of the Earth. Music was the 'speech' of man, useless perhaps, and even 'toxic', but the 'speech' of man.

So he was horrified that it was a useless symbolic system; that it was powerless against the 'essential occupations' resulting from interpersonal relations. The Romantics generally considered it a sort of contemplation, which – in the language of Aldous Huxley – allowed man to knock a door in the Wall of Perception. Had Chopin adopted that viewpoint, he would have added at once that it was contemplation which – even if it did enable one to see into the essence of phenomena – was not able to illuminate us in the matters imposed upon us by matter and body, history and existence, neighbours and homeland. German Romantics sought in music a mystic 'is-ness', *Istigkeit*. Chopin wanted it to 'speak' about the world of everyday experience. To use the beautiful words of Master Eckhart, whom the German Romantics so frequently quoted, one might say that Chopin would have preferred a musician to descend from Seventh Heaven and not barge his way into Plato's Really Existing Reality, but give a cup of water to his misfortunate brother. Be it only to one Julian Fontana. And that does not mean at all that Chopin ceased to be a Romantic. Quite simply, he was a Polish Romantic.

During the sojourn in Marseilles, the problem of real, concrete usefulness continued to trouble Chopin. In Paris, Wojciech Grzymała had just fallen ill. 'How I would nurse you!' Chopin

261

wrote to him on 12 April 1839, '[…] I've never been of any use to you, but now perhaps I could be capable of nursing you' (KS i: 345). The problem of the usefulness of music must have continued to bother him, since in another letter to Julian Fontana, after arriving in Nohant, we find a completely different and surprising solution.

On 20 October 1841, Chopin, who was still in Nohant, had just finished one of his astonishing works, the Fantasy in F minor, Op. 49. So he threw down his pen and went to the window. Or perhaps he remained at his desk and looked at the window. All at once he saw the sky, which always made a great impression on him (KS i: 327, 329). He described this moment to Fontana: 'Today I completed the Fantasy – and the sky is beautiful, there's a sadness in my heart…' (KS ii: 45). So he had the feeling of completing a task he had set himself. He was dazzled by the beauty of the world. But in spite of that, instead of joy he felt sadness. Thus he heard the fixed note that accompanied his life, all the more intense in that it was strengthened by a typically Romantic reaction to the beauty of the cosmos. Such an irrational descent into sadness, brought about by an epiphany of the beauty of nature, has been characteristic of many artists, but the Romantics experienced it with particular intensity. Almost in ecstasy. In October 1836, Juliusz Słowacki stood at the side of a ship heading for Alexandria. Beyond the watery abyss, the sun was setting.

—

Smutno mi Boże! – Dla mnie na zachodzie
Rozlałeś tęczę blasków promienistą:
Przede mną gasisz w lazurowej wodzie
    Gwiazdę ognistą…
Choć mi tak niebo Ty złocisz i morze,
    Smutno mi Boże![305]

---

[305] Słowacki, *Dzieła wszystkie*, v:182.

(Lord, I am sad! – For me in the west
You have spread forth a radiant, glittering rainbow:
Before me You extinguish in the azure blue water
    A fiery star…
Although You so gild me the sky and the sea,
    Lord, I am sad!)

—

With Chopin, something similar occurred, except that the sky he beheld extended above the trees of the park that surrounded the property of the remarkable Mrs Sand. We can only speculate on the character of Chopin's sadness, but let us just remember that in those days poets described sadness in a most exact and matter-of-fact way. Already in his early youth, Juliusz Słowacki had known an identical sadness, which probably meant that this was an insistently monotonous feeling. He also knew that sadness can engender hatred and bring an overpowering indifference down upon a man. From what we have learned from Chopin, it would be very similar to *żal*. This indifference can at times be so great that in sadness even eternity ceases to be of significance. Moreover, in sadness the mind can lose all orientation. Zygmunt Krasiński, meanwhile, was of the opinion that the temporal character of human existence made sadness an indispensable companion of our earthly journey.[306]

It is not surprising, therefore, that when, on 20 October 1841, this unusual feeling fell upon him, Chopin also pondered the sense of his life. 'Today I completed the Fantasy – and the sky is beautiful, there's a sadness in my heart – but that matters not. If it were otherwise, perhaps my existence would be of no use to anyone' (KS ii: 45).

In the eighteenth century, the word 'egzystencja' in Poland meant primarily everyday life. By the time of the Duchy of War-

---

[306] Krasiński, *Czas* [Time], in *Dzieła literackie*, i:98.

saw, in the journalism of the day, it equated to 'existence'.[307] Maurycy Mochnacki sometimes understood it to mean simply 'life': 'The means of existence interest me not in the slightest…' he wrote to his parents from Auxerre on 6 November 1834.[308] Sometimes, he used it to mean not so much everyday life as the very phenomenon of existence. 'For us, external things do not exist; we know nothing about them until we become convinced that they are. We become convinced of the existence of external objects only through science, or by grasping reason in the mind, that is, through reasoning'. Or this: '…an entire nation that acknowledged itself in only its own, indivisible existence would be like a fortified monad, closed on all sides…'[309] Similarly, Walenty Zwierkowski in his translation of Joachim Lelewel's French study *Korona polska…* [The Polish crown…] (1840): the madmen 'who render their love and attachment for their homeland by calumniating the institutions which were the mainstays of the existence of Poland, which, although they engendered misfortune, were nevertheless the source of the nation's greatness and glory…'[310] So for Chopin, the verb 'egzystować' meant to exist (KR 146), and the word 'egzystencja' denoted the endurance of existence from its coming into being to its annihilation.

'[…] there's a sadness in my heart – but that matters not. If it were otherwise, perhaps my existence would be of no use

<hr>

[307] e.g. Adam Kazimierz Czartoryski, *Myśli o pismach polskich* [Thoughts on Polish letters] (Vilnius, 1801; actually 1810), 159; Hugo Kołłątaj, *Uwagi nad teraźniejszym położeniem…* [Remarks on the current situation…] (Leipzig, 1808), 180; Wawrzyniec Surowiecki, *Korespondencja w materii…* [Correspondence on the subject of…]. See Józef Ujejski, *Dzieje polskiego mesjanizmu* [The history of Polish messianism] (Lviv, 1931), 113.

[308] Mochnacki, *Dzieła*, i:266.

[309] Mochnacki, *O literaturze polskiej w wieku dziewiętnastym* [On Polish literature in the nineteenth century], ed. Ziemowit Skibiński (Łódź, 1985), 79, 75.

[310] Joachim Lelewel, *Korona polska i jej królewskość* [The Polish crown and its majesty], tr. Walenty Zwierkowski (Paris, 1840), 105.

to anyone'. So on 20 October 1841, Chopin understood that his existence had a sense and was useful, although for the joy of usefulness he had to pay with a continual immersion in 'painful things', in the sadness from which he could not be freed even by the beauty of the world, since the condition of his talent were the *aerumna* of existence.

Mrs Sand, who for many years observed Chopin with a penetrating eye worthy of a great psychoanalyst, had an exceptionally accurate understanding of her friend. That concerns not just her woman's judgments of the composer's character. Those two minds analysed one another quite exactly and... reached the same conclusion: that an artist's talent is dependent upon the way he experiences the world. Were it not for the sadness, irritation and depression – so Sand asserted – that now and then extinguished the 'cheerful and quite robust ideas' that erupted in Chopin, his genius would not have risen to such dizzying heights and his piano would not have spoken in 'the language of infinity'.[311] The worries and cares of life were the form-generative power of his talent. 'Whenever he feels a little strength in himself', she wrote to Charlotte Marliani on 24 July 1839, 'he is cheerful, but when he is overcome by melancholy, he hurls himself at the piano and composes beautiful pages' (KGS ii: 44).

So on 20 October 1841, Chopin finally grasped the conditions of his talent, and he finally filled in the gulf between art and life that he himself had dug in the years of national misfortune. Just two years previously, he had been unhappy with the status of an artist, because he considered that his music could offer nothing to a person who had trouble with existence other than worthless appearances and poisonous beauty. Now he had arrived at the conclusion that the musical works he created 'spoke' about the anxieties triggered by existence and were thereby use-

---

[311] Sand, *Story of My Life*, 1092.

ful, in the simplest sense of the word. His music, although not verbal information, helps to solve man's existential problems.

In some sense, this was an unusual view, since the Romantic theorists had already managed to lead music beyond existence. In the eighteenth century, its source was still a person, who addressed it to another person, although there were already voices asserting that it was actually a presentiment of eternity and of the 'distant realm of the spirit'.[312] During the Romantic era, instrumental music became a symbol of eternal harmony and paradisiacal existence, an anamnesis of the pre-existence of the soul, a reminder of original chastity and happiness, a heavenly element and a bearer of subconscious feelings that had nothing earthly about them. It was treated as a reflection of the order of the spirit world. It cleansed the soul of its 'earthly dust', giving it a foretaste of paradise.[313] And suddenly there appeared an artist, more romantic than the Romantics, who for several years tortured his mind with the terrifying thought that in earthly matters music could do little to help anyone. A hard-working artist, tormented by life, who shut music back up within our four-dimensional cage, in our human space-time, having pulled it from the 'paradisiacal space', brought it from the domain of the soul's pre-existence into the earthly existence of a corporeal and historical human being.

---

[312] Dahlhaus, 'Karl Philipp Moritz i problem estetyki muzycznej klasycyzmu', in *Idea muzyki absolutnej*, 303–304; Ger. orig. 'Karl Philipp Moritz und das Problem einer klassischen Musikästhetik', in Friedrich Mielke (ed.), *Kaleidoskop. Festschrift für Fritz Baumgart zum 75. Geburtstag* (Berlin, 1977).

[313] Münch, 'Raj utracony i odnaleziony', 175–176, 180–181, 185–186.

5. PHILOSOPHICAL SCHERZANDO

Having stated that it was to his sorrows that he owed the meaning of his life, Chopin immediately wrote a very curious and mysterious sentence, suddenly suggesting to Julian Fontana: 'Let's hide ourselves away till after death' (KS ii: 45–46). In the meantime, then, there must have been a flash of an unwritten thought of the artist's immortality. The call to Fontana was clearly a periphrasis of that thought. It was written down in an unusual way and consequently gives rise to many questions. Why did Chopin begin to think of himself and Fontana together? Why are the two of them to hide? From whom? Where? What does that original phrase, again so beautifully couched in Polish, mean? How does one fathom the deep meaning of that sentence?

This sudden sense of togetherness with Fontana appears to attest not so much a surge of friendly feeling as concern for the fortunes of an artist. In life, nothing good lay in store for either Chopin or Fontana. They had to hide themselves, or rather their existence, beyond life. The question therefore arises: where? In Polish, the preposition 'na' that Chopin attaches to the verb 'schować', 'to hide', may concern a place: 'schować się na strychu', 'to hide in the attic'. But it can also concern a time: 'schowajmy się na kilka dni', 'let's hide for a few days'; or 'schowaliśmy się na jakiś czas', 'we hid for a while'. Chopin is probably speaking of a hideaway in time, considering death to be primarily a temporal phenomenon. So the two artists should hide their existence in posthumous time. Today, the deep meaning of the sentence 'Let's hide ourselves away till after death' reads 'Let's aspire to immortality'. The human lifetime is filled with anguish and suffering, but an artist finds consolement in art, which enables him to break the law of the destruction of being. He can enter immortality in time. And that is probably what Chopin meant by 'till after death'. In Słowacki-speak, this was an '*outre-tombe* brightening of his fate'.[314]

And immediately after this admission, Chopin allowed himself a joke at the thinker Pierre Leroux, a well-known philosopher of romanticism. He was a utopian socialist, highly productive and sought-after, particularly during the 1840s. He exuded a specific kind of religiosity. He linked his faith in progress to the idea of a new Kingdom of God on Earth. His programme for social reform also posited the need to work on the redemption of one's soul. He began, of course, by proclaiming a fight for the universal emancipation of humanity from poverty and humiliation, and ended with almost theosophic religiosity, so nebulous that he was dubbed a propagator of faith in metempsychosis.

George Sand quite soon became an advocate of his ideas. On this occasion, her fascination bordered on exaltation. Essentially, she saw him as a prophet. She wrote a number of novels under the sway of his views, proclaiming the equality of the classes, solidarity of the wronged and the right to happiness for all. She studied his greatest work, *De l'Humanité* (1840). 'I did not feel particularly enlightened', she would later recall in *Story of My Life*, 'when [Pierre Leroux] spoke to us about the "ownership of tools", a problem he was then turning over in his mind, which he has since elucidated in his writings. His philosophical language was too arcane for me, and I did not comprehend the wider implications of the words; but the logic of Providence appeared to me in his reasoning, and that was a great deal; it was a groundwork laid in the field

---

[314] *Korespondencja Juliusza Słowackiego*, ii:13.

of my inquiry.'[315] Heinrich Heine, whom one cannot but love, considered that Leroux's ideas had muddled Mrs Sand's head, and he may well have been right.

It is understandable that in such circumstances the philosopher became an acquaintance of Chopin, who in his native tongue called him Rudy [Ginger], as indeed did Zygmunt Krasiński.[316] He met him occasionally in Paris or Nohant, when this luminary travelled to the country home of his adorer and promoter. Chopin must have been familiar with his views on immortality, but that is hardly surprising. The philosopher's books and articles lay on the coffee table in Mrs Sand's salon. Moreover, the writer herself may have given him a brief exposition of the socialist's 'system'. He could have drawn this knowledge from her novels. Ultimately, Mrs Sand dreamed that Leroux's ideas might, through Adam Mickiewicz and Izydor Sobański, reach the Polish Tovianists[317]. Apparently, Chopin was 'full of unusual fervour' for this project (KGS ii: 90), but this is hard to believe, knowing his views on that religious sect.[318]

In order to understand Chopin's joke, let us first acquaint ourselves with Leroux's ideas regarding immortality. Above individuals, he placed humanity, in continual forward progress. This was the first transcendence of every person. In this abstract value, imagined by the mind, human beings participate in a necessary way. Every person, just like every generation, is necessarily a link in the great chain called humanity. A person is just a part of that 'extended beingness'. In the potential state,

---

[315] Sand, *Story of My Life*, 1050.

[316] See letter to Wojciech Grzymała of the summer of 1843 (KS II: 81). Zygmunt Krasiński, *Listy do Cieszkowskiego…* [Letters to Cieszkowski…], ed. Zbigniew Sudolski (Warsaw, 1988), i:105.

[317] Followers of the messianic ideas of Andrzej Towiański, linked to the political situation at that time (tr.).

[318] Or perhaps because Chopin held a high opinion of Sobański's mind (KS ii: 36). Izydor Sobański, together with Mickiewicz, was one of Towiański's first adherents.

this beingness is inhabited by an ideal entity, humanity – something that scholastic philosophers once called the substantial form of man, which is absolutely perfect and immortal. In this conception, death enables a person to pass from the state of potentiality into the state of true reality. 'We gravitate spiritually to God through the intermediary of humanity', wrote Leroux in *De l'Humanité*.[319] Thus individual existence turned out to be a link in a chain leading to God, the ultimate Transcendence. For Leroux, man, while ceasing to be – as in the popular metaphor – a cog in the machine of the world, revolving without any great purpose, nevertheless became part of a chain forged by death, which, endlessly growing, like some cosmic snake, slithered towards God, concealed in eternity. Thus was progress, a continual surging forward, deified. The present became inferior to the future. The constantly extending chain of Humanity became Man's immortality. Father Alexis, from George Sand's novel *Spiridion*, called this idea immortality on Earth, *l'immortalité sur la terre*. Sand summarised it in a letter to Marie-Sophie Leroyer de Chantepie of 28 August 1842:

> I believe in eternal life, in eternal humanity, in eternal progress, and since in this respect I have embraced the beliefs of Pierre Leroux, I refer you to his philosophical utterances. I do not know if they will satisfy you, but I have nothing better to offer. As for me, they have resolved all my doubts and become the cornerstone of my religious knowledge.[320]

So nothing but Eternal Progress awaited man on this and the other side of the grave.

---

[319] Pierre Leroux, *De l'Humanité, de son principe et de son avenir* (Paris, 1840), i:95.
[320] Sand, *Correspondance*, ed. Georges Lubin (Paris, 1969), v:757.

The chief reproach of the Polish Romantics, who read Leroux most attentively, was that his idea of immortality blurred man's personal identity. Nowadays, learned historians assert that Leroux had nothing in common with metempsychosis. However, Zygmunt Krasiński considered that he was essentially promoting teaching on the migration of souls. 'Leroux bases his reasoning on that', he wrote to Delfina Potocka from Rome on 18 January 1843, 'and is content, demonstrating that if, at birth, we remembered our past lives, then we would not have sufficient freedom in our minds to live again; we would be like old men who do nothing but recall; we would not be eternally youthful! For him, eternal youth is *to forget and go on*; that is what true life involves! [...] Leroux errs in that – unable to prove that in our future fortunes, after death, there is a moment in which, having accomplished the whole of our human nature, we awaken and recall our entire past – he prefers to demonstrate that the maintaining of our "I" and its constant immortality in ever higher epochs does not need memory as a principle'.[321] Juliusz Słowacki, in turn, hit at the mechanical character of the idea of progress, devoid of specific spiritual content. He criticised Leroux for linking man's immortality to his incessant communication with his fellow creatures, instead of showing that it is the soul's communication with the spirit of God. For this reason, according to Słowacki, that forging of a chain of humanity could not lead to any goal. Leroux's humanity was not at all able to perfect itself. His God was an insubstantial vapour, and so this progress without the King Spirit became meaningless and merely ostensible. '[...] he should first have shown that the soul [is] immortal – that it is creative – that it is justly rewarded – and then from this source, without any argument, *l'humanité perfectible* would burst forth as a neces-

---

[321] Krasiński, *Listy do Delfiny Potockiej*, i:689–690.

sary occurrence – that humanity which Leroux lays down as his cornerstone.'[322]

Polish poets reached for successive works by Leroux with the reverence due to a celebrated philosopher, and so they wrestled with his idea of immortality as with a false revelation. Chopin clearly avoided all speculation on critical questions and the improvement of the world. Here are his comments on Louis Jean-Baptiste de Tourreuil, a promoter of fusionism, a mishmash – as Georges Lubin writes in his commentary to Chopin's letter of 25 November 1846 – 'of the ideas of the Saint-Simonians, the theories of Pierre Leroux, a smidgeon of evangelical communism and a grain of mild madness'. The previous day, on Tuesday evening, Chopin turned up at the home of Mrs Marliani, who was just leaving in the company of three gentlemen 'to listen to the new prophet'. As he subsequently wrote to George Sand:

> I do not know the name of that prophet (not an *apostle*).
> – His new religion is fusionism – it was *revealed* to the prophet in Meudon Forest, where the Lord God appeared to him. The happiest thing is that in some eternity or other there will be no sexes. This idea was not overly to the liking of Mrs de Montaran, but the Captain [Casimir Stanislas d'Arpentigny, one of those three gentlemen] is *in favour* and whenever the baroness pokes fun at his *fusionism*, he accuses her of being *tipsy* (KGS i: 165).

He treated Pierre Leroux, whom Mrs Sand held to be a prophet and apostle in one, with a similar pinch of salt. He knew his mundane foibles: the philosopher was fond of joining in the rumours that were scandalising his circle of friends (KS ii: 81). Yet Leroux often aroused Chopin's interest. Here is

---

[322] Słowacki, *Dzieła wszystkie*, xv:456.

what he wrote to the Jędrzejewiczes from Nohant at the beginning of August 1845:

There were a dozen or so familiar faces here, including Ler[oux], of whom Ludwika was enquiring. At present, he is here some 8 miles away in Boussac, a village where there is also a sous-prefecture, like in Salliatre, in the depart. de la Creuse. A very old village, with an ancient chateau on the Creuse. There are druid stones nearby; the surrounding area is known for its beauty. He is a chartered printer there, and prints a daily newspaper edited in the town here which is called 'Èclaireur'. However, that printing press does not yet employ his new *procédé* [most probably a reference to a form of cooperative endorsed by Leroux – Krystyna Kobylańska], because, as everyone has their *but*, so it is a characteristic of his that he starts, but does not entirely finish. Once he's cast forth some grand idea, that suffices him. The same with that new machine, which he has not finished, or which he's not sufficiently completed. It *works*, but not precisely enough. It has already cost him and his close friends (including, in particular, the owner of Mr Koko [George Sand]) tens of thousands: he would need as much again, besides the desire, and especially the perseverance, and all that together at this moment in time is unlikely. However, the thing exists, and he will soon take to it as an *exploiteur* [user], arm himself with someone else's pens and show it to the world. There have already been, and still are, those who wish to purchase an invention that he does not want. Besides the two volumes on Hum[anité], there are plenty of his articles in the *Encyclopedia* and the *Revue*, where *Consuelo* is published. Everything he's written is coherent. In the *Revue*, there are several very valuable

273

discourses, not finished. This was all on the table on the Square d'Orléans (KR 146).[323]

All of this explains, to my mind, why, on the margins of a thought about the immortality of artists, there suddenly appeared a joke about Leroux's doctrines on the transfiguration of the human being into a link in the eternal chain of humanity, so heatedly discussed in Mrs Sand's salon: thus Chopin enjoined Fontana, 'Let's hide ourselves away till after death', adding 'NB, not in Leroux's sense – since then the younger one kills oneself, the more one is right' (KS ii: 45–46).

The actual content of the jibe is comprehensible. Chopin considered that the idea of immortality promulgated by Leroux was tantamount to inciting people to commit suicide. The sooner a person passes through death's door, the sounder is their judgment. It is worth remembering that youthful despair is something different to the speculation of a professional prophet. We have difficulty in understanding, meanwhile, why he ascribed this reasoning to Pierre Leroux. It should rather have been attributed to Father Alexis from Mrs Sand's novel *Spiridion*, who portrayed existence beyond the grave as a real life in a better world, *dans un monde meilleur*, offered to a person for his services rendered during his sojourn in this vale of tears. But who would wish to attack a platitude issued forth by ingenuous catechists? If I have understood the texts well, Leroux did not promote life beyond the grave at the cost of sublunar existence. As George Sand rightly noted, Leroux's idea of immortality was rather directed against 'materialistic philosophy', which the idea of death transformed into something quite absurd. He was suggesting to

---

[323] In Krystyna Kobylańska's edition, we have the following version: 'Besides the two volumes about hidr. [?]…' (KR 146). Sydow guessed that he was referring here to Leroux's fundamental work *De l'Humanité* (KS ii: 513). This inference seems correct, since the philosopher's work was indeed published in two volumes, both in 1840 and in 1845. Hence the signalled emendation.

educated people, *aux hommes illustres*, an idea of immortality filled with some spiritual and enlightened content. But perhaps Chopin noticed that, for Leroux, eternal progress, put forward as an absolute value, rendered our earthly time so futile that one might indeed long for a rapid transmogrification into a link in the chain of humanity. Perhaps he fathomed that Leroux treated death as emancipation from one's 'I', which is associated, after all, with nothing but suffering; that the movement of eternal progress, like every utopia, offered man the transfiguration of his miserable existence into an existence without misfortune. That is why he presented his idea of immortality as a race to death. And in order to reassure Fontana, who might have thought he was thinking of suicide, he threw him a characteristically Chopinian trifle: 'Take from this no bad thoughts; I'm off to dine' (KS ii: 46).

The pan had been struck, and the residents of the manor at Nohant began to descend for the main meal of the day. However, before taking his seat at the table, Chopin jotted down a few thoughts, from which one may infer that on 20 October 1841 he grasped the conditions of his talent and understood wherein lay the sense of his existence. Life filled with 'painful things' proved to be the source of the creative work that led him to eternity in time. He stated this as if in passing, with the clarity that his music emanates even in the moments of its most frenzied raptures. For such is the sense of musical beauty: to suppress the terrors of existence with the wisdom of melody and harmony. One does not always know how, but one always knows why.

6. Musical thought

In January of that same year, 1841, there took place between Chopin, Delacroix and George Sand a conversation which the writer noted down 'live', so to speak.

> Chopin speaks little and seldom about his art; but when he does, it is with a wonderful clarity, a soundness of judgment and of intent that could annihilate quite a few heresies were he to speak his mind openly. But even in private he is reserved, and only at the piano does he really open his heart. Still, he has promised to write a *method* in which he will deal not only with technique, but also with theory. Will he keep his word?[324]

He did not, although he tried. He left us some sketched remarks with a 'piano method' in mind. These were most probably sketches for a piano playing 'school'. In those times, handbooks of this sort were often called *Méthode des méthodes*. In 1837, the music scholar and critic François-Joseph Fétis published a *Méthode des méthodes de piano*. Three years later, together with Ignaz Moscheles, he issued a *Méthode des méthodes des pianistes*.[325] For the purposes of that work, Chopin wrote a few etudes. On 16 June that year, he placed a fragment of one of

---

[324] Sand, *Impressions et souvenirs* (1873; Paris, 1896), 88; quoted in Eigeldinger, *Chopin: pianist and teacher*, 4.

[325] On piano-playing schools in Chopin's day, see Irena Poniatowska, 'Artykulacja jako środek'.

these, in F minor, in the album of Jean-Pierre Dantan, and on 8 December in the album of Jenny Vény.[326]

The date of the writing of the above-mentioned sketches, occupying a dozen sheets or so, has not been established, but with a clear conscience one may state that the text arose in the wake of the conversation that Mrs Sand related, although it cannot be excluded that some things may already have been written. On sheet 11, there are about a dozen sentences with the character of aesthetic opinions. They cannot be overlooked in the present essay, since they concern the relations between music and human existence. In general, they are isolated sentences, and not always clear. Although the theories, ordered and formulated in an exhaustive way, are on the whole even more vague, in spite of everything I descend into that abyss not without a certain trepidation. For these are mysterious matters.

In romanticism, there existed at least two viewpoints on the relations obtaining between the word and pure sound. Even the most unreceptive man of letters would not be ashamed by the views of Wagner. At first glance – he asserted – the history of music appears to confirm the aptness of the Christian notion – as he put it – that music begins where the word proves powerless. But – he added – that is untrue. It is contradicted by Beethoven's Ninth Symphony, which proves the opposite, namely that where music proves powerless, the word appears. So the word is of greater worth than pure sound.[327] The Romantics were aware, of course, that music could not compete with the notional concreteness of words. Hence Wagner's view that the word was more important than the sound. They also knew

---

[326] Kobylańska, *Diariusz z lat 1836–1849* [Diary from the years 1836–1849] (KGS i: 55, 57). In the year 1841, Dantan produced a bust of Chopin from plaster and bronze, cast by Susse, whose warehouse was located on the Place de la Bourse. See KS ii: 21.

[327] Richard Wagner, *Nachgelassene Schriften und Dichtungen* (Leipzig, 1895), 135.

that the weakness of the word, in turn, resided in its inability to convey the emotional richness and subtlety of man's experiences. Hence Liszt valued the sound above the word. 'After the mighty and delectable shocks caused by other arts,' he enquired rhetorically, 'do words not always appear to us withered and poor, cold and arid?' Thus he concurred with 'a certain writer' (George Sand) who, although her pen 'described many things, painted many things, sculpted many things and sang softly about many things', often repeated: 'Of all the ways of expressing the world, the most perfect is the word'.[328]

Chopin did pass judgment on particular works and artists, but he did not judge an artist's tools. He defined their function or described their status. And his judgment on the relations between the word and the sound was of just such a character; written on the eleventh sheet of his notes for a piano-playing school, it simply stated that the sound existed before the word. This judgment confirmed the general conviction that in the beginning was sound, from which speech then emerged:

—

La parole naquît du son – le son avant la parole.[329]

(Word is born of sound – sound before word.)

—

---

[328] Liszt, *Gesammelte Schriften* (Leipzig, 1881–1896), i:168.

[329] Alfred Cortot published fragments of this text in his book *Aspects de Chopin* (Paris, 1950). A fuller text was published by Zygmunt Mycielski in the article 'Rękopis "Metody" Chopina' [The manuscript of Chopin's 'method'], *Ruch Muzyczny*, 1968/1). Here, we find 'sentences added at the side on the same page (11), omitted by Cortot'. (See '"Metoda" Chopina' [Chopin's 'method'], *Ruch Muzyczny*, 1968/12). I quote from Mycielski's publication, in which sheet 11 (Feuillet 11) appears as str. V. Through the efforts of Mycielski, a photocopy of the original found its way into the Biblioteka Towarzystwa im. Fryderyka Chopina in Warsaw, and manuscript access to this photocopy is possible with the permission of the current owner, Robert Owen Lehman. Since I am unable to move, Edward Boniecki agreed to check Chopin's original, which – so he states – is by no means as faded and unclear as hitherto believed. Admittedly, a photocopy always sharpens the image of a text.

Chopin elevated neither of the elements. When speaking of the origins of the word, he pointed out that it was also a sound, since it was born of sound.

Understandably, a sound in a word has a peculiar character.

—

La parole certaine modification du son.
(Word [:] a certain modification of sound.)

—

Since, for Chopin, pure sound was an 'indefinite word', then – we are entitled to infer – in articulated speech, the word was wholly and precisely defined. Linked to its sound was its meaning. The eminent Romantic-era linguist and language philosopher Wilhelm von Humboldt asserted that, regardless of whether we are dealing with a symbolic or an onomatopoeic way of signifying, the sound of a word in articulated speech does not arise as a result of actual physical or physiological processes. In this case, the crucial factor is spiritual activity aiming to express in a given sound some idea, and so verbal speech arises as a result of the soul constraining the organs of speech.[330] It is an expression of awareness, which reveals itself this time in the form of meaning. 'Thus', as Roman Jakobson writes, 'in approaching speech sounds we must take into account the fact that they are cardinally different from all other audible phenomena'.[331] So for Chopin, the basic element of articulated speech was meaning harnessed to a specific sound; that is, a definite word. This is speculation, but it is reliably documented by the content of the next sentence from sheet 11.

I am sincerely grateful to him for that, as it allowed me to establish the actual wording of the sentence 'L'expression de nos perceptions par les sons'. The word 'l'expression' was written by Chopin above the deleted word 'l'explication'. (The English translations given here are from Eigeldinger, *Chopin pianist and teacher*, 195 (tr.))

[330] Bolesław Andrzejewski, *Wilhelm von Humboldt* (Warsaw, 1989), 171.
[331] Roman Jakobson, 'Verbal Communication', in *Selected Writings*, vii (Berlin, 1985), 86.

Human awareness may manifest itself in sounds that are not burdened with meaning, that mean nothing, although they constitute a message full of content and sense. In a letter of 18 May 1833, describing to his father the dying moments of his younger brother, Kamil, Maurycy Mochnacki concludes: 'In writing this, I express the whole sum of my worries and convey in words that which perhaps only weeping could better express…'[332] Chopin called a sound which, eluding verbal signs, conveys information about the state of someone's awareness, an indefinite word. This could have been weeping, but it could also have been a sound produced by a musical instrument.

—

La parole indéfinie (indéterminée?) de l'homme, c'est le son.
(The indefinite (indeterminate) language [parole] of men is sound.)

—

So, for him, music was speech that employed indefinite words, or sounds not burdened with meaning. It is, therefore, non-verbal communication; if, that is, we reserve the term 'verbal' for words in articulated speech. Hence, on that same sheet 11 we find also the following opinion:

—

On se sert des sons – pour faire de la musique,
comme on se sert des paroles pour faire un langage.
(One uses sounds to make music
just as we use words to make a language.)

—

Man has several kinds of language at his command, and Chopin knew that there exists – for example – the language of gestures. After all, he was an occasional actor. At home and on the stage. In moments when he felt that words were insufficient or unnecessary, he offered a hug. 'I understand

---

[332] Mochnacki, *Dzieła*, i: 210.

you', he wrote to Tytus Woyciechowski, 'I penetrate your soul and… let us embrace, as nothing more can be said' (KS i: 143). Many people feel that verbal speech is at times not enough. As we read in Zbigniew Herbert's poem 'Podróż' [Journey], 'Odkryj znikomość mowy, królewską mocą gestu' (Discover the insignificance of speech, the regal power of gesture). 'Conceptual metaphorical speech is indeed adequate to the activity of thinking, the operations of our mind,' wrote Hannah Arendt, 'but the life of our soul in its very intensity is much more adequately expressed in a glance, a sound, a gesture, than in speech.'[333] Many people are convinced that various aspects of the life of our soul are better and more properly expressed in music than in notional speech. As Michał Bristiger states, however, language 'influenced "musical thinking", and the way the essence of language is understood must surely have played an important role in attempts to define the character of music. […] Over the course of historical evolution, music now came closer to language, now moved further away from it; in the moments of proximity, it turned out that it shared not all, admittedly, but some of its laws with language'.[334]

Thus during the Romantic era, music was treated as a certain kind of speech, doubtless with regard to the very possibility of aural communication between people. This is because speaking is a concrete and personal phenomenon, whereas language is an abstract and social product. It was widely written that this was the 'speech of the heart', which meant non-verbal communication, making contact without words, from heart to heart. For Robert Schumann, this was the most suitable way for people to communicate with each other,

---

[333] Zbigniew Herbert, *Elegia na odejście* [Elegy on leaving] (Paris, 1990), 24. Hanna Arendt, *The Life of the Mind* (New York, 1978), 31.
[334] Michał Bristiger, *Związki muzyki ze słowem. Z zagadnień analizy muzycznej* [The links between music and words. Of issues relating to musical analysis] (Cracow, 1989), 11.

since only thus did the human soul feel in its element.[335] For the Romantics, music was the expression of genuine spontaneity, not susceptible to the deficiencies of natural language. There was a widespread conviction that within that language, the mind was capable only of possessing opinions, and that every inexpressible idea consequently lies beyond its reach.[336] 'O lovers!' called Ludwik Tieck, 'never forget, when you would entrust a sentiment to words, to ask yourselves: what, after all, is there that can be said in words!'[337]

The Romantic era inherited its conviction of the affinity between music and speech from the theorists of the second half of the eighteenth century.[338] Everything suggests that Chopin had those ideas in his blood. Józef Elsner, his only teacher, wrote to him in a letter of 27 November 1831: 'Even the most excellent playing on an instrument, e.g. Paganini on the violin, Kalkbrenner on the piano [...] considered in itself, is merely a medium in the domain of music as the *speech of the emotions*' (KS i: 197; emphasis J. E.). Thus from an early age Chopin held music to be a phenomenon related to speaking. In a letter to Tytus Woyciechowski of 3 October 1829, we find the following passage:

> And how awful it is not to have someone to go to in the morning, to share with him your sorrows and joys; how abomi-

---

[335] Schumann, *On Music and Musicians*, 40; Ger. orig. *Gesammelte Schriften*, i:27.

[336] See Simone Weil: 'The mind which has learned to grasp thoughts which are inexpressible because of the number of relations they combine, although they are more rigorous and clearer than anything that can be expressed in the most precise language, such a mind has reached the point where it already dwells in truth.' From 'Human Personality', in *Simone Weil: An Anthology*, ed. Siân Miles (1986; New York, 2000), 69–70.

[337] Quoted in Alfred Einstein, *Music in the Romantic Era* (London, 1947), 21.

[338] Dahlhaus, 'Musical Logic and Speech Character', in *The Idea of Absolute Music*, 103–116.

nable, when something weighs, and there is nowhere to lay it
down. You know what I'm alluding to. I gab [*gadam*] to the
piano what I would have told you on occasion (KS i: 108).

In those days, the verb 'gadać' was not associated with
the vulgarity that we sense in its sound today. These days,
'gadulstwo' means a careless and even somewhat pathological
tongue-flapping. In Chopin's times, it meant simply to converse
or to speak. Mickiewicz began his evening conversation with
God thus: 'I gab with You, who reign in heaven…' Father Piotr
did the same in Part III of *Forefathers' Eve*.

—

Ale gdym Tobie moję nicość wyspowiadał,
Ja, proch, będę z Panem gadał.[339]
(Now that I have confessed to You my nothingness
I, dust, will gab with You.)

—

So instead of speaking to Tytus, Chopin 'spoke' to his
piano; that is, he created music. That is also how he 'spoke' to
Fontana in the Polonaise in C minor, Op. 40 No. 1. When he
spoke about the character of musical narrative, he used words
taken from the domain of verbal communication. 'I'm writing
here', he informed Julian Fontana on 8 August 1839, 'a Sonata
in *Si b mineur* […], a march and a little finale, perhaps about 3 of
my pages; the left hand gabs in unison with the right after the
march' (KS i: 353). He occasionally availed himself of rhetori-
cal terminology. Wilhelm von Lenz once played Chopin one of
Beethoven's piano sonatas. The master put his hand on Lenz's
shoulder and said: '[…] it is *fine*. But must one *always* speak
with so much passion?'[340] And Ignacy Krzyżanowski, during
his first audition, heard that: 'My music has its own distinctive

---

[339] Mickiewicz, *Dzieła*, i:255 and iii:189.
[340] Lenz, *Great Piano Virtuosos*, 57.

283

speech and mission'.[341] Hence it should be declared openly that the first-generation jazzmen who were convinced that the 'piano speaks' shared this view with Chopin.

Unsurprisingly, therefore, the sentences cast forth while sketching a preface to his piano-playing school included the following opinion:

—

La langue indéfinie de la musique.
(The indefinite language of music.)

—

Indefinite, because the sounds of which it consisted were 'indefinite words'. After all, the content of this speech cannot be expressed in the words of natural language. Today, we feel closer to the idea that music, as François-Bernard Mâche writes, 'is not the opposite of language, but a superlanguage'. It does not transmit to us 'this or that content, but – in cases where it reaches its peak – it [allows us] to participate in everything that is'.[342] The Romantics reasoned differently. Liszt opined that it was language 'that requires special work to comprehend'.[343] Thus he placed the emphasis on the fact that it served initiated specialists. For Chopin, meanwhile, music was non-verbal communication, speech without words, full of content and sense, although no meaning whatsoever could be associated with the sounds that form the essence of this 'indefinite speech'. The entries on sheet 11 show that Chopin by no means abandoned professional accents. Thus he wrote:

—

L'art se manifestant par les sons est appelé musique.
(The art that manifests itself through sounds is called music.)

—

[341] Michałowski, 'Nieznane wspomnienie', 206.
[342] François-Bernard Mâche, 'Muzyka a język' [Music and language], *Res Facta*, 2 (1967), 61.
[343] Liszt, *Gesammelte Schriften*, ii:140.

And a little further down, he gave another variant of the same idea:

—

L'art de manier les sons.
(The art of handling sounds.)

—

This brief definition is remarkably eloquent, since when an artist begins to treat his art like a craft, then he has clearly had enough of metaphysical speculation about it. He is tired of exalted and nebulous raptures. According to the dictionaries, 'manier' means 'prendre avec la main, se servir de'. In English, we say 'to use' or 'to handle'. A good ear will hear in this phrase a hint of impatience with the 'soulful' loquacity of the era, which saw music as resembling man's 'true' speech, the heavenly speech from before the tragedy of the Tower of Babel. To Chopin's mind, a musician was not a prophet from some extraterrestrial land. He was a craftsman. Wilhelm Wackenroder claimed that music was the language of pre-existential memory, 'which we do not know in this life, but learned without knowing where or how; it can be regarded, however, as the speech of angels'.[344] Ludwik Tieck considered it to be the 'vestibule of heaven', in which the soul shakes the earthly dust from itself. Chopin knew that music expresses only man, and only that which is in him on the Earth. Thus the composing of music consisted primarily of work and skill. Moreover, Chopin's definition is reminiscent of Malherbe's famous description, which also arose out of impatience with the Neoplatonic metaphysics of poetry and with poets' exalted utterances about 'divine madness'. 'You see, sir,' he told Racan, 'if our verse outlives us, at best it will be said of us that we are past masters in the arranging of syllables, that we have a great command of words, since we put them together

---

[344] Wilhelm H. Wackenroder, *Werke und Briefe*, ed. Friedrich von der Leyen (Jena, 1910), 168. Quoted in Münch, 'Raj utracony i odnaleziony', 185–186.

so accurately and aptly…'[345] Chopin was clearly of the opinion
that a musician should be able to arrange sounds, or 'indefinite
words', masterfully and appropriately. Hence he himself was
continually seeking the ideal shape for a work – a quest that
condemned him to torturous work on his score.

And finally Chopin sought to define the 'content' that
a composer transmits to us in the 'indefinite speech of music':

—

L'expression de nos perceptions par les sons.

(The expression of our perceptions through sounds.)

La manifestation de notre sentiment par les sons.

(The manifestation of our feelings through sounds.)

L'expression de la pensée par les sons.

(The expression of thought through sounds.)

—

These three sentences, as mysterious as they are explicit, can be treated in two ways. They may be three mutually
exclusive views, with the consequence that only one should
be attributed to Chopin. But one might also assume that each
of them expresses the composer's conviction, in which case
they would encapsulate, as it were, his aesthetic. The excellent
musicologist Mieczysław Tomaszewski has adopted the latter
standpoint: 'These notes, until recently disregarded, contain the
essence of Chopin's views on piano playing; the starting point is
his acknowledgement of music as speech expressing thoughts,
feelings and impressions, a speech that is undefined, but one in
which sounds are used as words'.[346] Other documents appear to

[345] Quoted in Philippe van Tieghem, *Główne doktryny literackie we Francji.
Od Plejady do surrealizmu*, tr. Maria Woczyńska and Ewa Maszewska (Warsaw, 1971), 21; Fr. orig. *Les grandes doctrines littéraires en France* (Paris,
1993). See also René Fromilhague, *Malherbe. Technique et création poétique*
(Paris, 1954), 133–134.
[346] Mieczysław Tomaszewski, 'Chopin' in *Encyklopedia Muzyczna*, vol. C-D
(Cracow, 1984), 180.

confirm this standpoint. And so given that music expresses our impressions, our feelings and our thoughts, it must be a non-verbal expression of man's earthly existence. It is neither the 'speech of angels' nor a reminiscence of our paradisiacal pre-existence, but testimony to our chthonic existence.

Although there was an awareness of the elusive nature of musical semantic factors, there were no doubts about the possibility of expressing in music the first two elements that Chopin listed on sheet 11 of his notes: impressions and feelings. The same did not apply to the question of the third element: thoughts. In this respect, opinions were, and remain, divided.

In general terms, there existed, and still exist today, two mutually exclusive standpoints. One of them posits that there is thought without verbal speech. The other proclaims that thought is wholly independent of verbal speech: the words of natural language are not the only medium of thoughts. Man has other ways of transmitting them, as well. In our times, one declared advocate of the former standpoint was the philosopher Maurice Merleau-Ponty.[347] According to Barbara Skarga, Merleau-Ponty referred to an old idea of Plato's, that thought is essentially only 'internal speech', taking place without a voice.[348] The opposite standpoint was adopted by Hannah Arendt. In her opinion, the life of the soul could not be reduced to that which a person is capable of expressing in the words of natural language. Thoughts contain more than speech. The inner

---

[347] Maurice Merleau-Ponty, 'Słowo i ciało jako ekspresja' [Word and body as expression], tr. Stanisław Cichowicz, in Merleau-Ponty *Proza świata. Eseje o mowie*, selection and introd. Stanisław Cichowicz, tr. Ewa Bieńkowska, Stanisław Cichowicz and Joanna Skoczylas (Warsaw, 1976), 85; Eng. tr. from Fr. as *The Prose of the World*, tr. John O'Neill (Evanston, 1973). See also P. F. Strawson, *Indywidua. Próba metafizyki opisowej*, tr. Bohdan Chwedeńczuk (Warsaw, 1980), 65; Eng. orig. *Individuals: An Essay in Descriptive Metaphysics* (London, 1959).

[348] Barbara Skarga, *Granice historyczności* [The boundaries of historicity] (Warsaw, 1989), 96.

life of the soul is expressed better by gestures and sounds.[349] Albert Einstein could therefore be invoked. Amused by the conviction of 'certain people' that 'their thinking is always in words', he wrote in a letter to the mathematician Jacques Hadamard: 'I very rarely think in words at all. A thought comes, and I may try to express it in words *afterward*'.[350] So for Einstein thoughts appeared before words and were completely independent of them.

The Romantics valued thought that was liberated from words. Hence in Chopin's day, the intellectual reduction of thought to verbal speech was simply out of the question. On 5 January 1811, Heinrich von Kleist wrote that a poet would be happiest if he could transmit thoughts themselves without words.[351] Adam Mickiewicz was not far from a similar view. It seemed, therefore, that the musician was in an excellent situation. Admittedly, when, in an impressive, but somewhat exalted, metaphysical frenzy, he began to claim that the 'last instance' of sense was 'that which went unsaid', both languages, verbal speech and musical speech – as we read in Carl Dahlhaus – proved powerless.

As Wilhelm Wackenroder wrote: 'Man is generally so proud to have been endowed with the ability to put a system in words and extend it, that he can set down in common speech those thoughts that seem finest and most daring to him. But... the greater man perceives only too well that his innermost thoughts are but a tool, that his reason and its conclusions are still dependent on the essence which is himself and which he

---

[349] Arendt, *Life of the Mind*, 31–34.
[350] Quoted in R. Jakobson, 'Einstein and the Science of Language', in Gerald Holton and Yehuda Elkana (eds.), *Albert Einstein. Historical and Cultural Perspectives. The Centennial Symposium in Jerusalem* (Princeton, 1982), 141.
[351] This admission made a great impression on Ludwig Wittgenstein, who was singularly aware of the limitations of language. See 'Uwagi różne' [Various remarks], tr. Feliks Przybylak, *Odra*, 1978/12, 55.

will never completely comprehend during this life. Is it therefore not irrelevant whether he thinks in instrumental sounds or in so-called thoughts?'[352]

Thinking in sounds, he could at least have the impression of approaching the essence: 'that which went unsaid'. However, when the actual work of art, treated as a sign, became more important than 'that which went unsaid', then the relationship between thought and the sound of a musical instrument took on slightly more distinctive forms. 'Some find it strange and foolish', wrote Friedrich Schlegel, 'when musicians speak of the thoughts in their compositions. [...] But whoever has a sense of the affinities among all the arts and sciences will at least not view the matter from the uninspired viewpoint of naturalness, according to which music is only supposed to be the language of feelings, and will not find a certain tendency of all pure instrumental music toward philosophy to be impossible of itself. Must not pure instrumental music itself create a text of its own?'[353] Carl Dahlhaus's comment on this was that Schlegel 'moved instrumental music from the sphere of the communal culture of sentiments to the exaltedness of an abstraction whose sense is derived from solitary esthetic contemplation'.[354] So when musical thought, and not 'that which went unsaid', became the 'last instance' of sense, the musical work – especially pure instrumental music – took on the character of aesthetic abstraction. The tonal raiment was exceptionally concrete, since musical structures were subject to almost mathematical laws; the effects on man were vast and penetrating, but musical thought remained elusive. Per-

---

[352] Wackenroder, *Werke und Briefe* (Heidelberg, 1967), 248. Quoted in Dahlhaus, *The Idea*, 106.
[353] Friedrich Schlegel, *Charakteristiken und Kritiken*, 1, in *Kritische Friedrich-Schlegel-Ausgabe*, ii, ed. Hans Eichner (Munich, 1967), 254. Quoted in Dahlhaus, 107.
[354] Dahlhaus, 107.

haps because, as Wilhelm von Humboldt wrote, without verbal language, our thoughts are by nature vague.[355] It is true that the Romantics valued music precisely for that elusiveness. On 26 January 1824, Eugène Delacroix wrote in his journal that music had nothing in common with verbalised thought, and 'hence it has the advantage over literature, through its vagueness'.[356] In the Romantic era, the vagueness of musical thought was far from a flaw, and so when Chopin wrote that music was 'the expression of thought through sounds', he was unwittingly praising an art form superior to poetry, in which – as Adam Mickiewicz wrote – ideas 'look out from words as if from prison bars'. Moreover, Mickiewicz had no doubt that sound, like colour, was an 'angel of thought'.[357] Chopin dwelt permanently in a mysterious cloud of non-verbal thought.

So 'musical thought' was a common term in that era, and Chopin was even accused of lacking it, when in 1834, during a sojourn in Germany, he appeared to Felix Mendelssohn to be an ordinary Parisian musical dandy, who had lost 'true musical thought'.[358] This judgment was both isolated and patently unjust, but it did reveal the fact that at the beginning of the thirties, musical thought was already a term used in value judgments. George Sand did not employ it in any other character. In her play *The Seven Strings of the Lyre*, one of the protagonists, Albertus, considered that music was incapable of conveying ideas, but eventually he too became convinced that the lyre, if it is 'magic', can govern the elements and 'governs also human thought'.[359] In her memoirs, she usually described Chopin's works as his

---

[355] Andrzejewski, *Wilhelm von Humboldt*, 159.

[356] Delacroix, entry of 26 January 1824, *Journal* (London, 2006), 24.

[357] Mickiewicz, *Dzieła*, i:340. This poem was not printed during the poet's lifetime.

[358] Quoted in Zamoyski, *Chopin*, 110.

[359] Sand, *Seven Strings*, 99 and 131.

musical ideas.[360] When he sat at the piano, he simply played his thoughts to his friends.

The conversation that took place in January 1841 clearly centred on the views expressed by Chopin in his notes for a piano school. As we will recall, besides the composer, the other participants were Eugène Delacroix, George Sand and her son Maurice. Towards the end of a lengthy and fascinating speech by the great painter, Chopin suddenly sat down at the piano. He did not notice that they were listening to him.

> He improvises as if haphazardly. He stops. 'Eh bien, eh bien', exclaims Delacroix, 'ce n'est pas fini!' 'It hasn't begun. Noth-ing's coming to me... nothing but reflections, shadows, reliefs that won't settle. I'm looking for the colour, but I can't even find the outline.'
> 'You won't find one without the other,' responds Delacroix, 'and you're going to find them both.'
> But if I find only the moonlight?'
> 'You'll have found the reflection of a reflection,' answers Maurice.
> This idea pleases the divine artist.[361]

This improvisation was music, but it contained no musical thought. By means of sounds, it expressed the impressions which all those present were attempting to verbalise in artistic terms. Chopin was rather fond of such improvisation. 'The Adagio from the new Concerto is in E major', he wrote on 15 May to Tytus Woyciechowski. 'It is not intended to be powerful, it is more romance-like, calm, melancholic, it should give the impression

---

[360] Sand, *Histoire de ma vie*, ed. Martine Reid (Paris, 2004), 1474, 1475; the collective translation edited by Jurgrau – the only full English translation of Sand's 'Life' – unfortunately fails to render this nuance (tr.).

[361] Sand, *Impressions et souvenirs*, 85–86. Quoted in Eigeldinger, *Chopin: pianist and teacher*, 282–283.

of a pleasant glance at a place where a thousand fond memories come to mind. – It is a kind of meditation on the beautiful springtime, yet to moonlight' (KS i: 125). Significantly, already during his Warsaw years, Chopin associated music with reflection, contemplation, thought. When Chopin sat at the piano on that January day in 1841, his improvisation slowly began to take shape. It prepared for the entry of a melody. George Sand expressed it in the following way:

> And then the note bleue resonates and there we are, in the azure of the transparent night. Light clouds take on all the forms of fantasy; they fill the sky; they crowd round the moon which casts upon them large opal discs, awakening their dormant colours. We dream of a summer night: we await the nightingale.
>
> A sublime melody arises.[362]

And only when the melody appeared did Sand realise that the musician was transforming music into a human matter.

> The master knows very well what he is doing. He laughs at those who claim to make beings and things speak by means of imitative harmony. This silliness is not for him. He knows that music is a human impression and human manifestation. It is a human mind that thinks, it is a human voice that expresses itself.[363]

George Sand had no illusions that the causes of human feelings could not be expressed through sounds. She also knew that 'the musical thoughts whose design stands out against the

---

[362] Ibid.

[363] Sand, *Impressions et souvenirs*, 86–87; quoted in Karol Berger, 'Chopin's Ballade Op. 23 and the revolution of the intellectuals', in John Rink and Jim Samson, *Chopin Studies 2* (1994; Cambridge, 2006), 78.

effects of harmony'[364] cannot be translated into any other language. Music is autonomous speech, which transports human thoughts into a realm of unlexicalisable abstraction, although like any language it possesses its own logic or rules for the expression of ideas. Here is how George Sand concluded her meditations on Chopin's improvisation:

> The beauty of musical language consists in taking hold of the heart or imagination, without being condemned to pedestrian reasoning. It maintains itself in an ideal sphere where the listener who is not musically educated still delights in the vagueness, while the musician savours this great logic that presides over the masters' magnificent issue of thought.[365]

While listening to Chopin, George Sand arrived at the opinion expressed in her friend's notes, that music was the expression of human impressions, feelings and thoughts.

The idea of musical thought ultimately resolved the antinomy between existence and musical abstraction. As we know, this contradiction tormented Chopin from the time of the Polish uprising against Russia that broke out on 29 November 1830. At the time the November Rising erupted, Chopin did not know that at J. Węcki's printing press in Warsaw, his friend Maurycy Mochnacki, one of the most wonderful minds in Polish culture, had presented a text that contained an explanation of why an artist, especially a Polish artist of the Romantic era, had to arrive at the conviction that music was 'the expression of thought through sounds'.

> Thought is the essence of our being: it bears our shadow, our likeness, our image. That shadow spreads out within us. In thought, we have the ground beneath our feet, and

---

[364] Ibid, 87; quoted in Berger, 78.
[365] Ibid, 88; quoted in Berger, 78.

within ourselves we have the expression of ourselves – that is like the central point of the entire sphere of our existence. Thought is like a limpid mirror: what you reveal will be revealed in it. Looking within, we see ourselves, we know ourselves, we become for ourselves an object of vision and like a thing apart. Until we approach this splitting, we do not have being. To be an object of vision for oneself is to think. To think is to live.[366]

History – particularly the rather black history of Poland – instilled in Chopin the conviction that music was powerless against the truly great affairs of man. However, the idea of musical thought enlightened him to the fact that, in spite of everything, it is not an unnecessary beauty. Music is not a poisonous mushroom, only seemingly edible, since it shows us the 'essence of our essence': thought. When sitting down at the piano, Chopin took possession of the central 'point of the sphere of our existence'. Thus he finally shed the complex of uselessness and arrived at an understanding of the human dimension of the art that he cultivated.

---

[366] Mochnacki, *O literaturze*, 57. Chopin most probably read this treatise, but in exile, of course.

Chapter IV

Black thoughts

The black thoughts invoked in a letter to Julian Fontana of 8 October 1839 descended upon Chopin very often, although – to imitate his moderation – it should be said that they occurred more often than rarely. They tormented him in particular during his successive bouts of illness, when his body gave him various anxious signs. And yet when your throat starts to bleed and a cough starts to choke you, then serious perils shift from the domain of foreboding to the domain of certainty. And in such moments, the thought of death fills your awareness entirely.

Before Chopin entered the trail of premortal blackness, he learned to come to terms with that terror during an abrupt bout of youthful melancholy. It was a valuable experience, but merely theoretical all the same. Later, his frequent illnesses made that dread of annihilation a very real issue. He was by nature a person who took up the fight against adversity and carefully concealed his breakdowns. 'Carry a bullet in your soul', he wrote to Fontana, 'and falter, but let no one see it on your face' (KS i: 233). So even if life has planted a bullet in your chest and you're barely alive, you must not betray yourself with your suffering. When he was writing this joke – *scherzando*, for it was, after all, a 'light little poem' –

—

Nieś w duszy nabój
I słabuj,
Ale z nosiwa
Niech tego nikt nie spostrzegiwa,

(Carry a bullet in your soul

And falter,

but let no one see it

on your face (lit. let no one notice it from your nose))

—

Chopin heard the well-known proverb that was at the same time also a musical metaphor: 'Spuścić nos na kwintę' (to make a long face; lit. to lower one's nose by a fifth). A person with a long face is clearly suffering. Chopin often joked about his own large hooter. His nose was too visible, beyond the decent norm, and became something palpably material, like objects that in Polish are designated by nouns with the suffix –iwo (genetive: –iwa). For the sake of the rhyme, he allowed himself an 'ungrammatical' form, such as Polish schoolchildren love having fun with. But that amusing form wrapped in 'discretion' a serious idea, a confession of faith that was clearly a motto of Chopin's. As we shall see, he expressed all his 'mottos' by means of a joke or a proverb.

So such a person never gave up fighting for himself and only submitted in a situation that was genuinely hopeless. In 1848, in London, when he was anxious that he might 'snuff it' somewhere in England (KS ii: 283), he continued to chase the darkest thoughts away: 'My soul is sad, but I'll shake myself out of it; I even avoid solitude, so as not to dwell, since one cannot be ill here for long...' (KS ii: 253). Moreover, he usually celebrated every victory over illness with a surge of hope, occasionally quite vociferous. 'I've already outlived so many people stronger and younger than me', he wrote to his family on the sad Christmas Eve of 1845, 'that I think I'm eternal' (KR 153). Yet his letters to trusted friends show that he actually lived constantly beneath a black cloud of agonal fear. I presume that one factor in this were his frequent attacks of nervousness, those 'neuralgic ailments' that George Sand so feared. When he lived with Jan

Matuszyński, who was in worse health than Chopin and indeed died earlier, the idea of death crawled into their dreams, which means only that it was continually stifled. In the night of 9/10 August 1841, he wrote to Fontana: '...today I bid you goodnight and may you not dream, like Jan [Matuszyński], that I have died, but may you dream that I'm being born, or something of the sort... [...] I once dreamed that I died in hospital, and it so stuck in my head that it seems to have been yesterday. If you outlive me, you'll find out whether one should believe in dreams or not; a few years ago, I dreamed something else, but it didn't come true. And now I daydream; *szałki-opałki*, as they say; that's why I write you such nonsense' (KS ii: 29).

Yet the conjuring away of dark thoughts by means of deprecating words, such as 'nonsense' and 'szałki-opałki', failed to help, because the memory of death turned Chopin's awareness into the poison of his life. Thus he arrived at the truth which made a Romantic of the artist. No illusions. Man's existence is tragic. That is why his life should be heroic. And irony should be a badge of heroism.

1. THE FACE OF GOD

On 27 October 1841, at Nohant, when preparations were under-
way for the return home to Paris, Chopin sent Julian Fontana
a letter that was literally bursting with instructions of a quite
peculiar nature. The matter at hand was to ready Mrs Sand's
apartment on rue Pigalle. The lady of the house had already
engaged the assistance of Lamartine's secretary, the journalist
and politician Eugène Pelletan, publisher of the daily *Le XIX*^{me}
siècle, who for a couple of months in 1837 had educated her
son, Maurice. With his help, but in such a way as not to cause
offence (God forbid!), Fontana was to escort her servant, Pierre
Moreau, out of the apartment, together with his wife, whom
George Sand could not abide. Admittedly, she was inclined to
keep him on for a couple of days to 'light the chimneys' and
'open the windows', but only 'without his wife'. Should he
decline that service, the porter, Mr Armand, and his other half
were to be asked.

These instructions exposed Fontana to nothing but un-
pleasantness. First, he had to deftly ensnare Pelletan. 'Speak
to him', wrote Chopin, 'about his *journal*, he is an honest and
learned man, and get on friendly terms with him and *don't get angry* with me, with *him*, with *yourself* or with anyone. As regards
the servant, keep them on their toes, but without constraining
anyone, because I don't know if he'll be pleased [...]. *En tout
cas* the arrival of the *porter*, good people and accommodating;
treat them *considerately* and give them to *understand* or better
still give them *in hand*, if they are to take care of the apartment,
and not Moreau' (KS ii: 47). So the problems were innumerable.

In the place of Fontana, I would have gone mad. And of the journalist, who had to be handled like a bad egg, and the servants, of whom one was offended and the other had to be bought in advance. It was all most complicated. And although Chopin had a great deal of faith in his friend's practical mind, he knew very well that he was burdening him with an exceptionally unpleasant task, which would undoubtedly entail some nervous decisions.

And at that very moment – after a dash, of course, marking a telling pause – he added by way of consolement, an adage: 'It'll be alright *somehow*. – my old saying' (KS ii: 47).

This declaration should be taken most seriously. Chopin was obviously not a philosopher, and in his letters, understandably, he did not philosophise, but that does not mean he had no opinions on the complex affairs of human life. An educated fool – of which there is no shortage in the human sciences in Europe – he left such problems as death, the meaning of life, the homeland and God to the great and famous thinkers, although, as we know, everyone has to struggle with them somehow. People talk of everything that preoccupies them, and wisdom, like the wind, passes wherever it will. Chopin, who liked a good aphorism and made plentiful use of them in his correspondence, occasionally spoke of existence by means of proverbs, and such an utterance – incidentally, rather uncommon – provides reliable information about his views.

Opinions greatly diverge regarding the functioning of proverbs in spoken language, and the language of Chopin's letters is written speech.[367] A proverb is generally seen as something like an approved quotation. It contains a certain wisdom,

---

[367] On this subject, see three studies in *Pamiętnik Literacki* 1978/4: Franz H. Mautner, 'Maksymy, sentencje, fragmenty, aforyzmy' [Maxims, dicta, fragments and aphorisms], tr. Małgorzata Łukasiewicz, 297–307; Algirdas Greimas, 'Przysłowia i porzekadła' [Proverbs and sayings], tr. Joanna Arnold, 309–314; Paul Zumthor, 'Przysłowie jako epifonem' [The proverb as epiphonema], tr. Joanna Arnold, 315–331.

which a community has acquired, formulated in such an apt and succinct way that everyone willingly employs it to express his own, at times very personal, thoughts. Polish noble culture had a soft spot for adages, particularly since they were popularised by the then numerous storytellers and much-liked calendars. We have all come across a 'rhyming' cab driver. In the Poland of old, one could meet a nobleman at virtually every manor house who uttered an endless flow of proverbs. Occasionally, this took a pathological form; thus Aleksander Fredro, a keen observer of life, furnished the titular character of his wonderful comedy *Pan Jowialski* [Mr Jovialson] with a carefree and cheerful mind, stuffed with nothing but sayings. The urban intelligentsia of Warsaw, which 'inherited' the noble culture, was wary of all its faults and whimsicalities, and so employed proverbs with moderation. Thus Chopin's father, who was a very conscientious man and tended to value acknowledged and universal wisdom, was rather partial to popular sayings. Chopin himself also employed them, but only when they expressed his own thoughts. In keeping with his inner injunction to 'discretion', that is, the principle of distance, above all in respect to himself, proverbs enabled him to conceal his own views behind a generally accepted cliché. That is the general view, and it is my view as well. It is a truth, but none too original. A proverb allowed him to make light of an issue. Thus it was, in some sense, one of his 'cloaks for secret feelings', to use his own wording – ideal, as usual (KS i: 125).

The classic form of the saying Chopin used to console Fontana reads: 'Somehow it'll be alright', and so he altered the order of the words, thereby emphasising the adverbial, which the addressee, the future author of works on Polish orthography, certainly noted and appreciated. The general opinion is that this is a typically Polish aphorism, which expresses on one hand our idiotic, but also admirably irrational, attachment to hope and on the other our astonishing insouciance, which, as life has taught

301

me, is by no means as inane as many rational authorities would have us believe. One must be well acquainted with despair in order to properly assess such life-giving recklessness. 'Dear, beloved Mama!' wrote Juliusz Słowacki just before Christmas 1834 [oh, those Polish Christmases!], 'just do not abandon me in your thoughts, for as things stand I am less lonely than many people, because I know that I possess something that people envy me – your attachment. When I think before falling asleep about my situation, sometimes my hair stands on end. Apart from my housekeepers, who are a great support, I have not a friend in the whole wide world. Somehow it will be alright…'[368]

As we learn from Chopin's letter, the saying 'somehow it'll be alright' was something of a life's motto for him. Meanwhile, he considered the 'greatest truth' about existence to be the opinion that human life itself is absurd and comical.

In the composer's family, the popular expression 'tere-fere', to some extent already proverbial, was often used. This comes from a wonderful rhyme undoubtedly derived from folk distichs, usually composed of two completely idiotic lines with nothing in common:

—

Tere-fere kuku
Strzela baba z łuku.
(Tweedle-deedle hallo
Woman shoots an arrow)

—

That woman could be Amor, fate or any old spiteful battleaxe. In any case, 'tere fere' signifies something completely meaningless, most often idle chatter or a frivolous trifle. Chopin's sister Ludwika erased a passage in a letter sent by Fryderyk to his family in which her illustrious brother wrote highly critically about an acquaintance he had just met in Paris. 'We

---

[368] *Korespondencja Juliusza Słowackiego*, i:275.

erased your postscript', she informed her brother in a letter of 27 November 1831, 'as soon as we had read it; the elders were itching to find out the secret, but to no avail. As I am no good at ex[cuses?], I admitted the erasure was my work and for what purpose. Mr Fred silly head, great big *terefere*'[369] (KR 81). But a variant of this expression was also used in the Chopin family, one that belonged rather to the family's own vernacular. On 8 May 1836, the same sister wrote to her brother, who wrote to his family too rarely and too briefly, the following comment: 'Our dear beloved Daddykins has written you a rhyme which will move you, I'm sure; but it's true that I have a good sense of how difficult it is for you be punctual, you would not believe, dearest Freddie, what sensations we get when… you know already, because I dare not bore you by writing out the word already repeated so often in our letters, to which, at times, and at this very moment, you might grimace or exhale with a stirring of your whole self an ah! more impatient than sentimental. It would not be *con fuoco*, but neither *con cuore*, and although *con anima*, I prefer sighing to us in another sense; long-winded *tere bzdere* that bores you in yet another way' (KR 113–114). In this variant, the writer had in mind something perhaps not so much absurd as simply frivolous, something banal, some item of news like 'queen Anne died'.

Well, at around the same time that he was confiding his life's motto to Fontana, on 25 September 1839, instructing him, incidentally, to furnish his own flat in Paris, Chopin wrote to him from Nohant: 'My life, my heart feels sometimes quite strange – may the L. God give what he needs. – But may he not be fleeced; though on the other hand… *tere bzdere kuku*. That is the greatest truth in the world!' (KS i: 357–358). It seems that, for Chopin, anyone who keeps in mind the absurdity and comicality of life will not allow himself to be fleeced by fate. He will not allow

---

[369] The letter 'e' pronounced, all four times, as in 'egg' (tr.).

himself to be cheated by the semblance of momentary stability in his life, since the idyllic life at Nohant will not necessarily last forever. Anyone who knows that our life on Earth is simply *tere bzdere kuku* will not lose sight of the truth that everything in it is only for now, for the time being.

So the adage 'somehow it'll be alright' corresponded to the idea of the frivolousness of 'everything' and defined Chopin's attitude to the past. So no concrete predictions. I don't know how it will be, but I believe that it won't be terrible and tragic. The future is indefinite, but probably not threatening. So in this instance 'somehow' means at least 'bearable'. Convinced that things would turn out alright, he was not so much trusting to fate as counting on its favour. This had nothing to do with hope, although Poles generally regard this as a proverb about hope. One way or another, Chopin was not yet admitting the thought of the cruelty of life. Let us remember this, as there will come a time when he ceases to count on its understanding.

Immediately after this declaration, Chopin reminded Fontana of another saying, admittedly not so popular, but which was clearly a striking 'cloak' for his 'hidden' views on existence: 'Moreover, time flees, the world passes, death pursues…' (KS ii: 47).

This aphorism was familiar in Europe, in various versions (at times startlingly different), from at least the Renaissance. Of course, I have no intention of tracing its history, since I am interested only in Chopin's thinking. It is enough to mention that it was based on a well-known ancient Roman saying about the constant flight of time. 'Sed fugit interea fugit irreparabile tempus' learned Chopin in one of his Latin lessons – like the rest of us, as it happens. This was a standard wise adage of the Renaissance. All the poetry of Lorenzo the Magnificent, a man typical of that era, impresses one with its continual variations on that theme.

—

Quant'é bella giovinezza,
Che si fugge tutta via!
Chi vuol esser lieto, sia:
Di doman non c'è certezza.[370]

—

Hence Pavel Muratov, when he came to write about the 'guiding idea' of Lorenzo's poetry, was able to cobble together a saying from similar fragments:

—

Il tempo non aspetta ma via fugge
Di doman non c'è certezza.[371]
(Time waits not, but hies away
And tomorrow is uncertain.)

—

Let us note that only two terms are mentioned here: time and tomorrow, that is, the future. Later, there appeared tripartite arrangements, which in the Romantic era enjoyed huge popularity, even among people who were unaware that they reflected an eternal truth: the Holy Trinity. Chopin clearly liked triads, but it is impossible to establish today whether he attached any importance to the symbolism of numbers. In a letter to Auguste Franchomme of 9 November 1846, he wrote: 'I'm working a little, deleting a lot. I'm coughing enough…' (KS ii: 177). This composition, as it is unquestionably a triadic structure, contains information about the three actions that filled Chopin's daily life at that time, with the degree of their intensity measured and specified: a little, enough, a lot.

The saying from the letter to Fontana also has a triadic structure. There are three sentences consisting of only a subject

---

[370] *Poesia italiana del Quatrocento*, ed. Carlo Oliva (Milan, 1978), 122.
[371] Paweł Muratow [Pavel Muratov], *Obrazy Włoch*, tr. Paweł Hertz (Warsaw, 1972), i:182; Eng. orig. *Images of Italy* (Berlin, 1924).

and a predicate. The geometrical form of this proverb is impeccable: three sentences, three nouns and three verbs. Each of the nouns is of one syllable, two verbs have two syllables each. In the Polish, if the first syllable can be considered an anacrusis, the phrase takes on an amphibrachic rhythm: 'czas ucieka, świat mija, śmierć goni'. The three nouns are at the same time, as Maurycy Mochnacki would have said, 'three chapters in the book of the self'. For Mochnacki, those were reality, dreams and death.[372] For Chopin, meanwhile, we have, in order, time, the world and death. The order of the 'chapters' is significant, since in the Romantic era this proverb generally appeared in a slightly different variant.

On 3 January 1852, Zygmunt Krasiński sent from Rome a letter to his good friend Stanisław Małachowski, who was at that time in Paris. 'Why are you idling so much time away in Babylon?' he asked peevishly. 'Why don't you go down to Marseilles and sail to Rome? Time scurries, the days fly by, eternity's at our heels: so hurry…'[373] Instead of the world, we have here only days, and instead of death, eternity. So for Krasiński, everything revolves around time. The measure of human existence here are days, and eternity – from my familiarity with this poet and thinker – is religious timelessness. Chopin's proverb, meanwhile, brings a picture of what happens in our three-dimensional cage. For there is time, the category of the perception of being; the world, in which human existence struggles; and death, which brings an end to the existence of every individual being.

The three verbs, meanwhile, create the impression of anxiety. Someone is pursuing someone, something is fleeing. And so existence is in motion, in which persecution pulsates. With Krasiński, the corresponding verbs do not make such a stir. Time

---

[372] Mochnacki, *O literaturze*, 44–45.
[373] Krasiński, *Listy do Stanisława Małachowskiego* [Letters to Stanisław Małachowski] (Warsaw, 1979), 303.

simply scurries, and the days just fly by. It looks like a game, as if boys were playing in a yard. But the set of verbs in Chopin's version transform motion into dramatic action. This is not playing. This is a serious and rather sombre spectacle.

Bearing all of this in mind, let us now consider, in order, the three clauses that make up that saying which was meant to make Fontana aware of how human existence really looks.

Time flees. In the Polish language, time is organised according to the metaphor 'time is a mobile object'. Perhaps we might not even have noticed that flight is always streaked with fear and anxiety were it not for the variant of this proverb written by Krasiński, for whom time simply scurries. To scurry is to leave a place quickly, but without drama. One scurries from someone who should be respected, but who is not hostile and threatening. One flees, meanwhile, from a persecutor, greater or lesser, malicious or bloodthirsty. And so from Chopin's saying, we learn first of all that time is persecuted and flees. We do not know whither, but most probably straight ahead. It cannot allow itself even the shortest rest. It cannot be conceived as immobile.

The world passes. In the middle of Krasiński's triad we have days that fly by. In Poland, days are said to fly by like pages from a calendar; monotonously and imperceptibly. This is essentially a complaint at the passing of life in a senseless grinding of the ordinary and the everyday. This time, therefore, we are dealing with the scurrying of empty time. Interestingly, we are still in the playground. 'Don't fly off!' ('Nie leć'), we shout to a boy who, at an order, hoofs it, as we say, without having heard why and to whom we are sending him. With Chopin, meanwhile, we are dealing not with days, but with the world, and so with everything that exists. Chopin's sentence resembles a variation on the theme of Saint Paul's famous *adagium*, 'For this world in its present form is passing away' (1 Cor. 7:31), which – as one commentator asserts – 'has not the least connection with the existence of the world and contains not the slightest eschatological-cal allusion, but all the cares, procedures, efforts and difficulties associated with human life'.[374] It would appear also that Chopin's saying is concerned not with the vanishing or dwindling of the cosmos, but with the passing of the things and events that make up the world of an individual person. The pleasant little things of my life and the grand sense of existence. Such an interpretation is supported by a later utterance from a letter to Wojciech Grzymała, written in Edinburgh on 30 October 1848: 'I barely still remember how they sing back home. This world is somehow passing me by, I forget myself, I have no strength…' (KS ii: 285). So again we have a triadic structure; again, the word 'somehow', attesting that Chopin's thoughts have become disorientated. And so when time fled him to somewhere unknown, the world passed him by in some unknown way.

Death pursues. We finally discover who is persecuting human time, who is the cause of that agitated motion which determines the substance of existence. In Krasiński's proverb, it is eternity in this place. This poet's views are quite well known, and so I can state with a clear conscience that he had in mind the Kingdom of God. Thus for Krasiński, human time is pursued by Transcendence, and our days fly by under the watchful eye of Providence. In Chopin's proverb, anxiety is aroused by death, an allegory of the end of every individual being. There is no transcendence. We live here, in ever-fleeing time. Death is constantly repelling from man the stream of things and events. Everything is in motion. Yet everything moves along behind man, although he is inclined to believe that everything still lies before him. Already in his youth, Chopin was no longer reckoning on the 'now' being realised in the future. '…why does it seem to man', he wrote to Tytus Woyciechowski on

---

[374] *Listy do Koryntian* [Letters to the Corinthians], introd. tr. and commentary by Eugeniusz Dąbrowski (Poznań, 1963), 203.

4 September 1830, 'that today will not come till tomorrow?' (KS i: 135). And he poked fun at such a stance, travestying the well-known proverb 'nadzieja matką głupich' ('stop kidding yourself'; lit. 'hope the mother of fools'). There is no 'is'. A fool is he who believes he'll find it in 'will be'. How similar he was in this to his friend Maurycy Mochnacki, who in that same year 1830 wrote:

> What hour, what minute or second should we consider a fixed point between those two poles of time, so to speak? Between the past and the future? – Is the present not illusion? Anyone who looks at it more closely will say: *there is no present time*.[375]

Pursued by death, time knocks life into the abyss of memory, which is like sleep. Chopin arrived at this truth as well very early.

A few years later, all these problems appeared before him in a somewhat different light.

He realised what a great difference there is between death and dying. Carl Gustav Jung, who followed the 'unconscious psychic activity' of people up to the 'immediate presence of death', stated that the unconscious appeared to be 'all the more interested in *how* one dies; that is, whether the attitude of consciousness is adjusted to dying or not.'[376] Whilst we have no information about Chopin's dream symbolism from that period, it emerges from his letters that for him dying began long before his actual death. He clearly worked on his 'attitude to dying'. We know that it is possible to 'somehow' reconcile oneself to death, but it is harder to live through the process of dying,

---

[375] Mochnacki, *O literaturze*, 42–43.
[376] Jung, 'The Soul and Death', in *Psychology and the Occult* (1977; Abingdon, 2008), 157–158.

especially if it is drawn out. Time, forever fleeing, drags beings into nothingness, but only at a certain point along the way does a person realise where God allows him to wander to. It is at just such a moment that the true face of God is revealed.

In the autumn of 1848, after travelling around England and Scotland, Chopin returned to London, where he became very seriously, and irreversibly, ill. The state of his health was alarming. Katharine Erskine, Jane Stirling's sister, began to prepare him for his final journey, consoling him with a vision of life in a 'different, better world', and so – according to the views of Zygmunt Krasiński – in Transcendence. The allusion to his impending demise was all too obvious, and only her deep Christian religiosity, which regards existence as a doleful sojourn in a land of exile, justifies her lack of tact. Chopin understood this and treated her rather benignly. 'M[rs] Erskine', he wrote on 18 October 1848 to Wojciech Grzymała, 'who is a very sincere, religious Protestant woman, perhaps wants to turn me into a Protestant – as she brings me the Bible and speaks about the soul – writes out psalms for me – religious, kind-hearted, but she's concerned more with my soul – she's always gabbing that the other world is better than this – and I know it all by heart and reply with quotations from the Holy Scripture, and explain that I know it and know about it' (KS ii: 287).

Of course he knew. We all know that this world is fit only for the devil to inhabit, and that in the other world one leads a blissful life. And what of it? Chopin would have had to have yearned with all his soul for Heavenly Jerusalem in order to master his fear while dying. He would have had to have stopped loving the material world for religious longing to be able to conquer his anguish in dying. This longing was clearly not there, since a great anxiety crept into his soul.

Two days earlier, on 16 November, 'rigged up' – as he put it himself – by Dr Mallan, a homoeopath, he performed in a benefit concert for Polish exiles. This was a grand gesture, but most probably wholly unnecessary. It brought only a great deal of bitterness. He played in a small room at the Old Council Chamber, from where 'noises of the dance band' could be heard. Members of the audience kept coming and going, many of them had come to dance, and not to listen to the playing of a pianist, even one as famous as Chopin.[377] It is difficult to say whether he played before innocent simplicity or the patriotic boorishness in which some Poles have always excelled. In any case, he did not complain. He noted that the 'Polish ball' was splendid, but added in the above-cited letter to Grzymała that 'straight after playing, on returning home, I couldn't sleep all night. My head is aching a great deal, besides the coughing and asthma' (KS ii: 286). He fell into apathy. The idea of the meaninglessness of existence, typical of people aware that they are dying, reared its head. He began to give Grzymała some instructions, but added at once: 'What for, why I'm bothering you with all this I don't know – since I don't want a thing' (KS ii: 287). Of course, the return to his Paris home felt like salvation, but then he immediately exclaimed: 'But what am I coming back for?'

And it was after this thought, still lacking a rejoinder after a century and a half, that he wrote something which attested that he had now seen the true face of God: 'Why does the Lord God', he neither asked nor asserted, 'not kill me straight away, but so piecemeal and through a fever of indecision' (KS ii: 287).

So Chopin's God suffered from irresolution. Instead of issuing a forthright sentence and sending him to his death, he appeared to have no clear opinion on the matter and allowed him to die slowly. He threw him into a cell to die without setting a date for his execution. He was unable, or unwilling, to deal the

---

[377] Maria Gordon-Smith and George R. Marek, *Chopin* (London, 1979), 213–214.

final blow, the *coup de grâce*. Perhaps he was cruel? Or perhaps he really was muddled by a fever of indecision.

When the nation was in agony, God appeared to Chopin in Stuttgart as a Russian with a knout in his hand. When Chopin himself began to die, he came to him in London as a devious brute. Each time, he manifested himself as a merciless Executor of the law, not so much stern as inscrutable in his rulings. This was certainly not the kind-hearted Father of Polish Catholicism, which likes to conceal Him behind the Mother's ample skirts. It was the God of those Polish Romantics who, in frenzied and beautiful flight, left our provincial narrow-mindedness behind.

On seeing the face of his God once again, Chopin understood that he could no longer count on the forbearance of fate. The future, in which – as we know – he never trusted, had previously been, in spite of everything, unthreatening, although even then he had no illusions that existence was anything other than death's plundered spoils. In any case, in 1841 the future was not yet pregnant with an irrevocable sentence. Something will turn up, and somehow it'll be alright. On returning from the British Isles, a month before his death, in a letter written on 17 September 1849 to Auguste Franchomme, still counting on surviving the approaching winter, but drowsy from enfeeblement, Chopin concluded his account, written in such a way that his friend not gain the impression that this was now a 'deathly sickness', in the following words: 'Cela ira comme voudra' (KS ii: 460).

And so no longer 'somehow it'll be alright' (*ça ira*), but 'it'll be as it will'. So what is fated will occur. No more counting on fate's good grace. The future stood before him like the God of the Old Testament. I'll be as I will be. And the three 'chapters of the Book of the self' took on a different character. Time hastened its flight, the world dissolved in morbid weariness, and death stood at the piano – pitiless, like all God's messengers.

2. The 'Living Corpse' of Music

People who hear the world often speak of life in musical terms. So musical metaphors are nothing rare. In Romantic times, when music was believed to be a primary principle of being, they were particularly readily used. But in those times even the laws of the cosmos were heard. Today, unfortunately, everything tends to be seen. Words are also seen instead of being heard, for which God, knowing Him, before he destroys this world, will pluck out our eyes by means of computers and televisions.

In April 1833, Maurycy Mochnacki was taking his younger brother to the south of France, as he wanted to extend his life by at least a few months. The state of the tubercular Kamil's health was grave, as the condemned man was well aware. 'What are you talking about?' he asked his brother. 'Can I not feel the disorder in my breast? Anyone, like me, who coughs 16 hours a day should consider every minute of his life as being stolen from death…' The two young men were musically trained, and so it is not surprising that characteristic metaphors appeared in their everyday language. 'On the way, stopping overnight in Auxerre,' wrote the elder brother to their parents, '[Kamil] woke me with coughing so violent he was shaking. I rose, lit a candle and ran to his bed. "In God's name! Kamil, what's the matter?" I called. "It's the music of death" – he replied cold bloodedly'.[378]

So behind Kamil's expression lay the metaphor 'man is an instrument'. When his body was 'in order', this instrument sang the praises of life. But when it fell into 'disorder', it began to produce the music of death: coughing. Let us remember this

---

[378] Mochnacki, *Dzieła*, i:229.

idea, that disharmony is linked to the disintegration of the body. After all, Chopin also coughed very often.

The Romantic era was also a time of great bemoaning over the demusicalisation of the world. In ancient times, and also during the Christian era, up to about the beginning of the seventeenth century, it was believed that the universe was something like a musical instrument, built according to mathematical rules, which gives out harmonious sounds. According to Pythagoreanism, all true movement emitted beautiful tones, and so an ordered universe fair resounded with music, which we do not hear simply because it is constant. After Plato, it was believed that in each of the eight spheres there were Sirens, whose joint concert created the musical harmony of the cosmos. The moment the secularisation of learning became a fact, when analytical rationalism smashed the cosmos up into pieces and chased away from it all 'spiritual laws', the myth of the harmony of the spheres was consigned to the history of cranky ideas.[379] This was essentially the work of Descartes, but the Romantics, who for some time held the achievements of scientism to be a Big Nothing and believed that music was magnificent proof that Providence kept a constant watch over the life it had created, ascribed the beginning of the demusicalisation of the cosmos to the 'godless Enlightenment'.[380] So they rejected the wisdom of the most modern times and returned to the archaic myth of Mediterranean civilisation.

It is understandable that various musical metaphors appeared at that time. Maurycy Mochnacki, brought up on the aesthetics of German romanticism, heard, during an ecstatic rapture, the harmony of the world in a chorus of the spirits that fill our three-dimensional cage to the hilt. 'Sometimes,'

---

[379] See Leo Spitzer, *Classical and Christian Ideas of World Harmony* (Baltimore, 1963), 138.
[380] Münch, *Raj utracony i odnaleziony*, 176.

wrote his friend Michał Podczaszyński, 'while out on a walk, he would fall into a sort of rapture and speak to the compatriots around him about the wonders of the other world, which he observed in the playing of spirits. "You do not hear it," he would say, "but I, who soon will join them, can already sense them, can already hear their harmonious playing, which fills the world".'[381] Death, which demusicalised the individual existence of Maurycy's brother, Kamil, opened up the possibility of hearing the harmony of the world, since it was created by the host of dead souls. 'The wind is always greater near churches', he told Antoni Walewski, ' – those are dead souls, and they emit tones in the air. I wish that my soul too would soon be such an airy tone. I believe in the spirits, in their pleasantest tones, I talk with Kamil, and I often see my father in my sleep'.[382] As we can see, he could best convey the essence of the soul, as well, by means of musical metaphor. Just like, incidentally, the essence of human thought: 'Our thinking is a tuneful, harmonious chord, sounding with the concordance of all the primary syllables scattered in nature'. Wishing to define the essence of man, in turn, he wrote that the 'I' was a dissonance in the harmonious concert of the world:

> Out of the childhood years grows a youth, playful, exuberant, then unchecked, passionate and tender, and full of raptures. He pulls away from the whole, tears himself away from the general accord in the existence of the universe. And then he sounds, he thunders like a note, like a particular tone, out of tune, at odds with the general tonic. Now he is a *person*, he is a particular, an individual being, an egoist – I.[383]

---

[381] Mochnacki, *Dzieła*, i:290.
[382] Ibid, 335.
[383] Mochnacki, *O literaturze*, 48, 60–61.

The harmony of the world could be heard not just during ecstasy. In order to receive that favour, in the Romantic era one sometimes had to go crazy. That is just what happened to the conductor, composer and music entrepreneur Louis-Antoine Julien. 'He would place his fingers in his ears', wrote Hector Berlioz, 'and listen to the dull roar produced by the blood passing through the carotid arteries, and firmly believe that what he heard was the cosmic A given out by the terrestrial globe in its revolutions through space. He would then whistle through his lips some shrill note – a D, an E flat, or an F – and exclaim with the utmost enthusiasm, "Listen – it's the A, the genuine A of the spheres! The vibrations of eternity!"'[384] It is to the note A that an orchestra tunes its instruments before a concert. Julien alleged that the note emitted by the movement of the Earth and discovered by him in the music of the human body was the basis for the harmony of the cosmos. And so the orchestra of being was tuned to the note of our planet.

Chopin also employed musical metaphors. Yet he was far from metaphysical exaltation, and so his expressions make no mention of the 'harmonious playing of the spirits' or the 'airy tone of souls' or even the 'A of the spheres' or the 'vibrations of eternity'. Chopin coughed, and so by means of musical terms he tried to capture the state of his health, determining his chances for living. Like Kamil Mochnacki, he often heard the 'music of death' and sensed, not without good reason, that the 'disordering' of his body by illness was beginning to 'untune' his thoughts.

Before that happened, during the years when he was not yet sensing the threat of death, a musical take on his own existence occasionally shed light on the traits of his own personality. In order to convey the necessity of going beyond the norms of the community, Chopin employed terms linked with the division

---

[384] Berlioz, *Memoirs*, 531.

into bars and with a break in musical narrative. He first stated that he had fallen out of the rhythm to which the life of the Polish émigré community lived in Paris. Here he writes to Tytus Woyciechowski on 25 December 1831:

> You know how easily I make acquaintances – you know how I like to daydream with them, well I'm up to my ears with such acquaintances, but I cannot sigh with anyone. – I am always, as regards my feelings, out of sync with others (KS i: 209).

Syncopation is the shifting of the natural metric accent to an unaccented note by extending the value of an unaccented note and holding it through the accented part. Thanks to its lengthening, a note leaves its 'mother' beat and 'hies' ahead. So this metaphor gives us to understand that Chopin was not in the emotional 'beat' of his compatriots, since among people who were able to talk about *tere bzdere* and knew only about neckwear, he could not and would not place his 'heart' on his tongue. Thus he skipped out of Polish society like a syncopated note out of the beat.

However, the beat that held sway in that milieu obliged Chopin to reckon with musical mediocrities. Chopin's portrait of one such good-for-nothing in a letter to Tytus, although a little long-winded, is so wonderful that I shall quote it here in full:

> Writing to you, I find it insufferable when my bell goes – and in barges a something with whiskers, large, overgrown, burly – sits at the piano and improvises he himself knows not what, pounds and thumps senselessly, hurls himself about, crosses his hands, rattles for five minutes on a single key with a huge finger that somewhere in the Ukraine was destined for

a steward's whip and reins. You have a portrait of Sowiński, who has no other merit than his good figure and good heart for himself. If ever I could imagine charlatanism or stupidity in art, then it would never be so perfectly as now. I often have to walk around the room while I'm listening and put a good face on it. My ears are turning red – I would shove him out of the door, but I have to be accommodating, even mutually sensitive. You cannot imagine such a thing – but since they regard him here (they who know of nothing but ties) as something, I have to fraternise (KS i: 209–210).

In Poland, when an adult man is spoken of as 'such a thing' or 'it', then he is clearly considered a complete pipsqueak. Such visitations could indeed cause Chopin irritation. Suppressing that anger must have been very painful. Hence his longing for a break in the mode of living established by the émigré norm, requiring that a fellow countryman be respected even if he is stupid and insolent. Chopin's great tactfulness exposed him to the torment of rubbing shoulders with people who thought that the music of a barrel organ, mixed with the gaggling of courtyard geese and a parish organ, was that sought-after national style, since 'it' played for him 'in a tavern, barrel-organ-gaggling-parish-organ style'. And so the weary Chopin craved just a break from that 'music of life': 'That's why I'm suffering, and you'd not believe how I long for some respite, for no one to call on me all day and no one to say anything' (KS i: 209).

When his health worsened frightfully during his stay in England and Scotland, the metaphor 'man is a musical instrument' came into Chopin's head, somehow relating to the 'music of death'.

This comparison of a person with a well-tuned or poorly-tuned instrument was highly popular during the Romantic era. It was spread by German music theorists, inspired by the seventeenth-century mystic Jakub Boehme. Chopin made use of this popular concept and imparted to it such a brilliant shape that, setting about a description of this pearl, I sense a fear of whether I shall manage the task that I have set myself.

First, this metaphor appeared in a rather strange form. Chopin identified his spiritual state not with a whole instrument, but only with a part, with a violin E string, and so the highest, albeit strung on a… double bass, a huge string instrument that sounds extremely low and deep. 'The park here is very lovely,' he wrote to Auguste Franchomme from Calder House, a stately home some twelve miles from Edinburgh, 'and so the owner of the house – a most kindly person – feels as well as is possible. – There is no question of any musical ideas – I am utterly derailed – I feel like, e.g. a donkey at a masked ball or a violin E string on a bass…' (KS ii: 257).[385] So Chopin had not yet heard the 'music of death', although he coughed, but through the image of the peculiar stringing of a double bass he tried to convey the idea that his state was quite dire, and his nerves strained to the utmost. Of course, this was also a joke at his own expense, since Franchomme received information about Chopin's 'demusicalisation'. A violin E string, from which a high range of notes are produced, strung on a bass instrument precludes any meaningful musical utterance. For a musician, the idea of that string having such a status, if one may put it like that, is quite simply comical – as comical as a donkey at a masked ball. This all should have communicated to Franchomme that the creative inventiveness had dried up in his friend's soul and that Chopin found himself in the situation of a human wreck. Admittedly, it is difficult to say whether the joke this time was intended to blunt or to sharpen the truth: the music had gone out of Chopin.

---

[385] Chopin's French text does not name the violin E string, but only 'une chantrelle de violon sur une contrebasse' (KS ii: 440).

Before setting about an exact analysis of Chopin's meta-phors, let us just take on board the fact that in the Romantic era, man was compared to instruments that are generally perceived as refined, noble and spiritual. No common or, let's say, folk instrument came into the equation. The comparison was usually aimed at discovering some semi-religious, semi-metaphysical truth about man in general. Thus it always concerned Romantic anthropology. A person was compared to an instrument in order to formulate some idea. Let us take one example. Novalis held man to be an active being, subjected at the same time to other activity.[386] As an active being, he can 'accelerate' or 'deceler-ate' the emanation of the particles of his essence in thoughts, words and deeds, since his mind enables him to consciously set in motion the mechanisms of the expression of his own 'I'. For the idea to be better conveyed, Novalis turned to comparison. Just as a flautist opens and closes the tone holes, so a person ju-diciously regulates the process of self-expression. So the object of comparison was indeed not the instrument itself, but the way it was used. On the other hand, as a being that was subject to the actions of outside activity, a person – according to Novalis – experiences first and foremost the effects of transcendent Breath. This term was associated very often with the New Testament Spirit or Wind. For Novalis, this signified Divine Energy, or per-haps the Spirit of the Cosmos; it is difficult to ascertain exactly. This breath produces 'the incredible diversity of tones of the Aeolian harp'. The simplicity with which this Force strikes the strings is astonishing. 'The same with man – he is, or should be, a harp'. The instrument named after Aeolus, son of Zeus, ruler of winds and storms, was constructed in the mid seventeenth century. Through the action of puffs of wind, it emitted a range of harmonious tones with a characteristic, piercing, 'immate-rial' sound. In the years 1780–1860, it was highly popular and

---

[386] See Münch, 183.

was often put on roofs and in castle ruins.[387] It was supposed to remind people of the musical primary principle of being. In Poland, Juliusz Słowacki transformed the Aeolian harp into a symbol of the nation, and this was connected – so it seems – with some form of messianism, since the Transcendent Wind striking its strings played the world the melody of God's truth.

Chopin was indifferent to all these exalted comparisons. He was concerned with his own adversity, which he treated quite ironically. Thus, when he thought about his own catastrophe and about the misfortune of his friend, Julian Fontana, there appeared before his eyes... a dulcimer.

His imagination suggested this image to him for two reasons. Firstly, it was in Poland a 'low', even common instrument. The rural band that Mickiewicz described in Book XII of *Pan Tadeusz* comprised a violin, *kobza* (a lute-like instrument) and dulcimer. The dulcimer was also a favourite instrument of Jews. An incomparable concert was given in *Pan Tadeusz* by Jankiel. Dulcimer virtuosos like Jankiel could also be found among itinerant Hungarian Gypsies. So even if no other circumstance had appeared, a comparison to a dulcimer would be a suggestive signal of distance in respect to the vicissitudes of fate. But, secondly, the Polish word for dulcimer, *cymbały*, also means slow-witted simpletons. It is not known when or why such a transferral occurred. We know only that this word was lent just such a figurative meaning in the sister language of Czech, as well. Aleksander Brückner rightly wrote in his dictionary that a *cymbał* was a *głuptas*, a simpleton, since this form sounds a note of indulgence. After all, a *cymbał* is neither a *głupiec*, which tends to evoke irritation, or a *głupek*, which usually arouses contempt. A *cymbał* is not necessarily stupid. He does stupid things because he is light-minded. He cannot be blamed. To a large extent he is a frivolous person.

---

[387] See Curt Sachs, *The History of Musical Instruments* (1940; New York, 2006), 402.

In Chopin's correspondence with his friends and acquaintances, this word appears in a figurative meaning several times. It is used, for example, by Julian Fontana, in a letter to Stanisław Egbert Koźmian of 6 June 1851. First he quotes an excerpt from a letter written by Chopin on 29 September 1839: "'Have Moscheles, if he's already in Paris, be given an enema of Neukomm oratorios, seasoned with *Cellini* and a Doehler concerto'" (KS i: 359). He then adds, from himself: 'In order to understand [this excerpt], you must know that Moscheles, in spite of his talent, is an inordinate pedant, and Neukomm ditto, minus the talent, *Benvenuto Cellini* a famous fiasco of Berlioz's, and Doehler we regard as a *great cymbał*...'[388] Teodor Doehler was court pianist to the Prince of Lucca. From 1829, he trained in Vienna under Carl Czerny. For some time, he travelled around the great European cities giving concerts, and when, in 1846, he returned to Lucca, the prince bestowed upon him the title of baron. Doehler's compositions were exceedingly mediocre. Chopin heard him play works by Czerny while he was in Vienna (KS i: 175), and it cannot be excluded that it was then that he acquired the conviction that he was a simpleton of the piano. It was an opinion that stuck.

This word also occurred in a letter written by Teresa Wodzińska, Maria's mother, to Chopin in Dresden on 5 February 1836: 'My dear Fryderyk! [...] Wishing to send a small sum to Antek, for various reasons I was unable to do what he asked and I happily fell upon the idea that I could do no better than to approach someone who has continually and constantly given us so much evidence of his good favour towards us. So you know the reason. Please now be so kind as to bring the rest to fruition

---

[388] 'Wybór listów Juliana Fontany do Stanisława Egberta Koźmiana z lat 1844–1868' [Selection of letters sent by Julian Fontana to Stanisław Egberg Koźmian from the years 1844–1868], ed. Józef Fijałek, in *Rocznik Biblioteki PAN w Krakowie* [Annual of the PAN Library in Cracow], i (1955) (Wrocław, 1957), 226. For more on Chopin's attitude to Doehler, see Kornel Michałowski, *Nieznane wspomnienie*, 207.

and hand the enclosed to my Cémbał' (KS i: 274). How much we learn from the very spelling of the word here. In those times, a so-called tilted 'e' next to the letter 'i' was read as 'ee'. Suffice it to mention Chopin's 'biéda' or Mickiewicz's 'kobiéta'. In those days, these words were pronounced 'beeda' and 'kobeeta' instead of 'byeda' and 'kobyeta'. In other positions, however, it was read as a Polish 'y'. For instance, 'czerwonym' was spelt 'czerwoném', but pronounced the same. Mrs Wodzińska most probably put a tilted 'e' instead of a 'y' because she associated the word 'cymbał' with the instrument called in Italian *cembolo*, and so with the harpsichord or *klawicymbał*. Harpsichords stood in palaces; Jews and Gypsies did not play them.

What did she understand by this word? Her *cémbał* was first and foremost a light-minded loon, committing unbearable acts of stupidity, rather out of reprehensible idleness than out of ill will. 'My dear Freddie, do not refuse him your friendly advice, encourage him to find some occupation there, for an idle life causes much unhappiness' (KS i: 274). Wise words wrote Mrs Wodzińska. Indeed, in 1836, while residing in France, probably out of boredom – as we read in Krystyna Kobylańska – 'he enlisted in a regiment of Polish lancers that, as part of the French assistance, took part in the civil war of succession in Spain on the side of the infanta Isabela. When he ended up in Saragossa, after being wounded in the Battle of Huesca (24 May 1837), Chopin was an intermediary between him and his family in the sending of correspondence and money'.[389] Wodziński's mother regarded the whole escapade as a series of ridiculous antics, albeit nothing too dreadful. Her *cémbał* was simply an overly light-minded simpleton.

With Chopin, this word sometimes denoted an irritating fool. His senior colleague from the conservatory, Józef Nowakowski, the same Nowakowski who – as he wrote to his family

---

[389] Kobylańska, biographical note in KGS ii: 345.

in 1847 – 'didn't wish to go with me to Legouvé for the evening, where among a host of the learned world he would have seen and heard up close e.g. Lablache', a well-known singer, was a good-hearted man, but such a great *cymbał* that 'may the Lord protect him' (KR 160–161). Occasionally, Chopin used the word *cymbał* for a devious swindler. The London publisher Christian Wessel, who allowed himself such caddish behaviour, was described as a cheat and a *cymbał* (KS ii: 42). Meanwhile, in a letter to Fontana of 11 October 1841, the meaning of this word took on an unexpected shade. The oversensitive addressee took it into his head that Chopin was intending to sell some furniture that he had previously given him for safekeeping with the right of usage. 'You're stupid', exclaimed his famous friend bluntly, 'if you think that I'm reckoning some debts of yours. If you'd had some estate in Cuiavia, then I might perhaps have reminded you – if it had been thousands. As regards the selling of furniture, I would be a swindler, a Jew in the mode of doctor Wołowski, to sell the old lumber – may it be of use to you. By degrees, as you buy yourself better things, you can let me have these; moreover, may it not upset your English bile; and I'm not such a *cymbał* as you think, and neither would I do anything that might cause you embarrassment or something of the sort' (KS ii: 43). Judging by this, a *cymbał* was a person who out of stupidity may become a bit of a rotter. Incidentally, this whole affair was probably due to Chopin's tact. So as not to offend Fontana, he most probably said that he would only *lend* him this furniture for while.

Then, in the summer of 1848, the same Fontana, who since 1843 had been living on the other side of the Atlantic, visited the Old Continent.[390] In July he was in Paris, whence, accompanied by a delegation from the Historical Society, he travelled to the capital of the British Empire, where, together with fellow

---

[390] Aleksander Janta, 'Amerykański rozdział w życiu Juliana Fontany' [The American chapter in the life of Julian Fontana], in *Nic własnego nikomu*, 169.

countrymen resident in London, he awarded Lord Palmerston, an advocate of Polish exiles in the British parliament, a medal struck in honour of Prince Adam Czartoryski. While in London, Fontana made contact with his friend, who was staying in Scotland, and from that same Calder House from where a week before – as we recall – those notable words were dispatched to Franchomme, on 18 August 1848 Chopin sent him a letter in which, employing the metaphor 'man is an instrument', he spread before him a moving image of his personal catastrophe.

> My life. Had I been of better health, I would [...] have travelled tomorrow to embrace you [in London]. Perhaps we will not see one another so soon. We are old dulcimers, on which time and circumstances have played out their miserable trillettes (KS ii: 259).

This was not the first time Chopin had identified his wretched situation with the misfortunes of Fontana. He always treated this parallelism of their fortunes most seriously, in the conviction that the differences in their talents, which he naturally never mentioned, had nothing to do with it. In such instances, 'we' meant 'we, who have been going through the world together since our youth', 'we musicians', 'we, upon whom personal catastrophes are constantly falling', 'we, cast out of our homes and our homeland'. Such was the conviction that he harboured, and that is why Fontana took upon himself various domestic services, without demeaning himself.

Such a 'we' allowed Chopin a play on words, thanks to which the word *cymbały* could mean both a musical instrument and also two simpletons. In a word, each of them was both a dulcimer and a simpleton.

So first there appeared an elaborate metaphor, which enables us to understand how Chopin summarised his life thus far. An instrument is for playing, and so it implies a performer. As it turned out, there were two players. The first was time, which for Chopin – as we recall – had already taken the role of an eternal fugitive tormented by death. Yet this fugitive managed to grab an instrument – a person – and to play on him at will. My imagination suggests to me a vision of old Saturn, a timeless – if you'll forgive the pun – allegory of time that was popularised by great art and numerous prints as, having set aside his scythe, he holds a beater and plays a dulcimer. The other player was 'circumstances'. This word denotes a set of conditions, always concrete and even very detailed, constituting the real cause of a particular situation. Most often, it denotes a situation in a person's life which is strongly grounded in time and space. It is legalistically tinged, as it is used in the language of jurists. A court usually examines the circumstances of every case. Only with a knowledge of those circumstances can it issue a just verdict. Hence in Chopin's conception, the life of the two friends had been shaped by time and by circumstances, by specific events that befell them alone and determined their personal fortunes. We are dealing quite simply with the affairs of life, what the Italians call *vicende della vita*. Fontana had gone through similar or even the same events. Today, we may find the anthropomorphisation of this notion somewhat annoying, but let us remember that the metaphor 'man is an instrument' implies the idea of a user and a maker of that musical utensil.

The music performed by these players symbolised the whole of Chopin's life hitherto. As it turned out, it comprised mostly 'miserable trillettes'. A trill is essentially an embellishment. It is like an intriguing setting of a principal note. Sometimes, it is a 'turn' entwining a particular note. The use of a quite disdainful diminutive form and an unequivocal epithet produce a striking impression. Time and circumstances have meant that the content of Chopin's life has thus far comprised pitiful little adornments. Nothing of substance. *Tere bzdere.* The most important thing, the principal note, the note of life, has been lost amid trifles. It has been neither homogenous, nor continuous, nor clear.

Therefore, in the next sentence Chopin numbered both himself and Fontana among the community of light-minded simpletons. 'Yes, old *cymbały*, although you'll defend yourself against such company' (KS ii: 259). Chopin's thoughts had again turned to metaphor, in order to state that he was a ruined instrument that can no longer be used. 'It disparages neither beauty nor respectability: the perfect *table d'harmonie*, just that the strings have snapped, some of the pegs have popped out' (KS ii: 259). So the soundboard remained intact, but these dulcimers cannot be played. As yet, we do not know who destroyed them, since the strings simply snapped. The same was true of the instrument in George Sand's play *The Seven Strings of the Lyre*, although there the lyre did not symbolise a 'thinking body', like the dulcimer for Chopin, but only the soul itself, '…as you are now, abandoned, loosened, set on a pedestal to please the eye […] a well-worked case, a cadaver…'[391]

In order to emphasise the idea that every artist is an irreplaceable and non-interchangeable individual, Chopin expanded his metaphor: 'The only trouble is that we are the work of a famous violin maker, some Straduari *sui generis*, who is no longer around to repair us' (KS ii: 259). I suspect that Chopin had in mind a Hidden Luthier, who in his secret workshop builds extraordinary instruments: artists. He gives them to humanity, unrecognised, and woe be it if such an exceptional specimen is smashed, since no one will be able to repair it, just as no one is capable of mending a violin by Antonio Stradivari.

So neither time nor circumstances will be able to produce any music from such mutilated instruments any more. Moreover,

---

[391] Sand, *Seven Strings*, 11, 17.

this is now a different, worse time, and the circumstances are also different, clearly unfavourable. 'We are incapable of producing new tones beneath poor hands and we stifle within ourselves everything that, for want of a luthier, no one will now ever get out of us' (KS ii: 259–260). The man-instrument fell silent. And so music is stifled in Chopin's mind. Not brought out into the open, it is smothered in his 'heart', in the centre of his identity. Like a lamp in a Roman grave. Not 'uttered', it falls into itself and goes out. So Chopin understood that he had now become a 'living corpse' of music. He could have quoted in this letter his own words, which in 1831 he wrote into his album: 'Why do we live such a miserable life, which devours and serves only to make corpses out of us!' (A 34).

—

Na świecie ciągle, ale nie dla świata:
    Czymże ten muzyk? – upiorem.
(Still in the world, but not for the world:
    What's this musician? – a phantom.)

—

Responsibility for this heart-rending catastrophe lay with death: 'I can barely breath, *je suis tout prêt à crever*, and you're doubtless going bald and you'll stay yet over my stone like those willows of ours, remember? – that show their bare head' (KS ii: 260). When Chopin was beset by the thought of death, contemptuous words immediately appeared in his letters. He was barely breathing. That is how we speak about a person gravely ill and dying, who arouses our pity. The French expression even had brusque ferocity: '*je suis tout prêt à crever*' – 'I'm just about ready to die'. Help also immediately arrived for these incantations of terror – for incantations is what they were – from ridicule. He saw Fontana standing over his grave, his head as bald as his elbow, like a Mazovian willow betwixt: betwixt life and non-being.

So this decomposition of a person was caused by a continual experiencing of departure. Now, his prematurely deceased friends and acquaintances stood in line for nocturnal conversations, so as to line his path to nothingness. 'I don't know why', he wrote in the same letter, 'the late Jan [Matuszyński] and Antek [Wodziński, that *cémbał*, who had died in the meantime] are now in my thoughts, and Witwicki, and Sobański! Those with whom I was most closely in tune also died for me; even Ennike, our best tuner, drowned. So I no longer have a well-tuned, according to my usage, piano in the world. Moos died, and now no one does me such comfortable shoes. If another 4 or 5 go up to St Peter's gates, my whole more comfortable life will be *ad patres*' (KS ii: 260).

Like every person cast into a similar situation, at the bottom of his consciousness he harboured hope. He dreamed. He planned. He joked. In a word, he kept up appearances. 'I'm vegetating, waiting patiently for the winter. I'm dreaming now of home, now of Rome, now of happiness, now of misery. [...] What's left to me are a big nose and an *unrefined* 4th finger' (KS ii: 260). He initially attributed this decline in his creative powers to tiredness, caused by his wandering lifestyle and the conditions accompanying that ill-fated tour of England and Scotland. On 1 October 1848, he found himself at Keir House, the property of Jane Stirling's cousin, where 'neither post, nor railway, nor any carriage (even for a short ride), nor any boat – nor even a dog can be *whistled*' (KS ii: 276) 'If I write you not jeremiads,' he informed Wojciech Grzymała, 'it's not because you'll not console me, for you're the only one who knows everything about me – but because if I start, there's no end, and always one thing. – It's not true that *one*, because the future's looking increasingly bad for me. – I feel weaker – I can't compose a thing, not so much for a lack of desire as for the physical impediments, as I'm roaming around a different branch every week' (KS ii: 277–278). So he saw himself as a bird that changes its location, and he still believed that when he returned to his Parisian nest, his health could be improved.

Towards the end of October that year, during a stay in Edinburgh, he stopped deluding himself. The majesty of death revealed itself, albeit somewhat shrouded in triviality. In the artistic circles of Paris, the rumour went around that Chopin was getting married. These 'caquets' attested that no one, not even Wojciech Grzymała, who 'knew everything', realised the gravity of the situation. Chopin assumed that such gossip was prompted by the protectiveness of Jane Stirling and her sister, Katharine Erskine, which all too often evolved into ostentatious adoration. 'My kind-hearted Scottish ladies', he wrote to Grzymała on 30 October 1848, 'whom I've not seen for a couple of weeks, will be here today; they would like me to stay on and knock about Scottish palaces, and here, and there, and everywhere they ask me. Kind-hearted, but so wearisome that may the Lord God protect!… I receive letters every day, I reply to none, and whenever I go anywhere, they come after me if they can. That might give someone the idea that I'm getting married, but some sort of physical *attrait* is necessary nonetheless, and that unmarried one is too similar to me. It would be like kissing myself…' (KS ii: 284).

Chopin was always remarkably matter-of-fact in assessing his own situation in life. When the verdict was fatal, he tried to mollify the cruelty with good-natured irony. In fact, this is the most splendid trait of a man, thanks to which all his judgments take on gravity and credibility. And so once more he attempted to explain to his friend why the idea of marrying was completely preposterous. 'Even if I could fall in love with someone who would also love me as I would like, then I still wouldn't wed, as we'd have nothing to eat and nowhere to sit. And a rich woman seeks a rich man, and if he's poor, then not a valetudinarian, but someone young and handsome. One can be hard up alone, but for a couple it's the greatest misery. I could die in hospital, but I'll not leave behind a wife without bread' (KS ii: 285). Chopin had a well-formed opinion on the duties of a man. It was passed on to him by his father.

Thus, having come to terms with the situation, he decided to prepare something like a will. 'Have you forgotten me,' he upbraided Grzymała, 'to conclude from my letters, in which I wrote you that I was ever weaker, more morose, without any hope, without a home, to conclude from this that I was getting married? On the day I received from you your dear, kind letter, I wrote a sort of arrangement to implement with my old lumber in the event that I should croak somewhere' (KS ii: 283). In this letter, Chopin twice wrote 'zdycham'[392] (I'm croaking) instead of 'umieram'[393] (I'm dying), which meant that he had more disdain for his own death than sorrow. In Poland, when someone says 'zdycham', then he is identifying himself with an animal. He is placing himself on the same level as the whole animated world, which – as we know from experience – is subject in a natural way to the law of the birth and death of particular members of a species. He is reducing himself to an anonymous specimen. A man dies. A horse or a cow croaks. But Chopin was not averse to trenchant expressions. He liked strong words. 'Tu me diras tout ce que tu voudras', his father wrote to him on 28 June 1832 from Warsaw, 'mais je n'approuve pas ton dégoût pour certaines personnes, je ne sais qui peut t'avoir indisposé contre elles, et gnoy ne me plait pas' ('Say what you like, but I do not approve of your aversion to some people, I do not know who might have turned you against them, and I do not like the word *gnoy*') (KS i: 381, 215). When we call someone 'gnój'[394], we

---

[392] Short 'y', as in 'Lynn'; guttural 'ch', as in 'loch' (tr.).
[393] Pronounced 'oom-yeah-ram' (tr.).
[394] Pronounced 'gnuy' (tr.).

consider him something disgustingly rotten, utterly base, a despicable, contemptible blackguard. It is a word still in common use today. So describing the dying of a human being with the strong word 'zdychać' was quite suggestive. 'Niech zdechnie'[395] ('May he croak'), we say about an enemy whom we sincerely despise. So a sober assessment of the situation brought Chopin loathing for himself.

Thus the 'balance sheet' of his life looked quite dreadful. 'Meanwhile,' he wrote in a letter of 30 October 1848, 'what has become of my art? And where did I squander my heart?' (KS ii: 285). The music was driven from his soul by the physical weariness brought on by his illness, since the 'disordering' of the body is capable of stifling any sort of creative idea. Discouragement was by now an ever-present effect of his mortal illness. And it was ultimately accompanied by a painful sense of the loss of his identity, since the heart – as we will recall – is a symbol of that which is most personal in a man, the one thing that makes him who he is. Thus Chopin reached the conclusion that he did not even know where – doubtless somewhere along his way through life, 'somehow or other', when the world, unnoticed, was passing him by – he had squandered the power that constituted the principle of his personal existence. Towards the end of our journey, almost everyone arrives at a similar conclusion. And that assertion in the letter under discussion was followed by considerable deletions, which meant that Chopin had said too much, or had not expressed himself as he had wished. He spared only the following admission: '…if I raise myself a little, then I shall fall that much lower. *I'm not complaining to you*, but you asked, and so I'm explaining that I am closer to the coffin than a marriage bed. My mind is quite calm'. Then more deletions, from which three terrible words can be deciphered: 'I am

---

[395] Again, guttural 'ch' sounds; 'nie' twice as 'n-yeah' (tr.).

resigned' (KS ii: 285). So he accepted God's sentence calmly, if cold despair can be called calm.

Mozart departed this world writing music with abandon, indefatigable and insatiable. As in opera, he died and sang music from deep within. He wrote the following to Lorenzo da Ponte on 7 September 1791:

My dear Sir,

I should like to follow your advice, but how am I to do so?... I cannot shake off the vision of this unknown man. [He had commissioned the *Requiem* from Mozart.] I see him continually, he entreats me, he exhorts me, and impatiently bids me set to work. I go on working because composing is less tiring than resting. Moreover I have nothing more to fear. I can tell from my condition that the hour is striking; I am about to breathe my last; I have come to the end of my life before having had the full enjoyment of my talent. And yet life has been so beautiful, my career began under such happy auspices. But one cannot, after all, change one's own destiny. No one can measure the length of his own days; one must resign oneself, all will be as Providence wills. I must conclude, here before me is my death song; I must not leave it unfinished.[396]

On returning to France, Chopin stated that the music had been gouged out of him. We find a sort of chronicle of this distress in the journal of Eugène Delacroix, who visited the composer quite often at that time. On 28 January 1849, he spent an evening with him, after which he arrived at the conclusion that 'his suffering prevents his taking an interest in anything, least of all in his work'.[397]

---

[396] Quoted in Annette Kolb, *Mozart*, tr. Phyllis and Trevor Blewitt (London, 1939), 335–336. Unfortunately, this is an English translation of a German paraphrase of the Italian original.
[397] Delacroix, entry of 29 January 1849, *Journal* (London, 2006), 90.

Perhaps he was even told as much by Chopin himself, since the entry is not entirely clear. At the beginning of March, Delacroix no longer had any illusions that his 'poor, great man'[398] was dying. On 14 April, when he visited Chopin again, the conversation turned to boredom, which is the poisonous fruit of idleness. It must have been a hymn to the great blessing that is weariness from work and the great curse that is weariness from illness.

> I found him in a state of collapse, scarcely breathing. After a time, my being there seemed to do him good. He said that boredom was the worst evil he had to suffer, and I asked him whether before he fell ill he had not known the unbearable sense of emptiness that I sometimes feel. He said he could always find some occupation or other, and that having something to do, however trivial, filled in the time and dispersed the vapours. Real grief is something quite different.[399]

The best thing in life, weariness from work, no longer affected him. On 18 June 1849, he wrote to Grzymała:

> I don't go out, just occasionally to the Bois de Boulogne – I am stronger, because I've had something to eat and thrown out the medicine – but I'm panting and coughing the same, just that I'm bearing it better. – I've not yet started to play – compose I cannot – I don't know what hay I'll soon be eating (KS ii: 298).

If he was intending to eat hay, then perhaps he saw himself as a donkey or an ass. But he more likely regarded himself as a horse, which is a symbol of hard work. He certainly feared that he would soon be eating dirt instead of hay.

---

[398] Delacroix, entry of 5 March 1849, *Journal* (Paris, 2009), 428.
[399] Delacroix, entry of 14 April 1849, *Journal* (London, 2006), 101.

So I leave Chopin with that 'black thought'. May he continue to die. After all, if you're dying, you must still be alive. I do not want to talk about what will shortly become of him, since I myself am already quaking in my death cell and fearful of my own thoughts about the moment when God leads us out onto the black courtyard of the Anti-Earth. Death ultimately stopped chasing time. It stood by Chopin's piano and slammed the keyboard shut, so that before leaving he would become a 'living corpse' and not regret life, which without work and music is indeed worth very little.

Warsaw, February 1986 – June 1991

Translated by
John Comber

Original Polish title
Cień Jaskółki (Cracow, 2009)

Graphic design
Ryszard Grzyb

Typesetting
Kotbury

Proofreading and editing
John Comber

Cover and endpapers illustrations:
Fragment of a letter sent by Fryderyk Chopin to his family, 10 August1824. Fryderyk Chopin Museum in Warsaw [M/4]
Fragment of Chopin's drawing-room (9 Square d'Orléans, Paris), unsigned watercolour. Original lost with the collection of
Laura Ciechomska in Warsaw. Photographic collection of the Fryderyk Chopin Institute [F.6267].

This translation is published by agreement with
Społeczny Instytut Wydawniczy ZNAK, Kraków

ISBN 978-83-61142-64-5

Publisher
The Fryderyk Chopin Institute
43 Tamka Street
PL 00-355 Warsaw
www.chopin.nifc.pl

Printed in Poland

CONTENTS

INTRODUCTION   9
Notes and words.   10

CHAPTER I. INITIATION INTO EXISTENCE   25
1. The antinomic nature of being.   28
2. The oracular romances of a Pole   35
3. The symbolic death of the 'I'.   53
4. The city of his youth in ruins.   77

CHAPTER II. SETTING HIS LIFE IN ORDER. 109
1. The attire of a spiritual aristocrat. 112
2. The forge of myths. 142
3. Epiphany of a Musical Idol 163

CHAPTER III. THE CONDITIONS OF HIS TALENT. 201
1. Espaces imaginaires. 203
2. Talent and the tone of life 229
3. Aerumnarum plenus. 239
4. Music and existence. 258
5. Philosophical Scherzando 267
6. Musical Thought 276

CHAPTER IV. BLACK THOUGHTS. 295
1. The face of God 299
2. The 'Living Corpse' of music 313

...atce porę moią, żeby nie Ma...

...ie dosyć iasno wystawiłem, ...

...by tylko Gerardot był w W...

...ni Dziewanowski o ooheuch...

...przesłał, a za pierwszym...

...by pozwolnie. W nadziei we...

...pozwoleniem Samey ludwi...

...pozwoliły, wnadziei maiące...

...ey materyi, moią dyssertacią...

...zefarni, Pan Podlowski, Pan...

...Szambelan, Siwicki, Pa...

...ia Wybranecki, z Białoo...

...Gulbinach w państwa Siw...

...Wybranieckiego. — Dwo...